YOURS VERY TRULY
GARETH KNIGHT

SELECTED LETTERS OF
GARETH KNIGHT
1969-2010

SKYLIGHT PRESS

© Gareth Knight 2010

First published in Great Britain by Skylight Press,
210 Brooklyn Road, Cheltenham, Glos GL51 8EA

Designed and typeset by Rebsie Fairholm
Front cover photograph by Mike Omoleye

Printed and bound in Great Britain by Lightning Source, Milton Keynes

www.skylightpress.co.uk

ISBN 978-1-908011-05-3

For Rebsie – true chip off the old block

LIST OF RECIPIENTS

Please note that these one line descriptions are simply my perception of those concerned and I apologise for any inaccuracies imposed by brevity and lack of wider knowledge.

Alan Adams — Old friend in SIL 1953-64. Leader of London Group. **76**

Dolores Ashcroft-Nowicki — Director of Studies SOL 1976 to present. **9 11 13 16 17 18 23 125 131**

Joan Baran — Co principal of Cinnabar Productions. **94**

Michael Beechey — Founder of Fellowship of the Valar. **53**

Katie Belle — Met at DF Seminar at Glastonbury. **126 128**

Wendy Berg — Head of Avalon Group. GK group member. **99 113 129**

Gillian Bourne — Met at DF Seminar at Glastonbury. **130**

Bernie Buedden — American member of GK group. **39 72**

Richard Brzustowicz — American academic, University of Washington. **21**

W. E. Butler — Writer, teacher and co-founder of SOL. **10**

Simon Buxton — Writer, teacher, bookseller, workshop organiser. **77 100**

Morag Cameron — Scottish enthusiast met at Glasgow workshop. **54 57**

Janine Chapman — Author of *The Quest for Dion Fortune*. **12 104**

Arthur Chichester — Warden of SIL 1946-79. **6**

Tom Clarke — Principal of Thoth Publications/Magis Books. **71**

Cinnabar Productions — New York based small film company. **68**

Carr P. Collins — Patron of esoteric projects, such as Sangraal Foundation. **24**

John Docherty — Anthroposophist, fellow enthusiast of Lewis Carroll. **47 49 50**

Michael Dummett — Professor of Logic, Oxford University. Tarot historian. **87 90**

Philip Dunbar — Senior member of GK Group. **32**

Paul Dunne — Prolific esoteric article writer. **118 124**

Anthony Duncan — Anglican clergyman and author. **4 7 8 44 74 75 107**

Steve Dwares — American attendee of Holy Grail week at Hawkwood. **65**

William Elmhurst — Founder and principal of Solar Quest. **111**

Mara Freeman — American esoteric teacher. **36**

R. A. Gilbert   Bookseller and esoteric researcher. **96**
James Hall   American Jungian psychiatrist. **80**
Mike Harris   Leader of Company of Avalon. GK group member. **52 93 97**
David Hicks   Member of original Tewkesbury house group. **22 25**
Ronald Hutton   Professor of History, Bristol University. **101 103**
Vivienne Jones   Hawkwood regular and esoteric networker. **33 48**
Jim Kaelin   Seeking advice on founding group in America. **66**
Warren Kenton   Author and teacher of Kabbalah. **92**
Terryl Kinder   Academic and historian of Cistercian movement. **89**
Donald Michael Kraig   Editor of *FATE* magazine, USA. **51**
Frann Leech   American enquirer. **60**
Diego Lipovich   Argentinian enquirer. **27**
Caitlín & John Matthews   Teachers, authors, founders of Hallowquest. **46 135**
Notis Michalitsis   Principal of Iamblichos group, Greece. **64**
Alistair Munro   New Zealand enquirer. **121**
Bernard Nesfield-Cookson   Principal Hawkwood College. **19**
Philip Newman   American enquirer. **67**
Mike Omoleye   Author, publisher, head of Divine Society, Nigeria. **122**
Alan Pert   Australian librarian and biographer of Anna Kingsford. **115**
Jonathan Poston   Member of GK group. **40 116 119 120 127**
Randall Prickett   Seeking advice on founding group in America. **79**
Kathleen Raine   Poet, Blake and Yeats expert, founder of Temenos Academy. **1 2 3 5 105 110 112**
Alan Richardson   Biographer of Dion Fortune and W. G. Gray. **26 98 102 114 123**
Billi Roberti   American enquirer. **85**
Ray Rue   American publisher's reader and book cover designer. **56**
Lance Slaughter   American enquirer. **59**
David Spangler   American esoteric author and teacher. **62**
Dan Staroff   American Tarot card designer. **81**
R. J. Stewart   Esoteric writer, musician, teacher, publisher. **14 15 117**
Paul Sugar   My host on trip to America. Former student of W. E. Butler. **35**

Dick Swettenham	General factotum of Marian Green's *Quest* magazine. **55**
Donald Tyson	Fellow contributor to *Golden Dawn Journal*. **69**
Libby Travassos Valdez	Artist, illustrator of my book *To the Heart of the Rainbow*. **109 133**
Andrew Walker	C.S.Lewis expert, contributor to the *Church Times*. **96**
Robert Wang	Associate of Israel Regardie in producing version of GD Tarot. **20**
Carl Weschcke	Head of Llewellyn Publications. My first publisher. **134**
Annie Wilson	Enquirer temporarily resident near Hawkwood. **58**
Mark Whitehead	Canadian member GK group. Writer and publisher. **28 29 30 38 41 43 70 73 83 106**
Peregrin Wildoak	Australian fellow traveller. **108 136**
Rab Wilkie	Canadian member of GK group. **31 37 42 45**
David Williams	Warden of SIL 1990 – 2010. **78 82 84 86**
Lynne Wycherley	Hawkwood attendee and esoteric networker. **34**

List of abbreviations, initials and acronyms commonly found in the text of the letters:

AA	Alan Adams, colleague in the Society of the Inner Light
CC	Charles Arthur Ulric Chichester, one time Warden of the Society of the Inner Light
CIA	Companions of the Inner Abbey *(when not Central Intelligence Agency)*, offshoot from the Gareth Knight Group
CTC	Christine Campbell Thompson, Dion Fortune's colleague and literary agent
CTL	C. T. Loveday, colleague of Dion Fortune
DC	David Carstairs, inner plane Master
DF	Dion Fortune, author, founder of the Society of the Inner Light
EIW	*Experience of the Inner Worlds*
FIR	Francis Israel Regardie, author
GD	Golden Dawn
GK	Gareth Knight
GM	Greater Mysteries
IGM	Inner Greater Mysteries
IPA	Inner Plane Adepti
LM	Lesser Mysteries
MCW	Maiya Curtis-Webb, a leading light of the Golden Dawn
MIMI	*Magical Images & the Magical Imagination*
MLB	Margaret Lumley Brown, medium for the Society of the Inner Light
MQ	*The Mystical Qabalah*
MQS	Mary Queen of Scots
MR	Master Rakoczi, inner plane Master
MS	Master Socrates, inner plane Master
MTH	Maiya Tranchell-Hayes, see Maiya Curtis-Webb
OGM	Outer Greater Mysteries
OTO	Ordo Templi Orientalis
PCC	Parish Church Council
PGQS	*A Practical Guide to Qabalistic Symbolism*
PW	Path working
SIL	Society of the Inner Light
SOL	Servants of the Light
TM	Thomas More
V&A	Victoria & Albert Museum
VMF	Violet Mary Firth, real name of Dion Fortune

FOREWORD

Having embarked upon writing my autobiography *I Called It Magic*, in the course of the search through my archives I came upon a number of letters written to a variety of correspondents that dealt at some length with my views on certain aspects of my life and work in the Western Mystery Tradition. It seemed to me that a fair amount of this personal verbiage was worth the dignity of print and also served to throw a more immediate light upon what I was up to or thinking about at the time. Thus providing vivid illustration for parts of the autobiography, and treating some topics at greater length than was possible there.

There used to be an old saying that "life begins at forty!" I don't know about that but certainly it is borne out in a certain sense in that the letters only start in my 39th year – anything before that is shrouded in epistolary darkness. However, my forty years since then, from 1969 to 2010, have hardly been devoid of recorded opinion or incident. This you are welcome to share with me in these letters to some 70 different people, that vary from learned discourse with academics, through exchange of strange experiences with esoteric colleagues, to providing answers to general enquirers who wrote asking me for information.

It is a book that must be the quickest I have ever written, having taken only a week to select and type up the contents. It is, on the other hand, the one that took me longest to write, in dribs and drabs over forty years. May you find it a worthwhile companion.

Gareth Knight

1. To Kathleen Raine

Dear Kathleen,

I feel after our long and most interesting talk on Wednesday that we know each other well enough to dispense with the formal mode of address. And thank you too for a most delicious lunch – your cooking rivals your scholarship!

Since we met I have asked John Hall, my colleague who runs Helios Book Service, to send you a complimentary copy of my book *A Practical Guide to Qabalistic Symbolism* and also the first five lessons of the Course. He will also probably take the opportunity to include a few other bits and pieces covering the work we do.

I hope you like the book. Looking back over the seven years since I wrote it, it seems a little naïve in places, but gives much of the material "got through" by the Society of the Inner Light up to 1961 and is based firmly on the Golden Dawn tradition of Tree of Life correspondences, which is what Yeats would have used. The volume on the Paths is more in the nature of meditations upon them than actual "Path workings" but can serve as a general introduction to each Path prior to working them, even if coloured somewhat by my own personal views – which is inevitable. There is some useful (I hope) purely academic research work contained in it by my close examination of the various varieties of Tarot design by different esotericals since the Marseilles Tarot – which is used to illustrate the work.

Since it was published Fr. A. D. Duncan has written his book (title not fixed yet)[1] and carried on a three year long discussion with me that has changed my views on Christ in relation to the Qabalah in the way in which I described to you. I have asked Tony Duncan to send a copy of his MSS to you as I think it an important work that will provide a basis of mutual approach for priest, psychologist and occultist. God knows how long Allen & Unwin will take to get it into print. By Christmas one hopes.

I am also writing to Gerald Gough[2] suggesting he contact you, but without mentioning any possibility of practical work.

We look forward to seeing you at Tewkesbury. If you should get stranded on the way to Forthampton do give me a ring and we will endeavour to get a car for you but I imagine Gerald Yorke will arrange to ferry you from the nearest public transport point, which is likely to be at least 10 miles.

[1] Eventually *The Christ, Psychotherapy & Magic*.
[2] Former librarian at SIL.

2. To Kathleen Raine   *11ᵗʰ April 1969*

Dear Kathleen,

Thanks for your note. Glad to have been of help.

There was one point in the article which caught my attention to ask you. You mentioned Dee and Agrippa as Christian Qabalists I believe. Do they have anything so illuminating to say as Robert Fludd? Was not Agrippa connected in some way with Thomas Aquinas?

With regard to *The Mosaicall Philosophy* what with family ties and other commitments I cannot say when I or Duncan will have a chance to get to the British Museum. I would be quite willing to have photostats made by them and sent to me if you could perhaps tell me which are the relevant parts of the book. As an alternative would the Bodleian be likely to have a copy available to the public? Oxford is much easier to get to.

I dropped in on Fr. Duncan the other afternoon and had a long talk with him which seems to have made some pretty hefty penny drop, because he wrote to me most enthusiastically the next day, and is seriously thinking of obtaining a dispensation to study magic at first hand by attending some of my group meetings. It is also possible we may write a book together, possibly called *The Mystic and the Magician*.[1]

Am busy at the moment getting a couple of little books of my own ready for press, on Occult Exercises and Ritual Magic. Also hoping to get a *New Dimensions Blue Book* on the presses by the year's end.[2] Apropos of this, in another long interesting article by 'F.P.D.' there is a question from a poem by Yeats, called "The Hosting of the Sidhe" from *The Celtic Twilight*, 16 lines, commencing with "The host is riding from Knocknarea" to "And Niamh calling, away, come away!" As Yeats died in 1939, this is no doubt still copyrighted material. Have you any idea to whom I should write for permission to quote?

Incidentally, I have been reading some of Yeats' drama, and been very impressed. One has tended to ignore this side of his work owing to prejudice built up against trying to wade through "drama" by other poets. Dylan Thomas got the nearest to success but the poet can never forget the sound of his own voice sufficiently to put characters instead of two dimensional puppets on the stage. Fry is a particularly vivid example. Eliot, from a promising start in *Murder in the Cathedral* drifted further into an emasculated type of poetry/ prose, and to my mind the heightened prose of Synge and O'Casey have been the peak of modern dramatic writing. (Giraudoux and Genet possibly in French, though my French isn't good enough to appreciate it.) These succeed because they are dramatists first and foremost, and poets second. But I had not realised before the extent of Yeats' practical involvement in the theatre, and some of the ideas he was putting across were years ahead of his time. For instance, quoting from Reynolds' *Modern English Drama*: first that the theatre should be "a place of intellectual excitement – a place where the mind goes to be liberated. In order to achieve this, more beautiful and more appropriate language must become the staple of modern drama." Second, dramatic speech must become musical. An actor should so "cherish the musical lineaments of verse or prose that he delights the ear with a continually varied music". Third, acting itself must be simplified. Fourth, in décor all representational effect, as of trees or hills, must be struck out. The "restless mimicries" of the contemporary stage were but signs of decadence and of "an art of fading humanity". He went on to find a sympathetic stimulus in the Japanese No drama.

These ideas are from articles printed in *Samhain*, which were reprinted in *Plays & Controversies* (1923). I must get myself a copy. The point about "the musical lineaments of verse or prose" cuts away, I think, an altogether false division between them that has been built up into axiomatic precepts by generations of academic critics. I am reminded of Pound's point that poetry is purer as it approaches song, and song purer as it approaches dance. In looking through Pound's *Literary Essays* in a vain endeavour to find this I have just come across his remarks with regard to prose and poetry: "The language of prose is much less highly charged, that is perhaps the only availing distinction between prose and poesy. Prose permits greater factual presentation, explicitness, but a much greater amount of language is needed". This, and his remarks about Melopoeia, Phanopoeia, Logopoeia, and the architectonics of form, seem to sum up pretty concisely the technical problems of dramatic writing.

Anyway, the thing is that Yeats has burst into my consciousness as a very modern, exciting and stimulating mind, rather than the obscurantist recherché mystagogue that he is often made out to be. My thanks to you for your article, which caused me to go to a little trouble to go to his original texts.

Forgive me for running on so, but the drama is close to my heart, a fact I usually keep quiet about, but after years of hammering my head against a brick wall, sustained only by my own cussedness and Roma's loyalty, a couple of plays of mine have just been read by a senior reader for The Mermaid who says "Whether the ordinary theatres will ever do you, one can't say. (Though if your work ever receives justice, it should be widely recognised). But, in the meantime, it is obvious that places such as The Mermaid or The Aldwych ought to get cracking on your plays." He is strongly recommending them to The Mermaid and if they won't play intends to hawk them around elsewhere in London for me.

So naturally I am very excited and encouraged, not so much by the fact that they may be produced (though this is obviously of importance) but because an independent knowledgeable assessor has confirmed that I have not been wasting my efforts in pursuing an entirely imaginary talent all this time. We do, of course, as you said, live in an uncongenial climate, and the dustbowl situation of the London theatre gave way, with the advent of the Royal Court, only to a social-realist clique in addition to the perennial commercial one that is always with us. However, as these plays have a raucous, superficially obscene and blasphemous façade (rather like Joe Orton, in depth) they may appeal, as long as they aren't misinterpreted in the direction, but in these matters one just has to trust in the gods.

Must close. Send any diary work direct to me, by the way, not to Toddington, where it will probably be shunted automatically down to W. E. Butler. You will of course be welcome to join us in a working again.

[1] [2] Never came to fruition.

3. To Kathleen Raine   *17th April 1969*

Dear Kathleen,

Many thanks indeed for your enthusiasm over *The Woman of the Rockery*.[1] Having had it rejected by 39 managements (and lost by a few) it is pleasant to hear an encouraging voice crying in the wilderness.

I take your point about the danger of getting bogged (a felicitous phrase in the context) in 'stage Irish'. It was the only way I could manage in the beginning to go on from Synge, O'Casey, etc. However, since then I have written another play called *The Pigeon Fancier*[2] in which I have tried to develop the line started with 'Mrs Knight'.[3] How successfully I am not sure, but Basil Ashmore, the reader at the Mermaid, seems to like it.

I won't send you a copy just now because I know you are going away. I passed on to Basil Ashmore your opinions about *The Woman* in order to encourage him to trust his judgement and maybe importune the Mermaid a little harder on my behalf because of it. Am also sending a copy to Patrick Hodgkinson as you suggest. Many thanks for everything.

We will look forward to seeing you on 1st June and will arrange accommodation. I will be pleased to transport you from Evesham and as it is a weekend hope you can come earlier in the day, so we can talk or get drunk or something.

[1] Subsequently destroyed.
[2] Produced at the Phoenix Theatre, Leicester, August 1969.
[3] Character in both plays.

4. To the Rev. Anthony Duncan *17th April 1969*

Dear Tony,

... ... The thing is that I see occultism as a science (albeit an inexact one, like medicine, psychology, etc.,) – a non-physical science. Therefore remarks of yours as to whether it is 'lawful' and so on really baffle me – they seem sweeping and arbitrary. I know there can be dangers and abuses, but so there can be in any sphere.

I have been very pleased to have sorted out in my mind the distinction between occultism and mysticism and religion with your aid, but it seems to me that you are now muddling them up again.

It may well be that there are aspects of occultism that seem hardly appropriate to a Christian calling, but the same thing happens in all walks of life – to the Christian doctor, the Christian salesman, the Christian PR man, the Christian soldier, and your remark that the devil works by compromise and subtlety is altogether too glib a simplification. He works equally well through uncompromising 'principles' very often. The Cross of conscience that the Christian has to bear surely is that of 'responsible compromise'.

... ... The thing that bothers me though is your preoccupation with the insinuations of the devil, which seems at times to verge on 'old maid's insanity'. I get the impression – I hope wrongly – that I stand a good chance of being cast in the role of the serpent offering the poisoned, or forbidden fruit. If this is the case then it would seem to put paid to any hope of fruitful communication between us.

5. To Kathleen Raine *17th April 1969*

Dear Kathleen,

Your book and letters came just as I was about to go off on a three day business trip, but I managed to put in the post to you a copy of one of my plays. Hope you like it, but no obligation to of course! There's no hurry for its return (if ever) for I have a few dozen more copies.

I liked the Calderon[1] very much – somewhat to my surprise. And my congratulations on having it produced this year. This is an achievement indeed. Let us hope The Mermaid favours the fortunes of both of us.

Thank you too for the guidance about following up Fludd, Yeats copyrights etc. I hope you have a fruitful Grand Poetical Retirement as it might be called following occult precedent, and look forward to hearing from you when you return.

We are making some interesting progress on the occult front on Sunday evenings[2] and we shall be happy to have you join us whenever is convenient. It will be interesting too to have a long talk on literary matters.

[1] *Life's a Dream* by Pedro Calderon de la Barca, trans. Kathleen Raine & R. M. Nadal.

[2] Private house group at Tewkesbury, 1965-9. Described in Chapter X of *Experience of the Inner Worlds* (1975).

6. To the Director, S.I.L.   *6th July 1970*

Dear C.C.,

I have recently been given a copy of the *Work and Aims* of the Society of the Inner Light, dated June 1970. It would now appear that the period of transition begun some few years ago is now complete and that, apart from the continued use of *The Mystical Qabalah* and *The Cosmic Doctrine*, the emphasis and direction of the work is radically different from that laid down in the late Dion Fortune's days and up to about 1960.

I would like to put to you that this original line of work is still of value and possible use to many and that it would be a pity for it either to be destroyed or to be buried indefinitely in the Society's archives.

As the work and aims of Helios Book Service and the complex of activities around it are more along this original line and we retain, I trust, a mutual respect for each other's specialised function, would you consider passing over to us material and archives that are presumably of no more than historical interest to you now?

Our intention would be to edit and publish any material that we thought was worth preserving, subject to any provisos you liked to make. For instance you would probably not want the Society of the Inner Light to be credited as the source but we could credit it to "Dion Fortune" or even "Gareth Knight" whoever the actual mediator or medium might have been. This would save you from unwanted and misleading publicity, and indeed if it were known that we had become custodians of this material it might be the best thing, short of changing the Society's name, to stop the flood of irrelevant enquiries to you that are mentioned in the last two paragraphs of your *Work and Aims*.

P.S. *The Cosmic Doctrine* is almost due for reprint, sales having been very good. We have asked the printers for a quotation and expect to be able to meet all the costs ourselves. If there are any changes you would like to see (bearing in mind it will be a photographic reproduction) please let me know.

The request was politely turned down on the grounds that the Group was still "on the lines Dion Fortune laid down but considerably further along them" and no archives were, or ever had been, available.

7. To the Revd. Anthony Duncan   *7ᵗʰ March 1972*

Dear Tony,

Many thanks for the last two letters and for the typescript of *Lord of the Dance*. It is quite some manuscript. I am hardly surprised that Allen & Unwin turned it down and I do not think you will have much enthusiasm from any other publisher either – short, of course, of direct divine intervention!

I must say that even I blanched at a first sight of it. It is very difficult to get anyone professionally involved in publishing to even attempt to read through page 1 of a manuscript of this type. There is no shortage of people willing to regale us with screeds of their personal philosophical wafflings about God and the universe. Unfortunately there is a considerable shortage of people wanting to buy it.

One has a similar situation in poetry of course – and indeed in most of the arts. Anything but the superlative tends to be strangled at birth by being swamped by the third rate, if you'll pardon the mixture of metaphors.

However, having read your typescript through, I am of the opinion that this _is_ of the superlative best, though that does not necessarily make the finding of a publisher, or a public, any easier. Your ordinary publisher will tell you, quite rightly, that the market for religious books, like the novel, is going through a major recession.

Your book is ahead of its time. We need to start – you and I – a revolution.

So rather than go knocking in vain from inn door to inn door I suggest you bring your little waif to birth in my humble stable. In other words, have it published by Helios.

… … You might, of course, find it professionally compromising to have your name on a Helios book. We could get by with a pseudonym ('Brother Herbert' or something similar!) though I think it would be a pity. I have a feeling that both the religious and the occult applecarts are going to go spinning over very shortly. It will be a divine boot that does it, but you and I, willy nilly, like it or lump it, are going to be mixed up there in the middle of it.

If I may quote from your own manuscript (how's that for one-up-manship?) "O Man! Will you be fearful? Will you hedge yourself about with law? I will teach you to be free with that freedom I won for you. I do not want you law-abiding. I want you as you are. I do not will compliance; I require integrity."

8. To the Revd. Anthony Duncan   *17th April 1973*

Dear Tony,

What a weekend indeed![1] I thought I would be fortunate if I escaped it without some physical repercussions and I am indeed struck down with tonsillitis – make what Daath symbolism out of that you like!

Crucifixion indeed too. I don't think that's putting too high a significance upon it. It certainly felt like it though there is a difference between Crucifixion with a large C – encountered knowingly and voluntarily with spiritual purpose behind it – and crucifixion with a small c – an agonising experience undergone without seeming purpose – and that is what a number of others experienced, the Helios crowd not least of all. If they reacted most strongly it was because they were more vulnerable and suffered the more.

I am aware of the seeming undesirable elements about them, particularly Mr. G, but in the light of later discussion with Dolores Ashcroft-Nowicki[2] and by what I 'feel' about the whole situation, I am confident that things will work out for the best. I hope that none will feel so ill advised as to take any magical action to try to halt the flow of the tide, for their own sakes.

I learned a lot about the Mysteries of the Crucifixion at the weekend, such as the acceptance and adsorption of suffering and malice, and above all the ministry of the holy angels who were, and still are, much in evidence. With such help and protection who needs astral magic?

I agree with you that we are launched on a long and exciting and rewarding ministry, that will see us well occupied until we shuffle off this mortal coil and probably for some period after. I look forward to the impending milestone when I get my current book[3] out and can present an occult system based firmly on valid Christian tradition and the properly differentiated inner realities of things – magical and mystical. As you know, it is based squarely on *The Lord of the Dance* and with a fair bit of general help from *The Sword in the Sun*.[4]

For the immediate future though, what about getting your weekend's lectures into print? Could you send me the typescript? I visualise a fairly simple litho job something after the fashion of the way the Helios monthly catalogues are done. We could possibly do two or three hundred and sell them at something less than a pound. Not a lot of money in it but that is not the main object. I feel it would help earth the forces that were manifest (if you will pardon the word) at the weekend.[5]

In the meantime, all the best for the move, and I will look forward to coming up to see you when you are comfortably in. Love to all the family, animal and human, and I think my special love and thanks to Helga who has not a little of the St. Veronica about her.

[1] Weekend of lectures at Hawkwood College by Anthony Duncan on "The Two Qabalahs" which upset a group of Helios Course supervisors present.

[2] Currently senior supervisor on Helios Course.

[3] *Experience of the Inner Worlds*, published 1975.

[4] Books by Duncan.

[5] Privately circulated in duplicated format.

9. To Dolores Ashcroft-Nowicki   *28th May 1973*

Dear Dolores,

I thought you might like to have, for the record, a transcript of the talks Tony Duncan gave at Hawkwood. I know you don't go along with all he says but as you may be asked questions pertaining to his views it will no doubt help you to have it on permanent record.

I wrote to Ernest about the weekend at Hawkwood, telling him that John and I were happy about his choice of you as designate Director of Studies, but also mentioning that things had been rather 'sticky' in that some of the Helios people were rather upset and also there had been a bit of bother subsequently on the astral.

He has not replied to this but I gather from John Hall, who saw him recently, that he has been having a busy and rather demanding time in other areas recently.

Unfortunately, I did not take a copy of the letter and I don't know whether he has passed it on to you to see, or has mentioned bits out of it, or said nothing at all.

It included a few reservations about your friend Mr. G, who struck me as well intentioned, though somewhat desperately introverted, but whom two independent witnesses had less complimentary things to say about, on the basis of psychic evidence. I don't take such evidence too seriously but felt it ought to be mentioned as he is a Supervisor. Any final assessment of the suitability and capabilities of supervisors and students is, of course, the responsibility of the Director of Studies. I would be failing in my own responsibilities however if I did not pass on to the Director of Studies all relevant matter that came to my notice pertaining to the Course.

The other point was that in the light of the subsequent astral kerfuffle I wanted to avoid as best I could well-intentioned Helios students being tempted to try to influence new trends in teaching by bringing magical pressure to bear. This has happened from time to time in SIL history and means that either the would-be-goods get hurt or somebody else has to spend a lot of effort breaking up the forms they persist in building or in absorbing the energies they send out so they do not get belted by the repercussion of what they misguidedly send.

I hope that my comments to Ernest in this matter have not been misunderstood as signs of Dennis Wheatley paranoia on my part or intention to interfere in the day to day running of the Course.

All this covers a lot of deep and indeed fascinating matter which we could discuss when the family come to Jersey in August.

I have just finished typing up the first half of my new book[1] and I hope to be able to send you a photocopy of what's done so far – so you can have an advance idea of what I may be up to. I am also asking John to send you photocopies of any public articles I do from time to time.

If, as a result of these, you have any queries or problems you'd like to sort out with me, please do write. As my own work diverges from the Helios Course lines there will no doubt be some difficulties caused but good will and ready communication will considerably ease the way.

As Mr Chichester[2] said once about the SIL – whatever the differences of opinion, there was the common principle of dedication to service – and this will ensure that the good will prevail. And often in a final way that surprises everybody!

[1] *Experience of the Inner Worlds.*
[2] Arthur Chichester, Warden of SIL 1946-79.

10. To W. E. Butler   *30th June 1973*

Dear Ernest,

Thank you for your very interesting letter. I should say that I am not entirely in accord with everything Duncan says, though it has become pretty plain to me that it is our appointed task to try, (according to our lights), to build a bridge between the Western Mystery Tradition and the mystical tradition of the institutional church.

The principle trouble is this business of Hindu monism. It may be that there are some, such as yourself, with a sound Christian background, to whom all this is no problem. But to those who have not this advantage, and it includes most these days, particularly in the younger age groups, the whole heritage of the Christian mystical tradition is being lost by default, and Hindu monist speculations are a poor substitute.

I would be interested to know of those Qabalists you mention who do not adhere to the Hindu view. And I would also be most eager to learn where I can follow up what you say about Christian monist philosophy. As I am in process of writing a book which may have some influence on a number of people for some years to come, I would be grateful if you could let me know your information on this as a matter of some importance.

As far as I am concerned the Hawkwood incidents,[1] in so far as they manifested on the level of personalities, are over and done with. I think your analysis is correct, and it all rather goes to show what a potent influence a concerted group mind can be, even by accident. It had not been our original intention to have the Helios Course form into a group, and if this is now a changed intention, I think we need to be aware of some of the risks involved. I am able to take care of myself but others less experienced who come up against this sort of thing might find they had more than they could cope with. The 'Tables of Seven'[2] would seem therefore to demand a pretty close kind of supervision if they are to be a pattern of the future. The Hawkwood incident was, however, rather special, in that there were some powerful archetypal forces to be earthed (pleasant and unpleasant) and most of those involved had little or no experience of this level of occultism before – it being on a par with former SIL Greater Mystery working.

With regard to the idea of 'two Qabalahs' I am glad you find this to be old teaching with which you have no quarrel. One's task then is in refurbishing that which has been overlaid by moth and rust rather than by anything radically new. However, some of the opinions expressed say by Dion Fortune in the early SIL Magazine, are, though Christocentric, of very wobbly theological validity – particularly when she gets on to the Trinity.

However, it is not my desire or intention to go heresy hunting amongst the writings of the past but to build up an approach to the occult that does not conflict with the traditional Catholic religious experience of the West.

There is one point of fact I would like to ask you about in relation to one of the early DF articles on the Guild of the Master Jesus (September 1931). "In the days when I was a member of the TS", she writes, "no attempt was made to develop the contacts of the Master Jesus. In fact He was never referred to as the Master Jesus, so far as my acquaintance with Theosophical literature goes, until I introduced the name. He was declared to be a virtuous Jewish youth, of mediumistic powers, who lent his body for the manifestation of the Lord Maitreya in the same way that Mr Krishnamurti is believed to do for the present incarnation of the same entity. The Liberal Catholic Church, though using Christian ceremonial, aimed at contacting, not the Master Jesus, but the Lord Maitreya; in fact, in Theosophical circles the Master Jesus was very much the poor relation".

Can you tell me if this is an accurate report of Liberal Catholic belief? It seems to me that if one does adopt a Christocentric (as opposed to Jesus reverencing) point of view one is bound to question some of the traditional Theosophical statements about Jesus being a man who embodied a 'Christ force'. This was an early Christian heresy, as I am sure you know well, that St. John went to some pains to eradicate.

I am aware of the reincarnationary ideas of early Qabalism, which differ somewhat from modern ideas, in that it was regarded as a relatively uncommon occurrence, rather than an essential universal means of 'spiritual evolution'. I think the traditional Christian view easily accords with this.

What is less easy is the mechanistic monism of such works as *The Cosmic Doctrine* and the various cosmologies put out by various groups of Masters. I suspect that they are maps of the 'inner creation' (which is to a large extent 'ideo-plastic' – to use Paul Beard's[3] felicitous phrase) and tend to ignore the mystical element, and thus a whole dimension, which is embodied in Duncan's *Lord of the Dance*, which perhaps should be read in conjunction with such intellectualised cosmologies to give a proper and fuller perspective.

As you say, the material of the past may present some problems in using them in *Quadriga*[4] – though it could prove fruitful stimulus to debate. However, I'm letting the idea gestate well before taking any action. I fancy the way will be made clear by the time of the Winter Solstice. I'd welcome the chance to look at anything you think of interest.

I'm glad you had an enjoyable Corpus Christi. Roma and I went to the little Deanery church nearby here on the Thursday. Let me know when you are likely to serve Mass at Glastonbury. I'd like to come. We are all looking forward to spending our summer holidays with Dolores in Jersey, and she has already given some indication of pleasures to come by sending the children some rock. Both of them are well. Richard has a new bike and has developed a deep and long standing interest in gem stones. He finds, grinds, polishes and sets his own stones in costume jewellery fittings and sells them. Made 60 pence at school the other day. Not bad for an eight year old. Rebecca is always full of beans and the biggest chatterbox in the whole county. Roma is very well and we have just bought her a power driven printing press so she can make a few bob printing leaflets for publishers.

[1] cf. Letter 8.

[2] A temporary form of organisation on Helios Course, soon abandoned.

[3] President of College of Psychic Studies.

[4] Student magazine run by G.K.

11. To Dolores Ashcroft-Nowicki   *30th June 1973*

Dear Dolores,

Many thanks for your letter and also particularly for the Jersey rock, which was consumed in short order by the recipients, who eagerly await their visit to the Big Rock Candy Mountain in the middle of the ocean. Only hope their teeth don't fall out at the end of it!

The Hawkwood weekend[1] had more to it than met the eye, as I have endeavoured to explain to Mariton Geikie,[2] who sent me a note of apology, which was very nice of her but really unnecessary as the involvement of *Quest*[3] was just what I wanted. There were a number of powerful archetypal forces, with various inner mediators and hangers-on, (good and bad), at work at Hawkwood that were 'earthed' by those present. This is a relatively deep type of occult working such as few there, I think, were accustomed to. It has an equivalence to SIL Greater Mystery workings of some years ago. All rather different from camping around the astral in romantic garb that newcomers to the subject usually think it to be!

Another lesson to be learned is the power of a closely knit group – and you will need to be a little cautious in formulating "Tables of Seven" because if things go wrong they can take a lot of getting back into control again and people can get badly hurt in the process. But this involves rather complex matters that can hardly be gone into by mail. We can talk about it all later.

Am pleased to say I've received a nice letter from Ernest and I hope to be able to continue a dialogue on one or two technical points over the new emphasis that I'm giving to parts of the traditional teachings. In the meantime I'm progressing with the book *Experience of the Inner Worlds* which I hope to complete by the end of this year and which will present these things in a more coherent whole, I trust.

My present task is to build a bridge between the traditional mystical tradition of the Western churches and the esoteric Mystery Tradition of the West. It is not an easy task, nor a role I would have readily cast myself for, and it involves a re-assessment of all one's terminology and preconceptions. You'll be able to make your mind up about it when you've read the book. It is, however, vitally concerned with the mainstream of the Mysteries and is not simply a question of an 'optional extra' for 'advanced' students.

But this will all take some years of debate and hard work of various kinds. It started in embryo as far back as 1961, began to be practically set up in 1964/5, and became a major commitment in 1969. So Rome is not built in a day, and it's hardly likely that anyone is going to be able to take in the implications in five minutes, or one weekend!

As I said, all are looking forward to their holiday. Do you have any gem stones or pebbles in Jersey? Richard is a committed rock hound and is making a small fortune finding, polishing, mounting and selling them. At least, I pay the capital expenses and he takes the profit! The polishing process, which takes six weeks, and is sited in my office because no one else will put up with it; is like the Chinese water torture but is, I suppose, good for training the soul – or something.

Roma is setting herself up with a printing press, so it looks as if they'll all have plenty of spending money. Rebecca is the only one not coining it at the moment – and she talks too much to do very much else.

We are none of us particularly good at swimming but quite enjoy splashing about in about three feet of water when it is not too chilly. I hope this does not sound too dilettante.

[1] cf. Letter 8.
[2] Helios Course supervisor, later founder of Ibis Fraternity.
[3] Neo-pagan journal run by Marian Green.

12. To Janine Chapman   *20th August 1973*

Dear Ms. Chapman,
I regret that Dr Regardie is slightly misinformed, as I never knew Dion Fortune personally. She was a little before my time.

You come a little late in the day [1] as most of her early associates are now either very elderly or deceased. I suggest you try Mrs Evelyn Heathfield, xxxxxxxxxxx, Lewes, Sussex, who was with her in the 'Land Army' in the First World War I believe. She may be able to give you the address of Mrs Helah Fox, who lives down that way and knew DF very well in the old days.

Mr Butler has been in delicate health for some time but is no worse now than he has been over the past few years, as far as I know. He tires easily, and has many commitments, and so occasionally is somewhat behind in dealing with correspondence.

I regret that this is the only extent I can really help you.

[1] She was researching a book subsequently published as *The Quest for Dion Fortune*.

13. To Dolores Ashcroft-Nowicki *2nd October 1973*

Dear Dolores & Mike,

I have not written before because I felt it best to let John, Mary [1] and Ernest have time to consider what we had discussed in Jersey. They have now done so and John has, I understand, been in touch with you.

It came as something of a surprise to me that John and Mary wanted to get clear of <u>all</u> the Course work. At first they had seemed rather against any change but on discussing it further between themselves came to this quite radical view of passing over even the production and distribution of lesson material. But I see their point in wishing to concentrate on their main concern, bookselling. The Course has now developed so far with its own success that it is becoming something of an administrative burden to carry on as a sideline. I would think that if you can take over all of it, including the revenue, it will be a viable little business apart from its esoteric benefits.

Unfortunately I think Ernest may be feeling that he and his work have been rejected. No doubt others will jump to similar conclusions – human nature being what it is – but I know and I hope you know that this is not the motivation behind it all. And I am quite sure that the steps we propose are in the best interests, material and esoteric, of all concerned, and the future well being of the work. I hope you will be able to reassure Ernest on this point – for his own sake.

Anyway, it seems we are now all agreed in principle and it really now remains for us to meet, I think, and hammer out the details for a harmonious transition.

Mrs. S.[2] has resigned by the way. John sent me a copy of her letter, which was far from complimentary as to my motives. One gets used to being misunderstood as soon as one comes into any position of prominence or authority though it always makes one a little sad. I think she is well rid of though, as far as the Course goes, and she has performed the useful function of a 'scapegoat', acting as a focus for the less charitable feelings of the student-group and taking them away with her on her back. The SIL has an interesting paper on this somewhere.

… … I am sending a 3-dimensional chess set for Carl.[3] It was given to me by my boss who had it given to him at Christmas but felt it was driving him mad. It has nearly driven me mad too so I'd be very glad to get rid of it. Hope you have a lot of fun with it!

New Dimensions[4] is now going out after much travail at the printers. I'll send you a free copy as soon as we're clear of the backlog of paying enquirers. It looks like being a success. Gratifying – but blooming hard work.

I enclose one of the snaps we took when we were on holiday. Roma and the kids send their love and we would like to thank you for doing so much to make our holiday a really enjoyable and memorable one. You know, of course, that you, or the kids, are very welcome to come and visit or to stay, at any time.

[1] Co-founders and Directors of Helios Book Service.
[2] Helios course supervisor.
[3] Son of Mike and Dolores.
[4] Small magazine run by G.K. Successor to original founded by Llewellyn Publications.

14. To R. J. Stewart   *30th October 1973*

Dear Mr Stewart,
I am writing to you at the suggestion of Mr W. G. Gray.

We have tentatively been talking about the possibility of issuing some tapes giving examples and instruction of various aspects of magical working that lend themselves readily to this form of medium.

In my belief Mr Gray could produce some useful material and I would hope to produce something rather better than other examples I have come across already on the market.

Neither of us are familiar with the technicalities involved although I am informed that it is relatively simple to hire a recording studio and to then buy dubbings to market oneself.

I would be interested to learn what expertise or knowledge you may have of this field. And in this I include the use of music without falling foul of copyright.

I am extremely busy just now with the launching of our magazine *New Dimensions* and so on so I have not been able to think through exactly what would be best for Mr Gray to record. I have indicated to him that I would not be able to proceed, because of this, before Spring of next year.

We could start to plan in outline now, however. Please let me know if you think it would be worth thinking in terms of a three way involvement with Gray doing the script and vocal work, yourself providing musical background, and Helios providing capital expenditure and marketing.

I would think – off the top of my head – that two or three cassettes with something on the lines of his Seasonal Rituals would be a good thing to start with and test the market.

Perhaps you would let me know your general thoughts.

15. To R. J. Stewart   *1ˢᵗ May 1974*

Dear Bob,
You will be most welcome on Wednesday 22ⁿᵈ to call for as long as you like. We will also make a point of arranging a baby sitter for the Sunday night so we can come and hear you at work. Folk clubs do not come into my usual ambit of haunts but as this one seems to meet at a pub we can no doubt find our way there.

Regarding the past disagreement between Bill and myself.[1] This is not a matter that rankles with me and it seems that new events have overtaken past ones, and we seem to have developed a mutual tacit agreement to take things from scratch as if the past did not exist. The good parts of it patently do exist of course, in that I learned a great deal from Bill and he got himself published, so it's probably best left at that. I won't bore you with the details, though if you are curious to hear my side of the story you can ask me when we next meet. Briefly it is simply that whilst working with Bill I felt that he had let his patriotism drift a little too far towards some neo-Fascist groups and so I told him I wished to cease working with him – at which he took great exception, seeing it as something of a betrayal.

I must say I left our last meeting very pleased that Bill had met up with some young people who could work with him, because he does have a tremendous lot to offer.

[1] Written up at some length in W. G. Gray's biography *The Old Sod* by Alan Richardson & Marcus Claridge (published by Skylight Press, 2011).

16. To Dolores Ashcroft-Nowicki   *10ᵗʰ November 1977*

Dear Dolores,
John showed me your recent letter to him, which I hope you will not feel is a breach of confidence, although I am flattered by your compliments.

In the interests of veracity and in fairness to Ernest I would like to clarify a point arising from our talk at the Festival Hall. Ernest did not in fact want to break from Helios; he wanted to break from any involvement with me on the Helios Course. In the beginning I had been Director of Studies and after asking him to take over writing lessons he took exception to my continued involvement. I had been training a group at Tewkesbury in ritual methods and had hoped this would be the nucleus of a Second Degree.

I respected Ernest's objections on the grounds that they probably resulted from our working on different inner contacts. The Alexandrian Mysteries, which seem to figure quite largely with SOL, are somewhat peripheral to me.

Later he said he would like to be appointed to the Helios Board of Directors. This did not make any administrative sense so, after my visit to Jersey, we suggested that he run his own show. The administration was beginning to be rather a strain on the bookshop resources, and we made the severance I think on quite generous terms.

Ernest seemed rather doubtful of the wisdom of this and, it seems, put it down to machinations of mine, though for what motives I find difficult to understand. He could however have developed some doubts about my general motives through my resignation from the Society of the Inner Light and my involvement with W. G. Gray. There were, in fact, very good reasons for both these actions but I concede that they could seem dubious or unwise to anyone not immediately cognisant of the inner plane factors involved.

In order not to cause any hard feelings (!!!) when I started my own Course and Group[1] we deliberately divorced it from any direct involvement with Helios Book Service, so that there should be no cause for anyone to think that we had ousted Ernest.

The correspondence you have should confirm most of this.

It is a pity Ernest should have taken this suspicious and emotional attitude, but if his dedication remains true to the Christ and the Mysteries any shortcomings should in some way be guided into ultimate good. As for us, we can but console ourselves that it is God and our duly appointed Hierarchical seniors who will finally judge our stewardship. Let those who seek similar responsibilities look to their own performance! It seems that the modern Mysteries do spread by splitting off from parent groups but it would be nice to see it done on occasion in a rather more mature and courteous fashion than is often the case. I am pleased to say that our own relations with the SIL remain cordial – although no doubt there have been some areas of misunderstanding and hurt feeling in the past.

[1] Originally entitled Gareth Knight Course on the Christian Qabalah, later becoming the Gareth Knight Group.

17. To Dolores Ashcroft-Nowicki   *23rd February 1978*

Dear Dolores,

Many thanks for your most welcome letter, and the slides,[1] and the cheque! A postal cornucopia of good things!

I had begun to get a little worried over the long silence. Wondering whether something dreadful had happened to you, or if, possibly that Ernest had resumed his pontifical crown and finally ordered me to be cast into outermost darkness! I might have known you were just up to your sahasrara chakra in overwork.

Have a good time on your trip. I don't think things will be too bad. A colleague at work has just returned from Haifa, sun tanned, and talking more about good swimming than political troubles. Roma went to Cyprus last year, and although there are signs of tension with the barbed wire barricades between Greek and Turkish sectors, as long as you don't take photographs of the troops things go well enough.

I am pleased to hear that the Mariton[2] business seems to be resolved amicably. I have not seen your exercises for the last seven lessons and would be interested to have a set – thank you very much. Your organisation seems to go from strength to strength and is, I think, a great credit to you. I would be interested to come along to your first conference at the Kenilworth,[3] if you don't think I would get in the way. I have to get round to running a similar kind of thing for my own lot before long and it would be helpful to come along and get some firsthand knowledge of what kind of things to do or to avoid. Nothing like profiting from other people's experience! If I can pay my way by giving a short talk or anything like that I would be glad to oblige, but only if you think it would be helpful. Also, I would like to take up your invitation of a quick trip to Jersey in the Autumn, but we can talk about that later.

My publishing activities seem to be entering a new phase. I am gradually winding up the Helios publishing as I feel it has served its main purpose and there are now other, larger publishers willing to publish books on the Qabalah. When I started, some 15 years ago, nobody wanted to know! I have, however, persuaded Longmans to enter the field in an oblique fashion, and have just commissioned Geoffrey Ashe to write a Guide Book to Arthurian sites in Britain, and Marian Green to do a book of Folk Festivals.

I think you are fortunate being situated in Jersey, and having an accountant for a husband. We are undergoing something of a cash crisis at the moment because the Inland Revenue are demanding three years back tax in a hurry and all the money we had is locked up in stock. They don't seem too keen to take payment in copies of occult books!

I think we will survive without their sending the bailiffs in to sell the furniture but it all leaves a rather nasty taste in the mouth and is somewhat disheartening to see the fruits of one's labours snatched away when one could put the money to so much better use than financing British Leyland etc. However, no doubt these things are sent to try us, and at least we still have our health and strength. I just hope that the Racial Angel is duly grateful for it.

Enclosed you will find a Mowbray's catalogue with an announcement of my book.[4] I think they have done me quite proud, with a front position and double page spread. There is also a copy of the dust jacket. This is just a proof, as the title has to be slightly changed. On the actual final version there will also appear a credit to Josephine Gill and a note saying that copies of the slides can be obtained from you.

I have high hopes for the new book and think it could prove something of a breakthrough across a number of boundaries. The I Ching was very enthused about it anyway, when it was first mooted, and the I Ching does not usually wax enthusiastic without good cause. Have also just had a request from the local Rural Dean to give him some instruction in the Qabalah – so something seems to be moving somewhere doesn't it.

[1] Set of Tarot Trumps designed by Josephine Gill.
[2] Breakaway Ibis Fraternity.
[3] London hotel near British Museum. Venue of 1st SOL Conference.
[4] *A History of White Magic*

18. To Dolores Ashcroft-Nowicki   *4th June 1978*

Dear Dolores,

You <u>have</u> been stirring things up haven't you! I must say I am rather surprised at Alan Adams over-reacting in this way.[1] We more or less went up through the grades of the SIL together and always hit things off pretty well together, though he always had a kind of rigid formalistic streak, which is partly to blame for the present situation I think. It made him a very good Ceremonarius of course, but I shall never forget, when I was librarian, complaining of being cold in the library, and Alan, who as an electrical boffin supervised the heating arrangements, insisting at great length with calculations based upon the thermal output of the fire and the cubic capacity of the room that I could not possibly feel cold. But I did! Though I don't think I managed to convince him.

I do not intend to take public notice of this argument in *Quadriga*,[2] and I rather hope that *Quest*[3] and the others will not either. This not because I want to sweep anything under the carpet but because the quality of argument and the way it seems to be being conducted seems conducive more to heat than to light. So if publicly aired at the moment I do not think anyone is likely to come out of it with much credit and the whole purpose of the original meeting will have been effectively reversed. A neat victory for the forces of darkness in fact. One can tell their hand is in it because of the amount of mis-emotion that is loaded around the matter.

Before much headway can be made I think that one has to define exactly what is meant by the term homosexual and what is meant by the term Mystery training. One obviously would not take in a raving deviate to a group that was doing high level work in purifying the racial archetypes, but there is a whole range of categories that seem to be lumped into the term homosexual, from those who are physiologically close to a sex change to normal people who in abnormal conditions may have had a minor homosexual adventure. Similarly Mystery training ranges from full participation in ritual magic in a closed Fraternity to elementary tuition in meditative techniques by correspondence course. I must say that I do not question my students about their sexual proclivities and have no intention of so doing. Although I am well aware that senior members of the inner plane hierarchy are much concerned about the problem of homosexuality [4] and some of the cosmic implications attached thereto, I must also say that my immediate worries as a practical supervisor of elementary magical training are more directed toward those with a history of drugs, neurosis or electric shock treatment. These provide most of the immediate problems.

My only other comment in this context would be that in my view it is the personal responsibility of each group leader to admit for training those whom he or she thinks fit. I would not attempt to lay down rules of behaviour for other groups, and I would not expect them to do so for me.

With regard to the Conference,[5] I would be pleased to help out and be the main speaker if you wish. I would rather welcome the stimulus to prepare a long talk on "The Mysteries of Isis".[6] If, however, you find someone else you would rather have for the main spot then I can do a shorter one in the morning, but probably on "A History of White Magic", a quick gallop through the topics outlined in my book, which should be out about that time.

I would also like to visit you in Jersey in September. Would a long weekend be OK? Thank you for the offer of a copy of Ernest's lectures in Devon.[7] I would much appreciate having a set.

[1] Furore over attempt by Dolores to convene meeting of group leaders to discuss homosexuality and Mystery training. AA thought them completely incompatible and thus unworthy of discussion.

[2] Student magazine run by G.K.

[3] Neo-pagan magazine run by Marian Green.

[4] As expressed in recent SIL paper.

[5] Impending inaugural SOL Conference at Kenilworth Hotel.

[6] Later incorporated into *The Rose Cross & the Goddess* aka *Evoking the Goddess* aka *Magic and the Power of the Goddess*.

[7] Under auspices of the Ibis Fraternity.

19. To Bernard Nesfield-Cookson   *14th January 1979*

Dear Bernard,

Many thanks for your letter and the interesting points that you raise. I am sorry that I seem to have been misinformed about Rudolf Steiner's original affiliations and will try to correct any false impression when opportunity arises, though the version I wrote seems to have gained pretty common currency. Anyway, we can talk about this and other matters when we meet, which will probably be when I come to talk.

I was not aware of Digby's book on Blake and will try to get hold of a copy, also Barfield's book on Coleridge. I had heard of the latter but somehow got the impression that it was a pamphlet! As you will gather from my book I am enormously impressed by Coleridge, and I also have great respect for Owen Barfield – although I have to read him several times to get somewhere near his meaning. He is mentioned quite a lot in an excellent recent book called *The Inklings* – all about C .S. Lewis, Tolkien, Chas. Williams, and co. I think Barfield and Williams between them exerted a profound influence on the popular writings of the more well-known Lewis and Tolkien.

I require no fee for the week-end (though presume you will pay my petrol to and from and provide free board and lodging while I am there). If there is any reason why you should want to allocate a fee perhaps it could go straight into Eileen's memorial bursary.

I have been asked to be certain to ask you to reserve a place for Mrs Dolores Ashcroft-Nowicki for my course. She has just had to rush off to Australia and could not get round to writing herself before she left. Her husband should be sending the money shortly and I can vouch for her willingness and ability to come and to pay. She is Director of Studies of what used to be the Correspondence Course side of Helios Book Service.

Things are quite hectic at the moment with the book[1] due out this week and quite a lot of media interest. Was on TV last week and have half a dozen radio chat shows to do, and Book Club rights sold too. The inner side of things seems to be making itself felt more and more these days.

[1] *A History of White Magic* aka *Magic and the Western Mind*.

20. To Robert Wang   *10th April 1979*

Dear Robert,

Nice to hear from you again. I received a complimentary set of the cards from Regardie and like them very much,[1] and in fact displayed them on a television show recently in connection with the launching of my latest book, *A History of White Magic*, which I understand Weiser will be publishing in the States. The questions you raise are not easy to answer but here goes.

I consider the Tree of Life and the Cube of Space as separate approaches but I do work them together in my own system. I see the Cube of Space as a kind of time/space capsule that one formulates about oneself before one goes journeying through the objective dimensions of inner time/space. The Cube of Space therefore seems to fit best as a construct within the Sphere of Tiphareth, from which one can then go up or down according to the general rough map of the Tree of Life Paths and Spheres.

It seems to me you may be making things difficult for yourself in the same way that the Golden Dawn people did, in trying intellectually to nail down every iota of symbolism in a complex system of correspondences. You can waste an awful lot of time this way and reap not much more than puzzlement and confusion. In my experience it is best to take the bare bones of the essential symbolism, for instance the three Mother Letters, Aleph, Mem, Shin, as a central axis around which to build the Cube of Space; and then the seven Double Letters as applied to the cardinal points (East, South, West, North, Above, Below) and Centre. Use this in practical visualisation work and allow the minor symbolism to fall in as it may on specific occasions.

Similar rules apply to the Tree of Life in my experience. Just use the Sephiroth in the Queen Scale colours, and let the other colours and symbols of the Paths show up and develop as they may. To do this is to allow the symbolism the opportunity to speak to you – as opposed to stifling it into silence in an intellectual strait-jacket.

To my knowledge the Society of the Inner Light never used the Cube of Space. My own experience of it developed from W. G. Gray's ideas about it plus my own experience. You can follow this up, if you wish, by reference to the seventh chapter in my *Experience of the Inner Worlds*. I also enclose one of the booklets used by the 1st Degree of my group which gives an idea of my approach to the Hebrew letter symbolism.

As regards sound, I have never been one to take a purist view on this. I am sure that few modern gentiles, if any, are capable of pronouncing the original Semitic sounds. The ability to "vibrate" ritual words in a reasonably dignified and dramatic fashion seems to work all right for me. I think W. G. Gray gives quite sound guidance on this kind of thing in his *Magical Ritual Methods*.

Some day I would like to get down to work out a neo-Pythagorean symbol system based on the mathematics of musical tones, working from first principles, but in the last analysis all these symbol systems are but pointers to another reality, and it is easy to miss the reality by concentrating on the symbols too much. As one of the old Zen masters has it: "Teaching is like pointing a finger at the moon. The inquirer must look at the moon, not the finger."

I regret that I have no information on Enochian chess or on the Enochian system at all. Enochian chess in my personal view is another instance of MacGregor Mathers' synthesising genius going rather too far. I am sure a system could be developed from it but life is too short for me to concern myself with it. As to the Enochian Calls, I am not given to scare-mongering over occult matters but I do think that these are dynamite, that we know very little about them, and that they are a doorway to some very powerful non-human, possibly anti-human elemental forces. Your own and Regardie's caution are therefore, in my opinion, well justified.

Like Regardie, I was not impressed with Saures, but as I grow older I tend not to spend much time on other people's systems. Having absorbed most of the basic literature I find that the important thing is for me to put what I know into practice, to develop my own thing, and train along anyone who seems to be sufficiently interested. Having opened one's own door to the inner, one is better occupied going through it, rather than examining the décor of other peoples' doors.

I hope this goes some way to answering the points you raised. If you want to raise any more – feel free.

[1] The Golden Dawn Tarot deck produced by Regardie and Wang.

21. To Richard Brzustowicz Jr   *27ᵗʰ October 1979*

Dear Richard,
Your letter gave me much pleasure. One gets the occasional eulogy and the occasional abuse. It is difficult to decide which is usually the more irrelevant. Once in a blue moon one has the satisfaction of receiving a letter from someone who has not only taken the trouble to read one of one's books with attention but also to have maintained a sympathetic and critical eye and then given one the benefit of the result. I am very grateful to you.

It was from similar circumstances that *Experience of the Inner Worlds* was engendered. Anthony Duncan, an Anglican priest, was sufficiently impressed by my earlier *Practical Guide to Qabalistic Symbolism* to get involved in a dialogue with me that went on for about seven years during which were spawned his own book *The Christ, Psychotherapy & Magic* and my *Experience of the Inner Worlds*.

One of the strange experiences of authorship is to have one's fresh ideas of yesteryear impaled like dead butterflies – some of them crumbling and going off a bit, others incorrectly labelled or mounted, and you just have to sit and make the best of it. Parts of *PGQS* I find somewhat juvenile and embarrassing after the passage of nearly 20 years but it is good for the soul having to live with it, though plenty of people seem to like it, so one has the consolation of the royalties steadily providing a little jam for one's bread and scrape, and likely to go on so indefinitely.

The most disconcerting thing I ever heard said about that book was from a lady who told me she kept it by her bed-side and lived her life by it and was extremely hurt and annoyed that I had publicly made a remark that parts of it were inaccurate. Another criticism was from a homosexual in California who said it was packed with sexual repression.

Experience of the Inner Worlds is still too close to me in time for me to have started having too many reservations as yet – apart from one or two factual howlers, such as King Arthur being a Saxon. However your own remarks indicate to me clearly where the yawning structural cracks are going to come. Just as *PGQS* was marred by my ignorance of real mystical dynamics, so *EIW* falls short by my superficial knowledge of the real Eastern tradition.

Heigh-ho!

Defence of a basically untenable position is, of course, pointless. But there are redeeming features that will, I think, outweigh the inadequacies. In the context in which it is written, that of trying to rid the modern Western tradition of some quasi-Eastern assumptions, I think it accurate enough. If I have overstated my case and tilted my lance at the mountain of the Eastern tradition instead of the mole-hill of Theosophy then it is a matter of elementary dynamics to tell who is going to come off worse! I think Buddhism and the Tao will survive my assault.

However, it gives the scent of a fresh quest to my slightly jaded nostrils, so I do not have to live with the debilitating thought that I know it all, and who knows, yet another book may come of it all. I reckon one book a decade is quite enough for any sage so that can be my effort for the late 1980s. After I've read a book or two. So I am also grateful to you for your suggestions as to reading matter; also for the other technical points you raised, which I will follow up.

... ... Your remark about hoping for a history of magic from the inside on the lines of Charles Williams' *Descent of the Dove* opened up vistas of possibilities for me. I had not thought of it before. The motive behind the *History of White Magic*, after the surprise of being asked to do it, and by a traditional religious publisher to boot, was simply to try to explain to ordinary intelligent contemporaries that I might not quite be the credulous nut that at first sight they might take me for on hearing that my main interest in life was magic. Whether I have succeeded or not remains to be seen.

In trying to promote the book, like a good author should, on chat shows on local radio between pop records, I began to doubt my own honesty and then even the possibility of being honest anyway. Stephen Skinner makes the point in a preface to one of his reprints of old magical texts. When one enters into magical apologetics these days it is so easy to try to deal with it all under the umbrella of psychology. This way people do not get frightened; there appears to be common ground; and modern accepted attitudes and prejudices do not have to be challenged. But it really isn't good enough. Firstly, magic is largely to do with concourse with discarnate spirits, human and non-human. Try that for starters on a chat show! And then there is the even more vertiginous ground of the nature of reality, etc., etc., which I have in any case, I think, as you say, fudged in the book.

Frankly I just do not think that I have the intellectual equipment to sustain a very deep argument in these matters. Though I might improve with age, should I live so long. I have been rather swept off my feet by Coleridge, with whom I am having a sustained intellectual love affair and it is fascination with his theory of the imagination which accounts for the largely psychological bias of the *History*. But even here I am beginning to get out of my depth. I do not have a very philosophical turn of mind, and although I might pass for a scholar or historian by those who know no better, I am principally an experimental occultist who hopes that the subject might one day merit the attention of real philosophers, scholars and historians. But if I can do anything to open a dialogue with such, without making a fool of myself or my subject, then I am willing to scribble a book or two.

22. To David Hicks   *9th June 1980*

Dear Dave,

I do not think my views on esoteric grades have altered much since I wrote the *PGQS*. They are for the most part an administrative convenience for those who run teaching groups. In this they are much like the classes in a school or the years of study in a university. It follows that, in a comparative sense, between one group and another, they have little meaning. A low grade in one group may be the equivalent of a high grade in another. Similarly they are akin to examination certificates or degrees. To have achieved a certain group may be like getting a 1st Class Honours in Classics at Oxbridge, or a Pass Degree in Sociology, Humanities and Needlework at North East Turdsville Polytechnic. Similarly, whatever the academic certificates of learning one may have, the real crunch comes in earning a living and making a contribution to the world outside academe and here those without any qualification whatever may do as well or better as those loaded with scholarly honours.

The SOL has no grades at the moment, which is causing some problems. A 50 lesson single degree tends to be unwieldy as compared to say the GK Course which has a 1st Degree of 10 lessons, a 2nd of about 15, and a 3rd of about 25, which are, roughly speaking, concentrating respectively on basic theory; practice in image building; and contacting mystical archetypal powers. All of which you have done in perhaps a less structured way over the past 15 years or so.

On completion of the 3 Degrees I administer a ceremony to my people where they can formally make the Unreserved Dedication to service of the Great White Lodge. However, in essence, this is a matter between themselves in their heart of hearts and the Great White Lodge. They do not really need my ceremony. It may on the one hand simply express a pious hope for the future, or on the other ratify something which came into effect years ago, perhaps in a past life.

There is an objective grade, or real grade, but I would not presume to identify it in myself or anybody else – but you will know from observation that some people have more spiritual and magnetic 'clout' than others, just as groups have, and there can be powerful people in weak groups and vice versa.

I hope this answers your questions, which, if you grasp what I am saying above, will reveal themselves as being largely meaningless, as based on misconceptions. (Learn to ask the right question and the right answer will become obvious!)

From what I said about the externalisation of the Hierarchy and the Aquarian type of 'open' group, and the development of the Hawkwood series, and the SOL semi-open conferences, it should become apparent that 'grade' does not have much practical import. We do the work in hand with whoever happens to come to hand. This may pull some people in over their heads a bit but I fondly hope that their own lack of development will be in some measure a protection – but it is a calculated risk.

There is thus equal opportunity for those who have been on the SOL Course five weeks or five years, or for any grade of my own group, or indeed anyone who has walked in off the street. The justification is in the parable of the workers in the vineyard, who all got the same pay whether they had been there since morning or just before knocking off time. Or Jesus walking into a crowd of fishermen and seeing who followed him. Who knows what the inner spiritual dynamics are? This also applies to Tewkesbury [1] and those who took part.

[1] See note to Letter 25.

23. To Dolores Ashcroft-Nowicki   *9th June 1981*

Dear Dolores,

Thank you for your news of the Igraine[1] contact. There seems to be a great deal happening on a number of levels all at once.

I have been sleeping as if drugged, since Hawkwood,[2] with odd flashes of vivid dreams – one of which was a long discussion with Margaret Thatcher! I have had a general feeling that somehow the King[3] takes over at night. But I have also been aware of a certain difficulty in their coming to terms with the conditions of the modern world. This seemed to be eased yesterday though when I was prevailed upon to go to Avebury stone circle and the little church (dating from 1000 AD) in Avebury village. There was a deep spiritual contact in the church and it and the stone circles helped to span the centuries. I had a very pleasant contact with the King and the Queen and have had the King in evidence since, in place of Gareth.[4] There is also a level of levity in all this in that they seem at one level to be very human 12th century characters. If I am somewhat awed at their military and equestrian prowess they are enormously impressed with my 'flying chariot' and my bravery and skill in using it. As well as the King, Sir Kay and Sir Mador de la Porte rode to work with me this morning. (All this must sound quite mad – but it does give a certain sanity to the otherwise portentous proceedings.) There are some strange theories being bruited about the technology involved. They insist on calling the accelerator the "spur"; and have a not too accurate but superficially plausible theory that the gear stick is a sort of magic wand, or rod of power, that conjures one horse, two horses, three horses or four horses beneath the bonnet! What is one to make of all this?

At a more serious level, work on the book[5] proceeds apace, and I have become particularly aware of the point Igraine made to you of the repetition of patterns. This happens particularly for instance in the mythology of the Celts who had their own race memories of being flooded out from their homelands around the Baltic about 500 BC, which coincide with the earlier Atlantean disaster.

[1] Archetype of mother of King Arthur.
[2] Hawkwood College workshop on Arthurian Legend.
[3] King Arthur archetype.
[4] One of several knightly archetypal contacts.
[5] *The Secret Tradition in Arthurian Legend*

24. To Carr P Collins Jr   *20ᵗʰ August 1983*

Dear Carr,

Just received your round robin about a possible 1984/5 party and felt moved
to write because of what seems to me its rather down-beat note. From where
I am viewing things the occult scene was never more alive and vibrant, even
if you were to go back a century and more to the days of the Golden Dawn,
the Theosophical Society *et al.* And much of this stems directly from the
foundation work laid down by Dion Fortune and her associates such as 'Kim'
Seymour and Christine Hartley in the late 30s and early 40s. Not that I think
it necessary to go back to the old rituals except in so far as they furnish seed
material for current growth. I think things only look depressing if one looks
at the scene in 'Piscean' terms; the basics in terms of 'Aquarian' type occult
groups are now growing strong.

The new type of group is not an enclosed formation of disciples
formed about a strong personality but an open forum that comes together
periodically, say once or twice per year, for a strong mutual stimulus – with
members going off and doing their own thing, individually or heading up
smaller groups. This is very much the kind of thing that has been happening
at Hawkwood over the past few years.

… … More importantly, the Hawkwood meetings see the coming
together of practising occultists from all manner of traditions in a way which
would have been inconceivable only a very few years ago, and, yet more
significantly, going away to work together and pursue a common end.

This is all done in perfect freedom and informality, which is somewhat of
a far cry from the encloistered and jealous disciplines of yesteryear.

In their way I think your parties have also been working along this
new and freer trend, and I think they have done much to break down old
prejudice. However their tenor is more social than esoteric and I do not
see an easy way on from this, for I fancy there is still a very great deal of
the secrecy and jealousy you mention. But this does not depress me, for it
is nothing radically new. And certainly I have no desire to try to pour new
wine into old bottles. Let those who wish to hang on to the old attitudes
do so. They have done good work and much of their work remains valid
and will remain in the future slowly to wither as it becomes out-dated.
Meanwhile the new growth will continue on the new wood. And it's all very
exciting.

25. To David Hicks   *21ˢᵗ April 1985*

Dear Dave,

Surprise, surprise! I hope it's OK writing to your work address but I fancy you've left Tarn Cottages and this is the only one I've got.

When last we corresponded we were not seeing things eye to eye too well, which seemed a pity given our sterling work together at Tewkesbury some twenty years ago.

However there are obviously such things as inner wheels and cycles or such like, and on the face of it you are, or have been, on an arc somewhat ahead of mine, because it has come in no uncertain manner to Roma and myself (via the old Sunday evening technique!)[1] that we need to be concerning ourselves now and in the immediate future with occultism as applied to the problems of the planet.

Having registered this and got furiously swotting into ecology, human geography, modern political history to throw into the cauldron of inspiration along with ley lines, astrological influences, alchemical transmutation, etc., etc. what should I find when walking into Longmans but a 'sign following' in the shape of your World Studies book, on the new publications shelf.

So, I don't know whether the esoteric aspect of things still interests you, but I thought the least I could do was write and say I think you had a lot of things right when you wrote before and if I was less than sympathetic to them, it was because I had other important things to do first, that faced in another direction, so to speak – towards the inner Earth. I've written most of this up in my recently published *Rose Cross and the Goddess* but the time now comes when a new phase commences for me and the destiny of the nations and humanity's treatment of the planet, acting as a single organism, becomes paramount.

[1] Refers to early private house group at Tewkesbury, described in Chapter X of
    Experience of the Inner Worlds.

26. To Alan Richardson   *21ˢᵗ April 1985*

Dear Alan,

Have received the folder of magical records from R. A. Gilbert.[1] It's obviously quite interesting material as far as the general occult public may be concerned but I must say it confirms the diagnosis to which other considerations have been leading me. This is that, at any rate at this stage of the game, Colonel Seymour was by no means a main spring or leading light of the SIL but 'doing his own thing' with C.C.T.[2] and others as an offshoot of the main thrust of Dion Fortune's work. There is no implied criticism in this – just that I feel one should beware of glamorised assessments of the work of this sub-group based on their own self-evaluations of the time, or since.

I find it difficult to write off the work of Dion Fortune in the early war years for instance, from the evidence given in her weekly letters that I've made recorded extracts from, in the way the report of 17.7.42 appears to do … "the Lodge has suddenly become vibrant and active; while it was merely passive, religious and intellectual it was not worth powder and shot. Now that K. has ????? it up…etc". [3]

I'm sure this is an honest opinion based on personal involvement of events at the time, but I think its objective validity somewhat wide of the mark. The work done by this sub-group that is reckoned to be causing such concern to the 'Black Forces' appears to be no more than searching the past for times when they were all together before.

Whilst this may make colourful reading, certainly for those immediately involved, and to a lesser extent for those with a taste for historical romance, it is by no means the stuff of the kind of occult work that causes Dark Masters to tremble. In fact it is a phase which most of us in the game go through, and, if we are lucky, it never gets published. When it is, as for example in some of Annie Besant and C. W. Leadbeater's writings (*The Lives of Alcyone* etc,) it all gets rather embarrassing sooner or later – there is so much subjective element and personality inflation, albeit in superficially disguised form.

I think in due time – they were obviously a talented bunch – they would have worked through this kind of stuff (as DF did in her earlier days) and got onto some work that was of importance. It is thus rather poignant to see the note of what may well have been an attempt by one of the senior I.P.A. behind the Lodge[4] to get through to them and divert them from their inward looking preoccupation with their own personalities, past and present. They registered this as an unwarranted interference from a disreputable entity.

I'm sure in course of time this would have been rectified, but it would seem that, for whatever reason (and this could have been the <u>inner</u> reason) the group ceased to exist as a functioning entity. Dion Fortune's work, on the contrary, has gone on from strength to strength, with temporary vicissitudes.

Thanks for letting me see this material. No doubt it will make good grist towards a generally helpful book one day, but I do think it quite important not to try to inflate its importance. It could lead many impressionable students into glamorously inviting cul-de-sacs.

I return it under separate cover.

P.S.

On material of this kind one frequently gets what scientologists used to call 'dub in'. That is, problem material of the present fantasised into a different milieu in time or space. This I fancy was what was at the back of the Avebury sequence with DF cast in the role of an oppressive baddy.[5] None the less truthful of course, at its own level, but how much is subjective and how much objective is anybody's guess though of course the former is always high, particularly in the sphere of personal relationships and where the scryer has a personal involvement in what is going on.

[1] Well known Bristol bookseller and expert on esoteric matters.
[2] Christine Campbell Thompson, aka Christine Hartley. Also Dion Fortune's literary agent.
[3] Letter indistinct. Obvious sense seems to be "livened it up".
[4] Apparently Dion Fortune's Socrates contact, responsible for *The Cosmic Doctrine* in 1922/4.
[5] Vision recorded in Alan Richardson's *Dancers to the Gods*.

27. To Diego Lipovich   *26th August 1985*

Dear Diego,

Thank you very much for your letter and for all the interesting information it contained, about yourself and also the Virgin of Lujan.[1]

I enclose a photograph of myself and my wife Roma when we were on holiday in Greece a couple of years ago. The building you can see in the background is the Parthenon on the Acropolis at Athens. The booklet I am holding in my hand is about Socrates in the Agora. The Agora is the old market place of ancient Athens and we are looking pleased with ourselves because we have just succeeded in locating the actual place where Socrates spent his last hours, as described in Plato. The site has recently been excavated and exposed by American archaeologists but so far no-one seems to be taking much notice of it, so we had the place to ourselves. No hordes of tourists. (Of course we do not regard ourselves as tourists!) Actually it was just like a voyage of remembrance for us, because we both have very strong esoteric links with ancient Greece. In fact we tended to regard ourselves as more Greek than the modern Greeks who live there!

You seem to have collected a good selection of books, and really you probably have all you need to make considerable progress. One fault of many occult students is to read too much. Actually there is no great harm in wide reading as long as it does not prevent you from putting into practice something of what you have read, but all too often the new student is so interested in reading the latest thing that he never gets round to actually doing any of it.

I do not much like Franz Bardon or Aleister Crowley as guides for practice. Of course they are both competent practitioners but although one may learn some interesting theoretical points from them they lack a sound moral basis, which makes them dangerous people to follow in practice. Crowley was much into drugs and perverted sexual practices and Bardon's attitude to Elemental creatures, binding and enslaving them, is just not acceptable to me.

David Anrias gives a good elementary introduction to the Planetary Hierarchy. Some of the portraits seem to look alike, and I have my doubts about some of the statements – particularly with regard to 'the Master Jesus' who is a great deal greater a being than Theosophists of his generation were inclined to realise. To my mind, Jesus is the Master of the Masters, Head of the Hierarchy – more like what the Theosophists tend to regard as the Lord Metraia.

Dion Fortune of course is well worthwhile and directly in line with my own tradition. *Esoteric Orders* is first rate. *Psychic Self-Defence* needs to be taken a little critically – it was an early work and marred by a little too much credulity and psychic 'glamour'. W. E. Butler is of course very sound. I knew him well, as also Dolores Ashcroft-Nowicki, whose little book on ritual is quite good. I have a great respect for Alice Bailey and *Telepathy and the Etheric Vehicle* is probably, in practical terms, one of the most important of her works – which is nice because it is also one of the shortest! Ed Steinbrecher's book is a good practical guide – the instructions on visualisation absolutely first rate. (Incidentally, there you will find the answer to one of your questions. You should not visualise yourself in these imaginary journeys. Rather should you concentrate entirely on <u>being</u> there. Take your own presence for granted and concentrate on what you can see, hear, smell, feel). I think the book deteriorates as it goes on, however. All the astrology and speculative material about 'aliens' and such can well be ignored. This comes from the fact that he is, first and foremost, an astrologer – and also because, like many people, he takes the old Golden Dawn symbolic correspondences too literally.

This leads to another of your questions – about the location of the Star and the Emperor. At the time of writing the *PGQS* I felt inclined to follow Crowley's theory and make the change, in parallel with the change between the cards Strength and Justice. However, that was over twenty years ago, and I am now inclined to think I was wrong. So I suggest that in putting the Tarot Trumps on the Tree of Life you put the Emperor on the 15th Path and the Star on the 28th. Also that you revert to the old order of the Marseilles Tarot, and regard Justice as Trump VIII on the 19th Path, and Strength as Trump XI on the 22nd Path. Though ignore this last advice if it confuses you.

To be quite candid, it really does not matter, because I have discovered in the last twenty years of practical experimentation that you can use any

Trump on any Path. However, when one is learning there is much to be said for starting with a fairly rigid symbolic structure, and the traditional one as given in the Golden Dawn derived books is as good as any. I am at present writing a new book on the Tarot – to be called *The Treasure House of Images* – where you can read all about this at length, but you will have to wait for this, I regret, until 1986 or early 1987.

Israel Regardie's *Art of True Healing* is one of the most useful practical books that there is, and was the first I ever published as an occult publisher when we set up Helios. Although the material is perhaps better developed in his longer book called *The Middle Pillar*. I don't know if this is still in print. Both though suffer, to my mind, with taking Golden Dawn symbolism – particularly the Hebrew Names – rather too literally. A little more flexibility and human warmth and common sense is called for.

Recently I have been advising members of my inner group to try working with a modification of the exercise as developed by some disciples of Alice Bailey's Tibetan in *The Rainbow Bridge*. I enclose a copy of my instruction sheet, as you may like to try it. Members of my group have reported very favourably on it. The key to all of this is the stimulation of the centre above the head – whether it be called Kether or the Thousand-petalled Lotus or whatever. It is quite easy to stimulate and once you get that going satisfactorily all else should follow more or less automatically.

In my last letter I spoke about starting a network of dedicated workers around the world all linked in common purpose for the welfare of the planet. I think the stimulation for this may well have come from Nuestra Senora de Lujan – but that is a little secret between us for the time being (and any of our friends). I propose to call this confraternity The Keepers of the Planetary Flame and I enclose an instruction sheet which I shall send to other possible co-workers in due course. I have people in mind resident in Canada, the United States, Mexico, France, Greece, South Africa, Nigeria, and Australia. No doubt others will follow. However, to begin with, I think we need to get the polar axis working, so to speak, between Braintree and Buenos Aires.

Ethel Contursi has also just written to me, as I expect you know, and I am sending her copies of these enclosures too. I note that she has a group of students, of which you are a member. As the greatest progress in occult work can be made through group work rather than in isolation it may well serve to help you best as well as others if I give practical advice to her on organising group work. Anyway, let us see how we go.

[1] Form of Virgin Mary, patron saint of Argentina.

28. To Mark Whitehead *16th January 1986*

Dear Mark,

Was fascinated indeed by the contents of your last missive which mirrors much that we are doing and realising here. Or perhaps we are mirroring you! Actually it must be that we are all reflecting the powerful new inner plane forces that are flooding in just now.

I have just completed a Star Ritual which we hope to perform a couple of times at choice times and places in the near future. Will send you a copy of it then, though as it requires eight officers you may not be in a position to perform it in the near future. However it could probably be adapted. More of which later.

Surprisingly the bear woman has been turning up here as well, so it appears she is not merely a North American phenomenon. I think the old Indian traditions have a message and application that will prove to be world wide. But this still means, I would think, that those of you who are on or near the actual territory have a special and important part to play in all of this.

The information about the second Golden Hind[1] is also fascinating. There is obviously a lot of worthwhile research, historical as well as esoteric, to be done on the Gilbert-Dee connection. Gilbert was a great researcher into magnetism was he not? I am being pushed very firmly into studying galactic astronomy at one extreme, and nuclear physics at the other, with a view to creating a new and extended vocabulary of images and number signification for the new age.

Am also, after due prompting, immensely enjoying Melville's *Moby Dick* which somehow seems relevant to it all!

[1] Full size replica of Drake's ship.

29. To Mark Whitehead *28th July 1986*

Dear Mark,

I enclose a report of the private meeting of the Greater Mystery group at Hawkwood recently. We initiated two more Dedicands and in the evening I conducted the group through the Path working that you had sent me. This acted not only as a link with the North American contacts which you represent but also with the ritual work of the following day which was the formulation of a star temple in Chokmah for the purpose of bringing down the redeeming power of "the Cosmic Christ of the Star Lords" to release all souls imprisoned in ancient sites as willing or unwilling sacrifices. This also was a resolution of certain problems that had been thrown up by the public Hawkwood ritual which you attended.

Just after the public Hawkwood I had a most significant 'synchronicity' in the form of an unexpected meeting with a lady from Toronto who had been conducting a party of Canadians and Americans round sacred sites in Britain and Ireland. She had had a powerful urge to make contact with me which was quite uncharacteristic she said, and when we met in Braintree she felt impelled to give me a moonstone egg that had been dug up in the Canadian Rocky Mountains. It is a most powerful magical artefact with a strong Dee element.

Roma and I continue to get Indian contacts – and they extend now to other members of the group. Latest one is with the State of Virginia and Pocahontas – who was an Indian 'princess' who came to England and died here in the early 17th century. Thus an important talismanic link.

We live in exciting times and ones of great magical opportunity.

30. To Mark Whitehead   *2nd December 1986*

Dear Mark,

Many thanks for your recent letters – and welcome back to the fold – not that you ever really left it. If it's of any comfort to you I did exactly the same thing in my earlier days in the Society of the Inner Light. However I hope you will not feel too hard about it as you are undoubtedly in a very exposed position and subject to fiercer pressures than most people in the group. The reasons for this you have already put your finger on – the dual nation problem for instance, but every problem represents an opportunity and it seems to me you are uniquely positioned and equipped to pull together divergent forces of a trans-Atlantic nature, which undoubtedly go very deep indeed and I for one would not pretend to be able to fathom just exactly what is involved in this cauldronful of forces, with its bits of Dee, Gilbert, Indian, European, Old World/New World, Lands of the Mystic West etc., etc., etc. It is my personal hope and hunch that in due time a pattern and grouping of you (Rab, Bernie, Janet, Chuck, Peter, etc.) may form with a clear sense of your own destiny *vis a vis* the group and the larger dynamics involved. You yourself will also have been particularly vulnerable to the consequences of the May Hawkwood disruptions in that you were also initiated on that occasion. So it is really hardly surprising that you have had a very rocky ride since then. It is really all too long, complex and personal to go into in detail in a letter but if we get the chance for a private chat in the future I feel that you are perhaps deserving of a more detailed account of events in May and immediately after. It was a real scorcher for many of us believe me, and I'm sorry that you too caught much of the brunt of this without our realising it. I'm glad your head pains were not of an organic nature. Sometimes (not often) unequilibrated forces hit the physical direct, as well as, or instead of, the mental and emotional levels. I have just had a basinful of this myself, with old back trouble recurring that had seemed totally cured a long time ago, coinciding with the latest Hawkwood meeting which, while successful, was very powerful indeed and slightly off balance in one of the workings. (To point up the synchronicity it was due to visiting the earthquake simulator at the Science Museum at the behest of Michael Bartholomew!)

It seems that you are quite psychically sensitive and closely tuned in to the group, which would account for the reactions you have been getting. This is all to the good and a cause of congratulation even if it has been rather too much of a good thing over recent months.

Anyway you now realise the subtle and insidious way in which inner plane pressures make themselves felt. It helps to have very open communication lines to alleviate this kind of thing which obviously isn't easy for you for geographical reasons let alone anything else. But feel free to let it all hang out. Contacted occult groups are by no means all sweetness and light on all the levels and human nature being as it is, due to the Fall, we spend much of our time in negative feelings about each other and events. Very often the best course is to let it run rather than try to repress it. Of course sublimation through prayer and spiritual recollectedness is the model precept – but usually easier said than done! In practical terms one learns to realise when it is happening and a good diagnostic indicator is when the reaction is out of proportion to the cause. For example when a trivial slight provokes profound outrage. And when all is said and done I have found the most useful sentence in the Degree Papers to be "Learn to fail well". We all fail, frequently and sometimes grievously. But one "fails well" by getting up, dusting yourself down, and staggering off in the right direction!

31. To Rab Wilkie
October 1987

Dear Rab,

Thanks for yours of 6th October. I went across to Arthog for their meeting of 20th September. It may be as no surprise to you that the Sirius influence was very strong. Also we are having difficulty understanding exactly what is going on. (I seem to be largely quoting from your own letter in what I have to say here!) However, it does all seem to be of considerable importance and to be under the aegis of quite high and capable inner plane hands. So we are content to be the pawns on the chessboard in a game that seems rather similar to *Alice Through the Looking Glass.*

Another remarkable event was a meeting at Hawkwood of the other 'main' Tolkien group, which I also attended together with two of my principal aides Kurt and Philip.[1] If we thought we were just going to give a helping hand to some relative beginners we soon had another think coming. Despite the lack of experience of most of those present, it turned into one of the most powerful magical events of my whole experience. Two major rites were performed: i) the 'Unmaking' of the Oath of Féanor; and ii) the Reconciliation of all the Elven Kindred. It struck back in its effect to the beginning of time, and the Luciferian fall. Quite incredible stuff.

As a consequence I trust you will not mind if I invite members of this group to 'tune in' to the joint venture of 8th November. Please let me know quickly if you do object.

With these kind of forces running, and general resonances into Lemurian and Paradisal times I am now no longer surprised at the unprecedented amount of misunderstanding, prejudice, and generally fouled communication that has attended the getting of the Tolkien material going. However, the key is contacting the Valar – under the will of Ilúvatar.

… … I also note your remark about rivers. The most evocative map I've ever seen is one of the British Isles that is completely dark except for the network of rivers. They are like veins and arteries in a human body with all their tributaries. And one realises how the land is segmented and shaped by the natural flow of the waters. At the French Revolution (which had its esoteric aspects apart from the unfortunate excesses) it was a remarkable move to rename most of the districts of France after the rivers.

The Round Table too I've been realising also has its application to the Periodic Table. Ritual being formulated!

[1] Launched as "The Fellowship of the Valar" under Michael Beechey.

32. To Philip Dunbar   *10th December 1987*

Dear Philip,

Thanks for your report. I enclose a copy of the working I did at Hawkwood, together with a rough diagram of the layout.

The basics of the altar arrangement is a circular schematic diagram of the first ten elements in the Periodic Table.

I find there is a vast amount of realisations relating to all this – from the Lords of Form or archangelic hosts (whatever term one chooses) who laid down the basic structure of matter (a special application of the Hermetic axiom – "as the created – so the Creators/Lords of Form/Elohim"– through to mankind's relationship to the various elements and common compounds during his history on Earth, from flint, through metals and explosives, to chemical fertilizers and radioactive materials. The structure of our own bodies (mostly H, C, O, N) and of the common life support systems (photosynthesis, structure of amino acids and biological macro-molecules) all comes into it.

And I find it quite astonishing that the Tarot Trumps as proto-god forms fit so easily into the system. As someone said, I think there is the foundation here for an occultism based on the material universe <u>as it is</u>, rather than as perceived by traditional pre-Baconian science.

Scope for a bloody great book here, but I'm taking my time. Have been getting strong hints of what's needed particularly of late by totally unexpected contacts from 'the Mahatmas' behind Blavatsky. There's a turn up for the book!!

33. To Vivienne Jones   *23rd May 1988*

Dear Vivienne,

Hope you had a good trip to Glastonbury. Nice to see you at the weekend, along with other members of the regular gang. It all went very well I thought, and I was particularly pleased by the way so many of the newcomers to it all took quite a powerful working in their stride.

Here is the MQS embroidery book. Like so much about MQS, the needlework bit is yet another aspect of her that connects up to deep archetypal goddess patterns. This book was bought at Holyrood, which was where she lived when she was Queen, in Edinburgh, and where Rizzio was murdered at the instigation of her husband Darnley. Though the tapestries are for the most part to be found at Oxburgh Hall, on more or less permanent loan from the V & A.

Roma and I, Vi and Alan Robinson visited there last year and I found the tapestries, which she did in captivity, very impressive. They used contemporary prints for their patterns and so there is also a trans-Atlantic link in some of them (A Byrde of America, for example). There are also a number of hidden messages, such as the ginger cat with its paw on a mouse's tail, which represents Elizabeth keeping her in captivity in a kind of cat and mouse game.

The juxtaposition of the various panels on the so-called Marian Hanging (p.100) struck me at the time of our visit – particularly the five going up the centre, like the central pillar of the Tree of Life.

At the bottom is "A She Dolphin Fishe" (she of course was originally married to the French dauphin). Above that comes the arms of Bess of Hardwicke, who was, in effect, her jailer. The centre piece is of two trees, one being pruned and bringing forth fruit (herself and the child Prince James) and the other unpruned but sterile (Elizabeth, the virgin queen). Above that comes her own monogram and surmounting all – a phoenix!

I'm sure there's a lot more that could be interpreted from much of these embroideries, although some I think are lost.

Anyway I think you will find this book quite an evocative source, as it tells much of the personal history and destiny of Mary, besides going into the detail of the needlework. No hurry to have it back – and feel free to show it around or loan it on as necessary to anyone who seems to be a valid part of this work of regeneration of that which has been repressed, despised and rejected.

You will find this quite a strong contact. Even as I write I get words and phrases pushed into my mind. However, if the work is done with right motive and good intention there should be no adverse reactions. Rather, the more it is worked with, the more balanced and fructifying should the whole thing become.

The main danger I think comes from an old karmic pattern surrounding Mary and maybe the Stuart line – and that is that others seem to want to break in and <u>use</u> them for their own ends. I think this equally likely in the present on the occult scene – therefore, as we have discussed, one needs to exercise a certain care in who wants to crash into this work for reasons of curiosity, personal aggrandisement, or glamour. If that happens, as with the consequences that result from the alternative problem of neglect and repression, you will have a very good chance of having a lot of flying claws of a Kilkenny cat fight about your head and ears.

If the opportunity arises, a visit to the MQS house at Jedburgh, on the Scottish borders, could be useful, but probably not essential. That's where her death mask is – as also a copy of the letter she composed (I think to the French king) on the night before her execution. But that should be obtainable relatively easily from other sources. I'll have a look through my history books and biographies of the time.

34. To Lynne Wycherley   *25th July 1988*

Dear Lynne,
Thank you very much for your Hawkwood report [1] and for so thoughtfully sending me the Tarot lay-out. The owl and the radio also was an absolute delight.

Was much interested in your Dee contact. He has been around intermittently for quite a long time, and at one of the early Hawkwoods impressed me to distribute snowflake obsidians – his black mirror in the British Museum being also of obsidian. On another occasion (or it may have been the same) I felt impelled to provide an empty chair for him! And of late things Elizabethan have been coming through with increasing steady energy. I know it's Armada anniversary and all that, but underneath all the tourist hype there is a genuine desire from the inner to make certain realisations conscious and Dee seems very much at the back of it. His four-fold injunction certainly seems very relevant in the light of the four-fold Tarot pattern I was teaching. Also I fancy there were typically Elizabethan double messages in his saying "Are you listening" – meaning the beacon towers are also bell towers, with all the connotations that that implies. And "twill be <u>fed</u> to you" suggests yet another mode of perception or ingestion besides the visual and the aural.

Your image of the figure with the lantern processing round the circle of Trumps like stained glass windows is very evocative – and I wondered why it seemed so important for me to pin up all those line drawings my daughter did. It was a kind of outer reflection of what you saw.

Indeed it suggests a whole new symbol complex to work upon – a kind to 20 seater Round Table. And no sooner did I draw out a sketch of it then I was hit by the image of an icosahedron – the 20 sided Platonic solid – forming a kind of glowing living crystal. But I've not yet had time to try to develop it any further from there.

Finally, your perception of Hawkwood as a spiral of energy seems very apposite – and I'm sure we did set a lot going at this very pleasant weekend.

[1] On Hawkwood Tarot workshop.

35. To Paul Sugar   *1ˢᵗ November 1988*

Dear Paul,

As regards trying to develop the Dee contact the enclosed might be of some help in providing a potted esoteric survey of what lines might be followed up. It is the script of a talk I gave at the annual Merlin conference over here last year and has since been published in a collection of conference proceedings called *Merlin & Woman*, although this particular piece is entitled *John Dee, the Elizabethan Merlin*.

You will note there are lots of trans-Atlantic connections and this seem to be quite an important issue these days. The three main lines seem to be the Dee/Canadian connection, in search of the North West Passage; the legend of Prince Madoc and the tribe of white Indians; and the foundation of the Virginia colony and in particular the initiation of Captain John Smith into the mysteries of the Powhattan tribe and the subsequent journey of the Indian princess Pocahontas to England, where she was presented at court but died before she could return home. Her grave at the port of Gravesend has in fact become a little known shrine of Anglo-American accord. There are some very strange threads in all of this including one of her descendents being closely connected with Woodrow Wilson, the League of Nations President.

This ball park is the one to concentrate on for a live and valid Dee contact, for he seems to be back of much of this. There is of course a great mass of rather dubious and spurious speculation and investigation into the Enochian Keys and Calls. The Golden Dawn rather made a mess of it in their general synthesising ardour and some of the contributions of Crowley and his followers we could well do without. My own instinct is to steer clear of this side of things although it has been strongly hinted to me that there is something to be gained in this general area in the province of numeric magic squares and the change ringing of bells. These have been described to me as "tongues of angels" and I think more likely to be so than the rather dubious elemental ambience of much of the so-called "angelic" language of the Enochian scripts. I fancy much of this was somewhat corrupted Kelley material and that although there is no doubt power in there, it is almost certainly safer, and probably easier, to start again from first principles. However, we have a long way to go yet before any of this becomes very intellectually clear and for the present the most promising and productive line to Dee seems to come from the trans-Atlantic links.

There is only one extant portrait of him, but it can serve quite well as an image. I was rather forcibly struck recently by the very close likeness there is between this and the statue of Melchizedek outside Chartres cathedral. And Dee is certainly more of a Melchizedek figure than a proto-Thelemite magician. I get quite a strong contact with him from a photograph of the River Thames that I took from just where his house stood at Mortlake, and where he must have gazed many times; and the river line in these parts is probably virtually unchanged since his times.

The figure of the Hieroglyphic Monad can, I think, be quite helpful, although I have not gained much enlightenment from reading the text. He undoubtedly thought highly of it, but it does go to demonstrate the great gulf there is between human mentation in the course of a few hundred years. And indeed I also think that in this kind of short hand version of *The Cosmic Doctrine* a lot depended on his verbal explanations that went with the diagram and its textual notes.

36. To Mara Freeman *24ᵗʰ January 1989*

Dear Mara,

Thank you for your letter. The story contained in *The Green Stone* did indeed look very interesting when it first appeared, and it was first brought to my attention as an item in a newspaper. However, I have to say that it is not, amongst the circle of my acquaintances at any rate, taken very seriously, and this includes a colleague whose judgment I trust who has met the people involved.

The general consensus is that it is a not unfamiliar situation of some inexperienced psychics getting rather overheated in their enthusiasm, hyping each other up, to the point of overstating the evidence. No doubt one or two objects were found although there is some reason to doubt the veracity of the find by the river. The sword in the bridge turned out to be a 19ᵗʰ century artefact and my own theory is that those concerned got themselves psychically mixed up with the residue of a nineteenth century magical group who had originally placed it there.

One does not have to scratch very deeply into the group soul of these islands before one comes upon all kinds of ancient grievances and causes, many of which tend to focus around the rejected Stuart line of Catholic kings, and in particular Mary Queen of Scots, who is a very charismatic figure to this day. From my limited experience of treading American soil there is not quite this tangle of psychic complexity just under the surface. In New York for instance there seemed to be a relatively thin layer of big city goings on, much of it not too pleasant, and then one was back through the founding fathers to more or less virgin Indian territory. In California the dynamics would be somewhat different due to the Spanish and Mexican overlay and different tribes of Indian but I would expect much the same. In Europe one is much more conscious of living on an historical compost heap, and this can be quite disconcerting for psychics who hit levels deeper than the trivial.

In all of this spiritual intention is very important, and so one tends to get what one expects, or takes for granted. Thus the very real difference between Jungian (or any other) psychology and magical work tends to be blurred over. The two are very far from synonymous because magical work is concerned with training inner sense perceptions to relay an awareness of a real inner objectivity. This is by no means the same as the unconscious or the subconscious mind. But the type of imaginative workings being published these days or conducted in various workshops is very much a Mickey Mouse operation if regarded as mere psychology. Path workings are not tame, believe me, if approached in the right frame of mind. The problem for writers such as the Matthews, or Bob Stewart, *et al*, is to prevent people getting in too deep too fast – rather like the writers of *The Green Stone* appear to have done.

Whatever the implications of this book and the lessons to be learned from it, it seems pretty safe to assume that it bears very little relation to the Holy Grail and the deeper levels of the Arthurian tradition.

37. To Rab Wilkie   *3rd April 1989*

Dear Rab,

I'm sorry to hear that you have been neglected to a large extent by all and sundry in spite of all your newsy letters that have been full of interest. I suppose you can at least feel what it is like to be "a lone voice crying in the wilderness" but we cannot let this situation go on indefinitely as, under these circumstances, I think even John the Baptist, in time, would have packed up his traps, said "Sod it" (or "Sod them") and gone home, maybe to start a locust and wild honey farm.

Anyway, whatever the others may or may not do by way of reciprocation, I can at least take account of my own share in this matter by putting pen to paper, now made easier by the fact that I have divested myself of all official position within the group now that we have the 3-fold magisterial system working with the UK group, with Magus for the year, Immediate Past Magus, and Magus Elect.

Not that this has meant any let up in magical work. We now have an Eastern sub-group in action, which meets every six weeks to do a Path working and a ritual, the main thrust of whose work appears to be centring on London as big city/psychic centre and the importance of the Saxon contribution to the Mysteries of Albion (the Celts up to now seem to attract all the public attention).

Added to this are various ad hoc jobs, from PWs undertaken at short notice from inner or outer instigation, to the re-opening of Bob Stewart's temple in Bath, where we go by invitation. Roma and I have also recently had our attention drawn to the esoteric importance of Belgium, which no-one ever seems to take much notice of but which has played a unique role in European and Anglo-European history from being the pathway or gate for incoming tribes in pre-history, through the strong Burgundian power to the site of massive blood sacrifice of a passing age in recent times and currently of course as the centre for the European Economic Community. We spent some evocative minutes up the high bell-tower in Bruges, famous for its shrine of the Holy Blood, and learned of other interesting natural supernatural sites that seem very evocative, in the Ardennes, a hilly forest region in the south of the country, with the largest underground lake in Europe amongst highly spectacular and vast caves, all under an area called the High Fens, where one is enjoined not to leave the beaten tracks by night to follow lights because they are likely to be will o' the wisps leading one into the swamps.

I've also got quite a workshop itinerary on for the first half of this year, that started with a lecture to the Arthurian Society at the University of Oxford and goes on to include two Tarot workshops in Bath and Bristol, a weekend on Alfred Noyes and the Popular Imagination at Hawkwood, and a day at Norwich on its importance as a psychic centre. (Which place isn't an important psychic centre I begin to ask myself these days.)

All this included a recent return trip to New York which went very well indeed, including a synchronous thunder storm while I was reading a passage from The Lady of the Fountain by Chrétien de Troyes. That seemed to impress the Manhattan natives all right!

It was nice too to have the opportunity to meet Mark and Bernie, together with Janet and Marina. Bernie took me up into N.Y. State around Carmel looking at megalithic sites which are very impressive indeed. I don't know why Americans bother to come across to Europe in search of such things. There are sites of at least equal interest and value on your side of the Ocean – and which, moreover, have not been messed about with, physically or psychically. I'll be writing a bit about it for *The Phoenix*[1] so won't go into it in detail here, except to say that the white horse continues to seem to be an important totem animal for us. Not only does our group have its most important centre at White Horse Hill near Uffington but at the other end of the world, so to speak, you keep popping up at White Horse – a kind of anchor man to the team it would seem, with your feet in the real wild. Anyway as another synchronicity, as Bernie and I were setting off on the old Indian trail in search of megaliths so were we accompanied by the very excited cries of a white horse in a nearby field – who got similarly wound up on our return.

In general it seemed to me that things are set to take off vis-à-vis the American branch of the group. I had over a dozen enquiries about further training or group work while I was in New York, which I have passed on to Bernie – and also a couple of offers of alternative bases for magical work that might prove more suitable in the long run than Lower Manhattan. Paul Sugar, with whom I stayed for the week, also seemed a powerful force for helping things along if we all get our act together. The general feel was indeed that there was a lot of power flowing and about to increase its flow, so, as I told Bernie, I feel that my recent release from formal duties with the UK group may well be part and parcel of a general inner plan to enable me to devote more energy and attention to getting things moving States side – although I should say that the woof and warp of the fabric of the Mysteries over there has got to come from those native and resident there. I can give the occasional push and shove to help get the boat floated – thereafter it's you lot who will have to man the oars. However I think much has been done by the three of you already that is highly commendable – and in by no means ideal circumstances.

Many thanks for the copy of the Song of Valinor and I hope it will at least stir Michael Beechey to responding. I have no direct communication with this group nowadays, having helped to get it going it now has to sink or swim by its own efforts. I think it will do all right though.

I've also a bit of writing to do in the next year and a half – about a quarter of a million words all told. Project 1 is *The Magical World of the Inklings* covering the magical dynamics in the work of Tolkien, C. S. Lewis, Charles Williams and Owen Barfield. Project 2 is a book version of my Tarot Course, extended to cover advanced work also. Project 3 is a major opus *Stars, Crystals and Heroes*[2] all about cosmic patterns and how they are formulated and expressed in manifestation through the agency of the Celestial Hierarchies.

When I get a minute I'll give some study to your form and sound ideas. Such principles are indeed the foundation of any magical system, from John Dee's to Tolkien's elven script. All the best with your endeavours.

[1] Small magazine founded and run by Bernie Buedden.
[2] Eventually abandoned.

38. To Mark Whitehead   *7th May 1989*

Dear Mark,

Many thanks for your recent letter. It is good to know that you have settled in in New York without too much trauma. I imagine it must be something of a culture shock for any normal human being to enter the maelstrom but I suppose its all right if you don't weaken. Plenty of raw energy around it would seem, anyway, if you can tap into it rather than be swamped or overwhelmed. It must be quite a help though being part of a pretty cohesive family.

Anyway I am sure it is good news for Bernie too, and for any aspirations we may share about getting the Work started on the eastern seaboard there, which would seem to be the logical place – apart from Canada itself. Although that again is I think a different kettle of fish which Rab seems to be plugging into at various levels – last seen haring over the Baring Straits I imagine on the way to Shambala and the Gobi Desert. Actually I have a feeling an oriental link might be coming in at some stage, but first things first. It's just that I was reading some Steiner wherein he was talking with some considerable respect for the Baghavad Gita, and then was coincidentally jumped by a young Indian lady from the Krishna temple who pushed some related material into my hand which struck a kind of chord. However I already have my quiver full of other arrows at the moment so I'd no doubt do best to get them fired off first before looking round for anything new.

I've set myself a pretty stiff itinerary the first half of this year and am just beginning to feel the strain. Just as well I gave up running the group otherwise I would have sunk I think. I've had one kind of workshop or another going on every month and with the opening up of another sub-group in Southend at John Selby's place, the magical working weekends are proliferating somewhat. Six a year for the main group, and eight a year with the sub-group, plus odd occasions such as invitations to work at Bath with Bob Stewart. I shall probably cut down on my public workshop activities next year, even perhaps bringing the Hawkwood sequence to a close. After about a decade or so it seems to have served its purpose, and it may be America that demands my attention in this regard for the immediate future.

The next phase seems to demand a return to concentration on book writing. I've just contracted to do *The Magical World of the Inklings* for Element Books, which will cover most of what I discovered (duly censored) in Hawkwood workings on Lewis, Williams and Tolkien – plus a philosophical stiffening from Barfield. Also I'm closing down the Tarot course and contracted to put that into book form with Aquarian Press, plus a new advanced section over more magical as opposed to divinatory aspects. Then there are two contracts in the offing, another with Aquarian for my much brooded over work on celestial hierarchies and such, to be called *Stars, Crystals and Heroes*,[1] and then a very practical book on working with patterns based on the Tree of Life for Penguin Books' Arkana imprint. I'd also like to do something Arthurian, although fairly small, for Gothic Image at Glastonbury, who are getting interested in doing some publishing. Added to this are new editions of *The Occult – An Introduction* and *A History of White Magic* which may be co-published by Llewellyn Publications in St Paul – which is where I first started in this book writing game. Can a wheel be coming full circle I ask myself?

You mention swapping notes on celestial hierarchies at some time. Pleased to do so when opportunity permits. However I do not have a lot to offer at the moment as on that score it is mostly swimming around in the back of my skull like a lot of luke warm porridge. However, as a basic structure, I've found the system of nomenclature of Dionysius to be a useful one, and it is elaborated by Rudolf Steiner in a couple of quite useful little books entitled *The Spiritual Hierarchies and their Reflection in the Physical World* and *The Spiritual Beings in the Heavenly Bodies and in the Kingdoms of Nature*. No doubt you have your source of Steiner books over there.

The 9-fold system ties up pretty well with the Tree of Life anyway, as an alternative to the Hebrew system generally in use. Mind you, it is all pretty arbitrary and relatively virgin territory. My line of attack is going back to first principles wherever possible, such as making inferences from the patterns in nature to discern the type of entity that would have been likely to have laid down such patterns – be they chemical elements or simple life forms or species, all the way up to types of astronomical body or the destiny of nations. Bit of a tall order really isn't it!

Your modifications to the Table Round formula seem to be absolutely fine, and I'm glad you have the wit to take the initiative in this way and to carry it out so obviously appropriately and ably. No doubt modified patterns are needed to suit different inner conditions on each side of the Atlantic. I will do what I can to help but at root it is up to you fellows who are native or naturalised there.

My visit seemed to have quite an impact one way and another, no doubt because a lot needed to be got into a short space of time. To add to everything else Paul Sugar just wrote to say that when he took me to the airport on the last day on his arrival back home all the clocks had gone on the blink!

[1] Subsequently abandoned.

39. To Bernie Buedden   *16ᵗʰ May 1989*

Dear Bernie,

Many thanks for the photographs, they look real fine. Pity about that one of me that seems to have been translated to another plane, however the one of the back of my head wandering off into the woods has a certain nostalgic charm. However, the pictures of the 'root stores' have come out very well and Roma could scarcely believe her eyes, as I think would be the reaction of anyone who is familiar with megalithic remains over here. We'll be interested to see what scholarship and popular recognition finally makes of them. I mentioned to Paul that he ought to buy up the surrounding real estate to erect some burger stands and other ethnic delights and a fortune might be made! However, he seems to have more than enough on his plate just now with pulling gradually out of one business (dentistry) and getting set up in another (infusion). Life as he lives it seems to be great as long as you don't weaken, but he and the whole family showed me tremendous kindness and hospitality so I'm very grateful to them all, and also to you for pointing me in their direction last year.

Too bad about the paucity of follow ups from my enquirers. This is partly due I suppose to the 'glamour' syndrome of wanting to deal only with the man himself and not bother with any intermediaries. You can guess what my reaction to that is. The other may be the general resilience of the American, or New York, mentality. They are certainly easy to work with in a workshop, as (when they aren't throwing bricks – or questions), they meet you more than half way, as compared to more phlegmatic British audiences. However, I fancy that when one has passed on to fresh fields, they are likely quickly to forget about you in their enthusiasm for the next guru who swans into view the next weekend. I don't know what one does about that. I guess that people like you and Mark and Janet and Rab, and even Reid, are in a special class, insofar that you showed a pretty firm commitment in the first instance by coming all the way to Hawkwood.

Anyway, you can never plan in too much detail in this game. It's just a case of sailing on, and seeing what hoves into view, and stays with you, or tries to sink you. I'll be interested to hear how you get on with your meeting with Cyra, and if you get any follow up after you have sent out a copy of *The Phoenix* to all and sundry.

Marilyn continues sending me Tarot lessons, and I have a great deal of time for her, but the Tarot may well be her main interest rather than the rest of what we are involved in. I also heard from Helene. It is not easy to see quite what her line is. She is a great esoteric tour organiser, which is not quite my scene. I must say I tend to cringe at the thought of bus loads of American tourists disgorging from their vehicles at Mount Sinai, the Temples of Egypt, or the Holy City of the Incas, to indulge in homespun rituals, meditations, sound vibrations and pendulum swinging. It seems a sort of insensitive trespassing on to others' domains. However maybe this is just my inherent snobbishness and insularity.

She says she is very keen on Dion Fortune, and she would like me to go there and do something some time. Much as the location attracts me for some irrational reasons I am not too sure just now. Fact is I am feeling somewhat jaded from quite a demanding programme of weekend workshops and lectures this year and I just can't even think of taking on anything new – in fact my thoughts are more inclined to seeing what I can do less. Partly this is due to my having entered into my book writing mode, which means waking up early every morning to knock out a thousand words or two, with the mind subconsciously working on the material for the rest of the 24 hours. As I've got a list of four or five books to get through I'm rather in the frame of mind of the camel regarding the final straw.

However, no doubt I will come out of this somewhat negative frame of mind when I have got the immediate programme of weekends out of the way. Only two to go now, Hawkwood in May and an advanced Tarot job at Bristol in July. Whatever happens, if asked, though, I don't think I should be able to resist another visit to Manhattan, as New York for some strange reasons seems a home from home – not that I would ever want to live there! Of course Roma and I love big cities, and New York is certainly all of that despite the violence and the squalor – which is what you get, to some degree, in big cities anywhere. If I can give talks or workshops that relate to what I happen to be writing at the time then the work involved is not too bad. My trouble is I always have to be original – which makes for quite exciting and unpredictable workshops at times, but which is far harder work than just regurgitating what one has written in old books.

40. Jonathan Poston   *22nd May 1989*

Dear Jon,

Many thanks for your letter. Yes, things can get very hectic indeed in the Work and despite your generous suggestion not to bother writing back I feel that there is sufficient that is important to say that is raised by what you wrote.

W. E. Butler should not be confused with Bill Butler – a different character altogether – who is best known for his scissors and paste job known as *The Definitive Tarot*. The one I'm sure you mean is Ernest Butler (the W I think stood for Walter). You can get a good contact through his books such as *The Training and Work of a Magician* in all of which the essence of the man and the initiate comes through quite strongly, and I imagine too that he would be up your street. Roma and I will be happy to fill in with any personal reminiscence that might be helpful to you when next we meet. Dolores Ashcroft-Nowicki edited a book of his essays and collected articles last year – which contains a picture of him (along with me and John Hall) and it would probably be helpful for you to get it. Unfortunately I forget its title – but it's done by Aquarian Press. Roma has also had one or two quite strong inner contacts with him over the years I think. I don't know his 'Mystery Name' and I'm sure would get no thanks form him if I did and passed it on, whatever the reason. I don't consider that astral projection etc. is outdated or outmoded. These things have their cycles and times and seasons and I think we are due for a swing back toward them in the group possibly. Certainly W. E. Butler would be your man for that kind of approach, allied to the highest motivations of Mystery work.

The theological speculation and discussion you mention can be a great bore (and when it starts at Hawkwood I take it as a cue to go to bed) but it does have a certain place, but perhaps in terms of interior reflection. I find it useful to check my assumptions from time to time against the writings of C. S. Lewis and Anthony Duncan, for example. Words are hardly adequate for noumenal realities but there is also a danger in going too much the other way and bathing in a vague glory – the holy glow rather than the Holy Grail.

As Wm. Blake always insisted, the spiritual realities are clearly defined – not draped generalities. So your statement that "One does not need faith in God and Christ – for the mystical occultist has gnosis" sounds alarm bells for me as insistently as those occasioned by the most opinionated hobby horse riding by our homespun theologians. All depends on what you mean by gnosis.

C. G. Jung is not one I'd have chosen as a glowing example, because when you get down to it, past the superficial similarities of his psychology with the inner realities, one finds him as materialist as the rest of the medical and scientific establishment, taking and misrepresenting ideas he's picked up from Mystery related sources. So, eschewing the intellect is all right as long as one is really transcending it and not just copping out from the problem of defining what is not easily definable. There is also, I think, a valid need for some at least in the group just now to ask and find answers to some pretty basic questions as to the fundamental dynamics of mysticism and magic and how they inter-relate. Indeed this might well be the growing point of the group. The final answer will come through direct magical and mystical experience, but I think it does no harm, and may well do some good, to air some of these matters intellectually – so long as intellect does not become a substitute for or limit on active experience.

41. To Mark Whitehead   *13ᵗʰ July 1989*

Dear Mark,

Many thanks for your letter. Yes you can say that again, about my always seeming to have so much on the go. The further one gets along the Way the busier it all becomes. This seems to be a matter of some envy from many who are at an earlier stage of things, at any rate in the current life, and I can remember the time when it would have seemed almost inconceivable to me that one day the time would come when I sometimes felt I had more than enough of it. Inner experience seems so infrequent and remote in the earlier days, but further along down the line it gets like trying to handle a busy telephone switchboard, and run messages and do odd jobs as the same time. However, not that I would have things any different, as it brings great fulfilment in many ways. All we need is about twice the number of hours in the day. Perhaps things are arranged a little better in Eternity.

You also put your finger on an important point about getting out from under the authoritative guru archetype. In passing on the leadership function of the group in this way – which is working out very well so far – I feel we have an important step forward in group dynamics, that hopefully will have a wider effect if it can be effectively implanted as a pattern on the inner. That is the distinction that needs to be drawn between an Office, or function, and the individual who may happen to be providing a vehicle for it at any particular time. A great deal that is wrong in human affairs stems from failing to make this proper distinction.

It was particularly instructive for all concerned to find that at the last group meeting which I was unable to attend (the first I've missed, ever) the power came in as strongly as ever, in fact by all accounts even more so. Thus the group realised that they did not *need* me, that they were capable of doing things on their own. And this was very good for me and also very good for the group. Also I feel I now have a bit of catching up to do on some practical living that I may have missed out on in earlier days with all the hassle of getting channels for inner things organised. Hence the shock that some people find when, at a lecture weekend, they find me in a quiet spot not reading books of higher philosophy but the mechanics of motor cycles or horse racing form! Which revelation is also as good for them as it is for me. The good earth and all its wonders cannot be denied, which is one of the abiding spiritual pathologies that often besets those with too strong a sense of destiny about the esoteric and the inner worlds.

Not that one is turning one's back in any way on the inner, but the deeper one gets into all this, the more one also finds that a kind of psychic pendulum has to be balanced up. The more one gets into the inner the more one has to be committed to the outer. In other words true spirituality has to be expressed on all the planes. So do feel free to approach me at any time on points of ritual or whatever. I am only too pleased to give advice, for what it is worth, based on the benefits of experience.

The outline working you enclosed seems very good to me and I hope that it grabs Mike Harris or Mike Waldron sufficiently to take you up on some kind of cooperative working. Therefore I think it best for me not to try to answer your direct question about four possible British sites to choose. There are in fact umpteen one could pick, with various nuances in mind, and in the last analysis it can be a fairly arbitrary choice, spiritual intention counting at least as much as psycho-physical detail (for the most part).

Incidentally it also seems to be the case that absolute temporal synchronicity is not a necessity in such hook ups. In fact I would go so far as to say that probably if one is within the same week, or even month or moon phase, that is generally speaking enough. Saves a lot of hassle over time zones too!

I would not worry too much about you and Bernie not coming up with exactly the same ideas. We do find that this is very often the case with the group over here these days, but it only comes from working together as a group entity for a long period of time. So things will need to be agreed between you on a more normal human basis of discussion and general give and take rather than the easier way out of getting inspired with the same ideas at the same time. If this seems disappointing remember that we had to go through this stage too, and over a number of years as well. It takes quite a time to form a group egregore, and it is very early days to talk about a group over there with you all.

Hope that all continues to go well on the home and job front, without which most esoteric plans tend to fall apart from lack of physical foundation.

42. To Rab Wilkie   *19ᵗʰ November 1989*

Dear Rab,

Many thanks for your recent letter and also for the most interesting bits of mammoth ivory. Never knew there was such stuff still around, but then who knows what might be buried under the tundra. I get a feeling that this Bering Straits connection between the Americas and Siberia could be of considerable importance in future work.

What makes me say this is the development of my own personal contacts towards a pan-European kind of Mystery focus centred off Denmark that might be regarded as a kind of synthesising centre for all the various European Mysteries, and which I am calling for the present the Hyperborean Mysteries of Europa. One might expect of course some kind of initiative of this kind in the present upheavals in Europe, east and west of the old iron curtain, aptly manifest in the Berlin wall – and there is manifestly quite a bit of pushing and shoving going on between various of the racial or folk angels on the inner planes. Getting involved esoterically in this kind of thing, as Roma and I have recently done on a trip to the traditional killing fields of Belgium (the Arthurian "waste lands" – home of King Ban of Benwick), is rather like being a beetle crawling out of the woodwork on the floor tiles of a cosmic *palais de danse* on a Saturday night.

The island incidentally is that of Ven, and that utilised by Tycho Brahe for his Uraniburg, or castle of the stars, where he investigated the stellar regions as well as conducted alchemical experiments. A fascinating character, who wore a gold mask, after being disfigured in a duel. Although a nobleman he married a peasant girl, called Christina, and had a dwarf, Jeppe, whom he credited with prophetic powers. His catalogue of 1000 stars and other observations enabled his protégé Kepler to eventually work out the laws of planetary motion. It is all evocatively recounted in Alfred Noyes' poetic sequence entitled *The Torch Bearers*. I did a weekend on it last May at Hawkwood and it has not stopped resonating since.

I mention all this because I get the feeling that the Mysteries of the Hyperborian Europa are but one third of a Mystery system that is concerned with the cosmic secrets behind the precession of the pole stars – hence HYPER-borean (that is, beyond the North). My hunch is that there is another centre somewhere in Asia and another somewhere in northern America. Beyond that, all is guesswork for the present, but I shall await developments with interest.

As might be expected bears have a large part to play in all of this. And it was something of a tingling shock to see on the newsreels last weekend of the opening up of the Berlin wall, a bear walking amongst the people. Apparently the bear is the totem or heraldic animal of the city of Berlin.

Added to this I had a pretty horrendous spiritual experience when Roma and I went to see the new film called *Bears*. I suddenly had a cosmic vision of the responsibility of the Fall of Adam for the fall of all nature, making it red in tooth and claw. As a consequence I have been unable to eat meat or fish since! (But that's my problem.) I'd be interested to hear if you get any vibes or intuitions along these lines.

43. To Mark Whitehead   *23rd November 1989*

Dear Mark,

The latest edition of *The Phoenix*[1] just arrived and it is good to see that it is still flaming away there. Actually the name itself is quite apposite at the present time as we have been getting the symbol of the phoenix coming through in other magical contexts. As you will have gathered from the newsreels things are hotting up, one way and another, on the continent of Europe – which has kept my own concerns tending to face eastward rather than westward over the past few months.

Nonetheless I was much taken with the linked ritual effort that was set up at this end by Mike Waldron. Rab, in his six monthly letter in my direction, tells me this was largely operated by you at the New York end. I trust that it all went OK, as by its very nature the amount of ritual accoutrements to take account of was quite formidable even for an experienced group of ritualists. I was also a bit nervous about the amount of horn blowing envisaged, as open horns can be difficult to sound, and often overly strident when they are successfully blown – thus tending to break up the subtle etheric forms, shake up the immediate participants from out of their meditative depths, and alert the whole neighbourhood for up to half a mile around! This kind of thing is best reserved for the climax of workings therefore, and then sparingly. In the event, following the lead from W.G. Gray's *Rollright Ritual* recording, we used a horn with a reeded mouthpiece, which worked very well.

[1] Small magazine founded and run by Bernie Buedden.

44. To the Revd Canon Anthony Duncan ***15th December 1989***

Dear Tony,

Thank you for your usual newsy Christmas card, which always makes an interesting read and brings back happy memories of yesteryear – particularly of the wild crew in the front pew.[1] It always sets me thinking along the lines of doing something similar for ourselves, but this always founders on the grounds that the recipients of our cards are such a divergent bunch of assorted cliques – all interested in different aspects of us, and with widely differing ideas no doubt as to who we are (ah – if only we knew that, as Schopenhauer said – or was it Kierkegaard? – but enough of name dropping of authors I haven't read!) – and so it becomes impossible to say anything more than to wish the joys of Christmas – but then I suppose, what more needs to be said? Anyway I have chosen to send you an unholy card this year, as I am sure you get plenty of the holy kind anyway, and besides I'm sure you don't need reminding that there is a religious side to Christmas in there somewhere.

You may be interested to know, though possibly keen to keep it dark, that a very flourishing white magical group is now operative, whose training is based on the foundation of the exercises in *Lord of the Dance*. I've given up active leadership of this now, although still very participative in an 'emeritus' capacity. It has a cyclic kind of leadership and the outgoing one found it a salutary experience to meet up with you (coincidentally!?!) when he was taking up office. I still wonder from time to time what white magic is all about, but it seems to be the thing that I was sent here to do and organise, so on the assumption that I am not being serpent led (perhaps an optimistic one) I just continue to get on with it. My latest definition is that it is Holy Spirit led active prayer. Much of what we are led (?) inspired (?) to do has its parallels in international events, from the ringing of the church bells in Russia for the first time in 70 years, to the tumbling of the Berlin wall, or in the other direction the restimulation of the sense of responsibility to the Earth that was the heritage of the American Indian. And on the home front there have been some very powerful goings on connected with the image of the city, and its cleansing, going back to the great impetus in the reign of the Restored King to rebuild the city of London after a new pattern after the years of fire (1666) and pestilence (1665).

As you get deeper into all this you begin to realise how closely myth and legend links in to 'popular' history and the aims and ideals that men and women have had over the ages, with historical figures as paradigms for present human endeavour – be they national heroes like Drake, Ralegh, or other great figures such as Wren, Shakespeare, Dee – or indeed the communion of the better known saints. (I should say from personal experience that there are some pretty uncompromising lesser known ones still about and looking for cooperation too – particularly of the Celtic and Anglo-Saxon kind).

All this has been going on with the background of writing a new clutch of books. The last six months has been taken up with the first draft of *The Magical World of the Inklings*, which has meant getting to grips with all the published 'mythopoeic' output of C. S. Lewis, J. R. R. Tolkien, Charles Williams, and Owen Barfield, the anthroposophist who had such a long term influence on Lewis in particular. I've come out of this somewhat 'mazed and fazed' (whatever that means) and with an increased respect for Charles Williams, who on close analysis stands, in my view, head and shoulders over the rest of them. In fact to read his novels in a concentrated fashion is a hair-raising experience – bringing angelic contacts and realisations that are a very far cry from the effeminate gentlefolk in white nightgowns of the Victorian imagination. More like the roaring wheels and fires and animal headed forms of the Vision of Ezekiel or the Revelation of St. John. He makes it all so contemporary too, and real. At times I felt a bit like a beetle that had crept up between the floorboards of some celestial *palais de danse* on a Saturday night. I remain uncrushed, but the experience leaves its mark I can tell you. Powerful as well as beautiful lot. They don't really need the kind of protection afforded by the evangelicals who have been jostling patrons on the pavement outside 'Psychic Fairs' (yuk!) or fire bombing an occult bookshop.

Actually a touch of what it's really like 'up there' might scare off most of the occult and mystical dabblers quite quickly, as well as somewhat amaze many of the faithful – whether fundamentalist fire raisers or deliquescent intellectuals like your local bishop. (I still prefer to see the lightning struck tower at York as an act of God – if he may be academically posited to possibly exist.)

I'm scanning through *The Celestial Hierarchies* for a few clues in formulating my following book, to be called *Stars, Crystals and Heroes*, which is to be an attempt to throw some dim human light on the shining angelic worlds but the main source of inspiration seems to be in very demanding texts on atomic physics, industrial chemistry, microbiology, Newtonian and quantum physics, and the history of the nations, for it is in these areas that we see the evidence of the activities of the angelic hierarchies most plainly – and "by their works shall ye know them", whether in the terminology of Cherubim, Seraphim, Principalities and Powers – or as Lords of Flame, Form and Mind, or as Folk Angels and Angels of Species. Makes you see the familiar domestic animals in something of a new light too. Is this how some of the angelic powers manifest, to bring their influence upon humankind?

Apart from all this I've got a more occultly conventional book on the Tarot coming out too, based on a little course I knocked out, which has some surprises because the Fool is in reality the *Lord of the Dance* and a way to him for those who can be approached in no other way.

My *History of White Magic*, originally commissioned by Mowbray's, is also due to appear in America in a new edition, suitably up-dated, under the title "Magic and the Western Mind". It's my attempt to make my consuming folly reasonably respectable – intellectually as well as morally. But the truly spiritual always was a great scandal, wasn't it, so I don't know what my chances are. But that's the hazy purpose to all my scribble.

[1] Tony & Helga Duncan's three children.

45. To Rab Wilkie   *7ᵗʰ February 1990*

Dear Rab,

Many thanks for sending me the copy of your January Full Moon report, which Roma and I read with great interest. I understand Roma is writing to you separately, which may or may not find itself into the envelope which contains this. There are so many balls to juggle in the air just at the present that coordination sometimes becomes difficult.

And flinging balls into the air is all that this letter is about really. Perhaps catching one or two you have flung up in your report, and maybe slinging up a few that you might care to make a grab for. I think this likely to be more of a useful exercise than trying to coordinate our efforts too closely. It seems to me that conditions, needs and opportunities, vary so much as between America and Europa that it is really a matter for those who are there on the ground to do what seems best at any particular time. However, there may well be use in general notes as to what we are doing, which can be picked up on, or adapted, or left alone, as seems appropriate.

You will have gathered I am sure from the news columns of the political events in Eastern Europe that we have more than enough to keep us busy over here, sorting out the manoeuvrings of folk souls and racial angels, which are a bit rumbustious just at the moment – even in the West where we have the common Economic Community coming up ever nearer as 1992 approaches, with political federalism being openly talked about rather than behind backs of hands and closed doors. Of course the position of Germany is crucial to all this, and its possible reunification, all symbolised by the Berlin wall, and we discover that a bear is the totem animal of that city. Our first inkling of that was seeing one being paraded with the crowds when the wall was coming down.

On your general points about land masses and configurations, the importance of major continental rivers has just been borne in upon me, as a consequence of a ritual we were recently called upon to do. This involved an opening up of the old gold route, which ran from the Wicklow Mountains in Ireland, across to Mona and Anglesey, the Druid stronghold, and thence across country to East Anglia, accounting for the incredible wealth of Queen Boudicca and the Iceni (which is no doubt why Roman cupidity caused a large scale revolt). Most of this is covered in a book published here recently *Life and Death of a Druid Prince* by Anne Ross and Don Robbins, published by Rider, all about "Lindow man" recently dug up in a high state of preservation from a peat marsh, having been inflicted with a sacrificial 3-fold death.

Anyway we were asked to renew this route magically, and also to extend it across Europe, so that it became the spinal column so to speak of Europa, after the fashion of the Charles Williams derived diagram in my *Secret Tradition in Arthurian Legend*. It came across also that this gold column should follow the route of the main river valleys. It was along these that the Celts came to Britain in the first instance. Also they made a practice of throwing their gold into water, whether rivers or lakes. (Although the Romans managed to dredge most of it up.)

Therefore we carried on the route down the Rhine, and then the short distance across to the fount of the Danube in the Black Forest, which winds its way via Germany, Czechoslovakia, Austria, Hungary, Yugoslavia, eventually to form the frontier of Romania with Bulgaria and then outpour into the Black Sea. Without going into too much detail this developed into quite a powerful working, aimed, it would seem, at getting the continental kundalini flowing and equilibrated. Something of a tall order, but it would seem to be of vital import in our present times. It brought about with it quite a lot of choppy astral waters too, which broke through into the physical, so not only did we have 'heavy vibes' and disturbed nights and vivid dreams to contend with but storms, hurricanes, blizzards, fires, and literal pandemonium from another group who were sharing Hawkwood with us. A very sedate lot on the whole, studying personal mandalas, but who broke out into most bizarre behaviour while we were doing our working, propping open their door while playing loud music, banging on the piano just outside our room. All very apologetic afterwards of course, but it needed all our technique and experience to keep going through it. Not that I think that it was a deliberate assault instigated by dark forces, but simply another manifestation of general turbulence that is around just now. After all if one elects to work with group-angelic forces when they are humping around then one must expect to get a bit of a bruising in the process.

Anyway, following through in the comparative calm since then, I have found it a useful exercise to trace through the routes of the great rivers, seeing them as psychic spinal columns so to speak, and taking note of the types of country and peoples and traditions they flow through.

By extension this must also be relevant to other continents and land masses – the Mississippi, the Amazon, the Volga, the Congo. All their tributaries forming nadis, or nerve complexes, or veins and arteries, the flow of water being determined by the configuration of the mountain ranges and valleys – in which the human psychic centres of cities are then formed.

I discovered incidentally in reading up about the lower reaches of the Danube that wolves and bears are still very much in abundance in the wooded areas, as the river runs between the Transylvanian Alps and the Balkan Mountains.

None of which need detract from the other area of considerable interest and I think future concern, the Hyperboreal complex, that leads out into the stars. Here I suppose a map of the world with the North Pole at its centre is the pattern to work from for inspiration. There is an important game of ring-a-roses to play I fancy incorporating Northern Canada, Alaska, Siberia, Scandinavia, Iceland and Greenland. And maybe the movement of Northern migrants such as the Lapps and the reindeer herds.

We have also been much impressed by the fantastic film coming back from the outer planets and their moons from the Voyager programme. There's quite a lot still to learn within our own Solar System back yard!

46. To John & Caitlín Matthews *10th September 1990*

Dear John & Caitlín,

I have, in a busy life, finally managed to get round to studying *Hallowquest* and the Arthurian Tarot in detail. I want to say I think you have done an absolutely magnificent job, and I think we have here the basis of a reconstituted Arthurian Mystery system, that many of us have been working towards for years. May the sapling grow into a very strong and mighty tree! I only wish the *Household of the Grail* book could have come out a little later, so that I could have put *Hallowquest* as the logical continuation of the stream of work and tradition I described in the last paragraph of my Dion Fortune article. Congratulations. Hope to see you John at the launch of the London book, and both of you at the Merlin event in Bath quite soon.

47. To John Docherty *January 1991*

Dear Mr Docherty,

Element Books passed on your letter to me and I would like to thank you for your interest and constructive remarks.

I must confess to complete ignorance about Barfield's *Silver Trumpet* and any information or guidance on how to get a copy would be most welcome. I am a little surprised that O.B. did not mention the fact when he read the MSS, but this may very well have been modesty.

The felicities or infelicities of Lewis's patchwork over details in the Chronicles of Narnia had not struck me as being of too much importance. I see myself as an enthusiast rather than a literary critic, but hope I have not done too blatant a whitewash job over any cracks.

As to George MacDonald, it would have been good to have dealt at some length with his influence, but it would have raised problems over the space I was allowed, and it seemed to me rather the subject matter for another book – not necessarily from my hand. Perhaps you could oblige? It seems high time this neglected figure was brought into greater prominence.

At the same time I was aware of other influences particularly on Lewis that would need to be considered once one opened the gates to admit those outside the immediate Inkling circle. I think for instance of David Lindsay's *Voyage to Arcturus* and one could go on further into writers of relevant literature, from E. Nesbit to William Morris etc., etc. In fact it seems to me that there is scope for quite a series of books on the importance of mythopoeic literature, and I hope Element Books or other publishers will do something to encourage it. Your mention of Lewis Carroll opens up another fruitful vista.

48. To Vivienne Jones   *14th January 1991*

Dear Vivienne,

You asked me a couple of times about the personal implications and application of what I wrote in Bob Stewart's book[1] about 'spiritual pathologies' and 'the Fate and the Ghost', and mentioned it had also caused some heart searching with Wendy and Peter.

If it has caused you, or anyone else, (as indeed it did me), to pull up short and re-assess what they are and where they are going then it is all to the good. Another step in the important process "Know Thyself". And as I said to Wendy, who rang me up in some distress earlier on, it is no small achievement to realise how badly one has performed as a human being – it shows a glimmer of clear sightedness and the beginning of practical spiritual wisdom.

The problem is that people most in need of this short sharp shock of self revelation and realisation will protect themselves well from it with a thick armour of glamour, self righteousness, self justification and various combinations of pride and dishonesty with which the occult/esoteric/New-Age scene is particularly rife. That is the reason why many are part of the scene – it provides an apparent escape route from their own inadequacy in terms of physically expressing themselves as rounded human beings.

Of course the occult scene does not have a monopoly in this regard, although different sectors of cultural expression are more or less prone to it. The arts generally have more than their fair share. For every genuine artist with the necessary talent, vision, and application there are many pseuds.

In another sense it is a phase we all go through, generally in adolescence or early adulthood. But the problem arises with those who never progress beyond that stage.

This is their personal misfortune, but gets worse when such sub-adults group together for mutual support and self-delusion. Hence my lack of enthusiasm for esoteric communities, festivals, and other foci – for the level of self-indulgent unreality gets pretty unbearable as far as I personally am concerned.

It is not my desire to make any detailed value judgments about how you, or any particular person in the group, conducts their own life – unless it seems likely to affect the work of the group, or I am particularly asked. It should be sufficient to state the principles, as I have done to the best of my ability in the article, and leave the application of them to individuals.

I would just say this however, in your instance it would worry me a bit how much you seem to be embroiled in a vast net-work of esoteric chit chat. But having said that, it is only you who can make the final judgment as to whether this is a) an expression of spiritual type or destiny as go-between and facilitator; or b) an obsession with other people's business as a substitute for lack of real substance in your own life expression. These are the extreme poles, it would seem to me, expressed bluntly – but in life things are rarely that simple, and one finds destiny or gifts occluded with various errors and distortions on the one hand; or quite appalling mistakes mitigated by high virtues or genuine spiritual intentions, on the other.

To illustrate this, is the Scarlet Woman archetype an expression of spiritual type or a 'ghostly' deviation? What is the motivation, and where does one draw the line, between a) an interconnector between individuals or groups, the willing free-lance servant, wishing to serve all, a kind of universal Martha figure, and b) someone whose sense of boundaries, or faculty of discrimination, is completely lacking – a very 'Aquarian' trait, but in many respects an averse one as often expressed on the New Age fringe.

[1] *Psychology & the Spiritual Traditions* ed. R J Stewart (Element Books 1990).

49. To John Docherty   *7th July 1991*

Dear John,

It was a pleasant surprise to see you at my Inklings weekend at Bath recently and I note your comment about my appearing to be held back to a marked degree. I was not all that conscious of this myself, but it was not the easiest of groups to handle, because of its diversity. One is all the more conscious of this the smaller a group is, certainly when it gets down to less than a dozen. With a good hallfull one just has to plough on anyway to the assumed general level of intention and comprehension, for better or for worse. With a more intimate group one becomes more aware of individual needs, preconceptions, expectations and limitations. Although it was a friendly and sympathetic collection of individuals it never really bedded down into a particularly coherent group mind. One for instance had come for creative writing stimulus, another expected a magical type workshop, someone (who did not last very long) just had a glamour about Gareth Knight, and another never read the newspapers (let alone occult novels) for fear of being contaminated with negative images. However all seemed to enjoy themselves, as indeed I did, and the organisers appear to have received favourable reports.

I am much obliged to you for the copy of the Marjorie Spock article, I must confess I have never heard of this lady but I found her *Art of Goethean Conversation* most impressive, in explaining much that I had come to realise by experience was the mainspring of discussion groups and similar activities when formulated with the right spiritual intention. Again, as you imply, there is really no substitute for the regularly meeting group, but no doubt public conferences and workshops have their place, for all their inadequacies, as a general stirring of the pot.

I do not think you need be too worried about the appearance of my Inklings book as "Back List Book of the Month", and I hope it does not have a similar resonance with booksellers' buyers. It appears there because I read the riot act to Julia McCutcheon about a general lack of professional promotional effort when the book first appeared. I should say that I find the staff of Element Books very pleasant to deal with, but there is a certain feckless amateurism that gives one the occasional sinking feeling. As a publisher myself I have a distaste for badgering the publishers of my own books with queries about promotion and sales but I await the first royalty statement with interest and not a little trepidation.

I think however that sales cannot have been too bad, otherwise they would not have suggested some kind of sequel. They received my tentative suggestion of a review of the major mythopoeic writers with considerable initial enthusiasm, after which silence. This is par for the course, though, as they kept me hanging about several months for a decision on the Inklings book and only came to contract (in two or three days flat!) when they heard I was going to offer it to Aquarian. Anyway I have not pursued the matter as I have quite enough else on hand at the present completing another book for Aquarian and editing some letters of Dion Fortune.

50. To John Docherty   *19th September 1991*

Dear John,

Many thanks for the revised synopsis and chapter specimen. These are OK as they stand and I have sent them on to Julia McCutcheon with a covering letter, copy of which is enclosed.

I take your point about the usefulness of a foreword on mythopoeia, and would be pleased to try to oblige. I would suggest that on the basis of providing such an essay, my share of the royalty be computed at one third, as compared to one quarter for editorial supervision only. This can be dealt with later when, as I hope, Element decide to take it on, and offer contract terms.

With regard to such terms, I think your generosity misplaced when it comes to publishers' advances. Shed no tears for them. They do very well out of authors generally. If you think in terms of discounted cash flow, the author has to do a lot of work on faith, for probably two years before the book is published, in initial writing and then proof checking in production, and even after that the publisher sits on the money earned before accounting for it six months or a year later. So any advance of royalties is no act of charity on the publisher's part.

We are in any case talking of relatively trivial sums in this kind of publishing, where anything in four figures is reckoned to be 'big money'. It is different with professional writers, who usually are paid the equivalent of the whole of the first impression royalties as an advance, or with big names in popular fiction whose agents claim and get vast amounts.

The kind of sum that should be offered to you as an advance ought to be around £1500, split into two or three parts, payable on signature of contract, delivery of MSS, and publication day. They might offer you less as it is your first book. But you ought to get enough to pay for your paper and a down payment on your new word processor, even if not much reward for your time.

So don't turn it down; in any case, it is very dangerous even to *think* of the possibility of the book not being a best seller, at this stage of the game. Publishers thrive on optimism, and wilt very easily at the very thought of a lack of confidence in anyone around them.

Having said this, I do hear that Element are having some cash problems at the moment. We can only hope that they pull through this. So one may have to expect any advances promised to be paid late, for the time being. This does not mean however, that one should offer to work for nothing. Sermon over!

51. To Donald Michael Kraig   *20ᵗʰ September 1991*

Dear Don,

Many thanks for yours of 22ⁿᵈ August. Sorry not to have replied before now but have been pretty frantic meeting various deadlines – I'm sure you know the feeling.

Glad to hear that the Dion Fortune article will suit, and the payment is acceptable. I would however like this, and any other articles by me, to be on a serial rights basis, so that I could, if occasion arises in the future, use the material in book form, in a volume of collected essays or some such, with due acknowledgement to *FATE* of course.

Interesting about the other Glastonbury article turning up so fortuitously. Maybe someone is pulling strings "up there". How does it feel to be a marionette?

As regards the Regardie Tatvas, I've been giving this some thought and as Regardie gave them to me, I do not particularly want to take money for them. I am therefore sending them to you as a gift. No strings attached. I think it is what the old boy would have liked. And you seem to me to be a genuine sort who will appreciate them.

I am sending them under separate cover, as "specimen artwork", but I enclose a note of gift and provenance herewith. I regret that I do not have any back-up correspondence with Regardie as all the old Helios files appear to have been dumped.

If you should feel like some kind of gesture as a *quid pro quo* there is an American book on star lore recently published which has been highly recommended to me, and which does not seem readily available over here. It is called *Beyond the Blue Horizon* by E. C. Krupp, possibly published by Harper, San Francisco.

And if you should at some time sell the cards on for a fortune, perhaps you might cut me back in for a small percentage!!

52. To Mike Harris   19th *October 1991*

Dear Mike,
Many thanks for your letter describing recent ecclesiastical events and the
write up of the Glastonbury working. This all seems highly significant stuff
and I appreciate your sending it to me. And as you say, some aspects of
all this could be of high portent. It would certainly seem sensible for us to
exchange notes on all the goings on, for I too have not been idle. If nothing
else it will also serve to get me to make a record of my own work and
experience at this time, which might otherwise go unrecorded apart from
brief mention in the GK Group monthly reports. And we ought to meet
up, as suggested, from time to time in the Malvern/Evesham area when
opportunity permits.

I did my workshop/lectures in Glasgow this last weekend. The first day
was on Tarot, and a useful warm up, the second day was obviously going to
be the more significant, ostensibly on the Arthurian tradition in Scotland,
but which was plainly getting tee'd up for a strong Merlin mediation.

This centred on Bob Stewart's emphasis on the Scottish Merlin, some
preliminary work upon which you will recall we had done under Bob's aegis
in Bath, and which he has written up in various books since. It all goes back
beyond that to the famed visit to Dinas Emrys as far as Bob is concerned
but to a little beyond that in my own Merlin related work at the early
public Hawkwoods, and the writing and publication of *The Secret Tradition
in Arthurian Legend*. This in turn of course stems from Dion Fortune's
Arthurian work which was seeded when she first went to Glastonbury in the
1920s but which came very much to fruition as a consequence of the Weekly
War Letters meditations – which, coincidentally, are to be published at the
end of this year, edited and commented on by me, and published by Arcania
Press, whose physical location is at Swallow Street.

Another dynamic in this was the discovery of the Altar Stone associated
with Merlin between Drumelzier and Stobo, which came as a result of Bob
telephoning us on the eve of our first trip to the Scottish borders, to ask us
to look into it, on the strength of an old Scottish book that he had found on
a Bath secondhand bookstall. All this led to our discovery of Drumelzier as
legendary location of the 'three fold death' of Merlin, Stobo as the conversion
place of a local Merlin by St Kentigern (who happens also to be patron saint
and first bishop of Glasgow), and the 'waters' meet', where the Powsail runs
into the Tweed, having overrun its banks in 1603 to make the connection,
in connection with a prophecy about "when Tweed and Powsail meet at
Merlin's grave/England and Scotland one monarch shall have", attributed, I
think, to Thomas the Rhymer, otherwise famous for disappearing for a time
into the Eildon Hills with the Fairy Queen.

Anyway, this was the first and main theme of my Scottish Arthurian day, to be followed up with the marriage of Gawain and Lady Ragnel (aka the principle of sovereignty), the many coloured quest of Gareth, and ending up with Uwain and the Lady of the Fountain – which had coincided with a certain amount of atmospheric disturbance in New York when I did it there. I also fed in a certain amount of related Merlin material from Nikolai Tolstoy's *Quest for Merlin*, which locates more Merlin territory just north of Carlisle at Hart Fell.

I used as a primary starter an imaginal introduction to Merlin as found in Bob Stewart's latest book *The Way of Merlin*. (This is a useful and more 'user friendly' practical handbook to the Merlin material than most of Bob's previous stuff.) It invites the party to ascend a hill along a path overgrown with trees (very much like the physical approach to Cadbury I found) and on a clearing at the top to seek entry to a dark tower. The door has to be opened with the help of a totem pig but then, up a spiral stair, one meets Merlin, in shamanistic guise, who shows you pictures from a great book. In Bob's account the pictures then shown are scenes from Merlin's life but I branched off here according to the needs of the day.

At the foot of the steep bank under Drumelzier church we witnessed the three-fold death of a shamanistic figure pursued by an uncouth crowd stoning him, and he fell and was impaled on a stake in the stream's bed and at the same time caught by a hanging branch or creeper by the foot so that he hung with head under water and was also drowned. The supposed victim then transformed into a shining child radiant with light, turning the waters golden as they passed down the stream to the waters' meet, where a dark figure stood on the bank, Mary Queen of Scots. This figure was very powerful indeed, as not only I but others found, but in a very dignified, queenly way. An aspect of sovereignty itself.

And if one let consciousness track up-stream of the Powsail, one was aware of it springing up at the forest glade of the Lady of the Fountain, by the emerald stone balanced upon four rubies according to the very powerful description to be found in Chrétien de Troyes. This figure, by means of a working later in the day, was in the company of the Lord of the Animals.

All this has a lot of cross references, with Merlin, the Lord of the Animals, the Green Knight, the Mabon, the Principle of Sovereignty, the Spirit of the Land, the Stuart line, and so on and so forth. At a third working in the middle of the day, in a fairly straightforward visualisation of Gawain and the Loathly Damsel story, found HRH the Prince of Wales being keyed in to the Gawain position, (Gawain was, also, in the ballad, heir to the throne), with the Loathly Damsel being not only sovereignty but somehow connected with the whole of the national mystery tradition in some way in its fullest sense.

(I begin to get a glimpse as to why the inner – specifically Wren and his Fedeli buddies – seemed so insistent about my attending the inaugural meeting of the proposed Temenos Academy in London recently, as HRH is apparently taking that under his wing on the quiet. The Temenos Academy is an initiative that stems from Kathleen Raine. It is all a bit hifalutin for me, but is probably an important marker on the periphery of the intellectual and artistic establishment to keep the banner of the inner tradition flying. Lectures on Dante and the Neoplatonic tradition and the like. A bit of a far cry still from our kind of caper, but going in the same direction).

Anyway, as regards the Scottish weekend, definitely a lot of clout to it. I forbore to pour waters from the bowl onto the emerald stone, recalling what had happened in New York, and also the tendency Merlin has to disturb the atmosphere on key occasions, notably laying on snow in April when we went to Wenlock Edge, and the storm that wrecked the Fastnet yacht race when we went to get a sample of the blue stones. Nonetheless the few days following have blown up quite a synchronistic lot of storm and gales. Another interesting synchronicity was *vis à vis* MQS. We have had dealings with this lady before and they are not always easily handled. However she seems to have got the message that basically we are on her side – or at any rate not Protestant Tudor yobbos. One of her favourite images of her long imprisonment under Elizabeth relates to a cat and a mouse, and this features in some of her embroideries of the time. On the train down from Glasgow who should get in the carriage and sit next to me but a man with a cat in a cage. In fact he let the cat out once on board and I travelled down to London with it on the seat next to me. Striking up a conversation with the man it turned out he was a warder at Lancaster jail.

But as to the future, I had the feeling that this ought to be a 'seeding' weekend, and my impression is that this is how it turned out. My immediate hosts were impressed by the way people came from a wide geographical area, and not just from Glasgow. We had your friends from Dumfries, and also others from Edinburgh, Ayr, the Borders and the Isle of Arran.

53. To Michael Beechey   *13th June 1992*

Dear Michael,
Thank you for your note and copies of the two versions of the communication of last December.

I agree with your first impression, and think you were right NOT to send them on to me in the first instance, and largely for the reasons you give.

As to your sending them on NOW, it seems to me that you are picking up on a genuine strong impulse that is coming through on the inner planes just now *vis à vis* the dynamic of the 'paradisal west' (to coin a large portmanteau term to cover a variety of elements). I think this to be largely incidental to this particular year which apart from being the centenary of Tolkien's birth is also the quincentenary of Columbus's voyage to the Americas and a number of other quite important events, and contemporaneously the Earth Summit in Rio de Janeiro. All this seems to bring an impulse to renew, refurbish, and dust off old contacts and work along these lines, and possibly to pick up on old opportunities missed or to correct shots that went variously astray in the past.

Having said that, it follows that I do not take at face value the detailed assumptions of the communication. And this is in no small part due to the fact that I have not neglected the work as is implied but have, amongst my other work, had and made contacts with various elven lords, not only of the Noldor, but also, somewhat to my surprise, of the Vanya. Also I have been aware of work and contacts being made by others, some closely associated with my group, others more peripheral.

Also, I have to say, I have made the not inconsiderable step of putting the possibility of contact with the Valar and the other powers behind the Silmarillion material, into the public domain, with the Tolkien section in *The Magical World of the Inklings* published in the Autumn of 1990. It is now up to various readers who feel sympathetic to this work to make their own contacts, and for the powers behind the work to reciprocate. I have made the links more readily possible and it is not my function to oversee each and every one of them.

All this is a logical follow up to my original experimental weekend at Hawkwood, dabbling magically with the Tolkien material, after which our association started.

As to this association, I have to say that I gave what encouragement and assistance I could to you during the following months, and rather more than I would normally expect to do in such circumstances. However the circumstances were somewhat out of the ordinary in that for various reasons a considerable amount of dust was kicked up and it was very difficult for anyone to find their way easily for some time.

Having given sufficient of my time and support to help you get an embryo group going I withdrew from close or direct involvement on the grounds that if you took all the opportunities that were available the group would go from strength to strength (much as the SOL did after the initiative set up by Helios) but that if you or the group so formed were not capable of carrying the force available then it would run into the sand and peter out, but that there was sufficient inner plane force around, associated with the material, for some other individuals or groups to pick up the ball and run, in whatever directions were deemed appropriate.

Credit where it is due, and I feel that a great deal of useful work was done as a result of initiatives picked up by you, not least the special working at Hawkwood. However, I have to say, (and I will not insult your potential ability by being anything less than honest), that for every grain of gold you are capable of mining, there is a very wearisome amount of dross to sift through. And I fancy that your work in this line will not thrive until you have learned to remedy this.

In other words, I think you need to refine and tune your intuitive perceptions more accurately. It may have been understandable, even acceptable, in the early days to have a high percentage of communication couched in crabbed pseudo archaic language, highly repetitive and inflated with bombast. Even so it put a lot of even quite discerning people off.

By now I think you ought to have learned to filter out all this dross, and concentrate on the gems that you are quite capable of getting through to. Get this right and the work, and particularly your part in it, will flourish. But if you do not, you are likely to remain in an ever more inaccessible and subjective ivory tower that does not do much good to you, or the work, or those on the inner trying to work through you.

The other point I have to make is that, with this line of work as any other, (Arthurian, for example), no-one has any monopoly on it. There is a vast amount of inner plane lore and power to bring through on any of these dynamics, (and often they overlap or resonate one with another), but it is great folly for any of us to regard ourselves as 'special'. Nor do I recognise any group as having a monopoly of authority in any line.

As far as I am concerned, anyone is capable of being an 'instigator', 'elf-friend', 'co-director', and I lay no special claim to any such office. I stand, as always, in trying to open the ways, for as much free traffic as possible, and have always stood also for as much free interchange of information as is practicable – hence my books, magazines of the past, and workshops. There is no lore of 'stars, crystals or heroes' that I am storing up as a private preserve, and as much as I know, and could communicate at the time, was laid out for all at the last Hawkwood.

I sincerely hope you succeed in setting your house in order and getting a Fellowship of the Valar type group thriving. But this is your initiative. I will offer whatever advice I am asked, but I wish no special relationship with it. Any more than I would with any of the other groups similarly dedicated, that I hope will spring up in time and may well be working well, without my knowledge, already.

54. To Morag Cameron   *17ᵗʰ June 1992*

Dear Morag,

I do not think you have the location of the Waters Meet quite right. I have marked in green on the map where I understand it to be, the stream evidently being too small to be shown on the map. However, it is very plain when you get there, as it runs alongside the track that runs northwest from the road, having passed under a bridge in the road. It flows right around the foot of the hillock upon which is Drumelzier church, which is shown on the map by a +. Walk along the track with the stream to your left. It is here that is the site (or one site) of the legendary threefold death of Merlin, falling down the bank from where the church now is, to be caught in the overhanging branches with his head in the stream. You will need to leave the track, by climbing a stile to a field on your left, in order to follow the bank of the stream, which will lead you in about 100 yards or so to the Tweed.

Although the ancient Egyptian imagery seems at first sight somewhat alien in the Scottish countryside I think it indicates that you are on the right lines, in so far that Sothis was very much associated with the flowing of the life giving waters as it heralded the inundation of the Nile which brought renewal of life to the land. And it is also a star which has high spiritual associations.

When I performed a working at the Glasgow meeting which incorporated the Waters Meet the most striking image for me was the unexpected figure of a dark queenly lady standing where the waters met, evidently Mary Queen of Scots. I subsequently had inner confirmation that this presence was more than just my imagination, and that there was a genuine contact with an important archetype in the national soul. The figure of MQS comes up quite a lot in workings of any depth, and can be somewhat two-edged if one is working from an English angle with Tudor dynamics! On this occasion it seemed entirely benevolent however, partly perhaps because of my part Scottish ancestry (my mother is a Sutherland) and partly because on that occasion I was deliberately trying to restimulate a Merlin contact for a Scottish based group to use.

All this may seem a bit deep but it is what you get down to eventually in any serious occultism, the interplay of archetypal figures from the past. It is as if they are complexes in the subconscious mind of the race, rather than actual "spiritualist type" contacts with the souls of dead kings, queens and well known figures in popular history and legend. It is seldom too clear, I also have to say, just what is required. Certainly no kind of overt or covert political activity. Rather I think, the recognition of these dynamics by spiritually minded, psychically discerning people, so that they do not fester and break out in uncontrolled ways, rather like a neurosis or psychosis on a national level. (We see something of what can happen if such forces get out of control in Northern Ireland, Yugoslavia, Armenia/Azerbijan and elsewhere). However, when one works with these images, they can and do behave to imaginal perception as if they were actual personages and it seems best to treat them as such. But at root I believe them to be foci for all kinds of national aspirations and frustrated lines of expression, particularly if they have been long brooded upon, or blood spilt – and God knows there is plenty of both in the history of the Jacobite movement and the turbulence of the Border country over the centuries, back indeed even beyond Roman times.

In connection with all of this it follows that the image of the Tarot Trump the Star is also very relevant. So I think you are along the right lines, and in these matters if your heart be pure, the beneficent forces behind, the racial angels, will see you do not go far wrong.

For myself I am not a great one for doing rites and ceremonies on actual sites. I prefer a visit to the site to pick up on the psychic atmosphere, and this physical visit will cause an actual etheric link to the place in anything you subsequently do in more appropriate or private circumstances in your own home or at a group meeting indoors somewhere.

If I can be of use in giving any further advice or information please do not be hesitant to ask.

Certainly there seems to be a strong current running just now for a restimulation of esoteric interest in the Tudor and Stuart period, intertwined with which is of course the mystique of the blood royal and the Scottish line. All of this I hope does not sound too much out of step with modern intellectual assumptions. It is, I know, heady stuff that feeds all kinds of crypto-fascist and ultra-nationalistic phobias, to say nothing of tourist trade royalism, but when you get down to it, it is all part and parcel of the heritage and wisdom of 'the ancestors', who seem to have a kindly interest in the progress of our civilisation and the destiny of nations, and at least offer some kind of counterbalance to the more materialistic and monetary concerns that seem to be the be-all and end-all of most modern political and social aspirations.

55. To Dick Swettenham   *25ᵗʰ June 1992*

Dear Dick,

Thanks for your outline of the lines you have in mind [*for an esoteric authors' cooperative*]. I have to say at the outset that I think you are in danger of walking into a quagmire. This for two reasons.

The first being a realistic sales projection, coupled with how much it is going to cost to obtain and to service those sales (i.e representation, trade discounts, advertising, mailing, warehousing, invoicing, postage and packing).

The second is the size of the cake that is left after such hoped for sales have been realised, and how it can be sliced – between author, financer, administrator, hired hands, and let us not forget the inland revenue who will want a look in at some point if anyone looks like making a profit.

There is also a third reason, but that is more subjective, in that I would not trust a cooperative of new age authors to run a piss up in a wine bar, let alone a publishing company.

... The plight of esoteric authors at present is I believe part of a general malaise, in part due to the dire state of the economy, which has depressed all the book trade, leading to some booksellers going out of business and some publishers looking as if they might well follow suit. In this state of affairs, if the professionals are having trouble there is not much chance of amateurs doing any better.

This is further complicated by the fact that I think we have seen a balloon of esoteric publishing enthusiasm that is now fast deflating, having burst its reasonable bounds. When I started off with Helios we had hardly any competition; in fact our greatest risk was that we were lone venturers in a field that few people had heard much about and were little inclined to tangle with. I speak of the time when 'meditation', if heard of at all, was likely to be regarded as some kind of kinky self abuse!

Come the sixties and seventies and Jack and his mates are all jumping on the band wagon, and latterly with the big financial operators getting involved. Witness the rise and decline of Aquarian Press. Founded and once run by a dedicated old second hand bookseller with one assistant in charity buildings in Vauxhall Bridge Road, then bought up by the upwardly mobile Young father and son, along with a clutch of similar small ventures, to become, as Thorsons, the most rapidly expanding privately owned publisher in the UK, until big enough and financially over extended enough to fall into the maw of international publishers Harper Collins. What do you see happening? Anything that is not fast selling, big selling, to the lowest common denominator, being slung out of print.

This argues that the wheel is about to turn full circle, with opportunity for small specialist publishers again – like Helios and Aquarian were. And I think one sees this beginning to take place with imprints like Gothic Image and Arcania, who can operate very usefully in niche markets where the big boys do not wish to, indeed cannot, compete. However, it does require ready access to a customer base, such as is provided either by a specialist book shop, or an esoteric society (e.g. Theosophicals or Anthrosophicals), or a small to middling operating friendly publisher.

To try to start up unaided by this, and undercapitalised to boot, is in my view financial suicide.

My advice to any author who is inclined to put money into his own works is to approach an existing small operator whom he thinks he can trust, and do a shared profits deal. Claiming a larger royalty in recognisance of his financial as well as editorial input. A small publisher might well welcome such an arrangement, although if wise would not accept self-indulgent rubbish from those with more money than talent, for that is only to debase his own imprint and sure as hell to lead to nothing but grief and recriminations as reality strikes home in the hard logic of the market place – in other words descent into the tacky world of 'vanity' publishing.

And if such an author were to ask me how best to try and make a living at occult writing, then although getting published is a large part of being taken seriously by the public, the money is not likely to come in very large measure from books, but from what can be spun off from them. In other words cultivate one's own fan club, with courses self produced and supervised and based on the books, and ancillary tapes and seminars and whatever else can be bolted on to the enterprise. This is what I have done in the past in small measure myself, although I have not taken it to its logical conclusion because I have always been fortunate in finding easier ways of making money.

As a publisher of successful textbooks for the past twenty-five years with a large publishing house I have to say that I know of only two or three of my several hundred authors who have been able to make a living out of it. And a publisher only pays his own salary by publishing a lot of books. In my case turning out about two dozen a year, with an ongoing back list of about a hundred and twenty. There is just not enough money involved in a single book, or even half a dozen books, to pay the average mortgage.

As for doing it all by direct selling. This can be done. Study the Finbarr adverts in *Prediction*, which must succeed because they are repeated time and time again. Generally they are selling a single title, from a whole page spread of dense copy, but it's pretty tacky old stuff. But I think the psychology of it is interesting. From looking at all the advertising in the psychic press, (and as an interesting parallel with the tipsters and betting system merchants in the racing press), people are quite happy to buy a pig in a poke for £15. (Sometimes this may be reduced to £10. Or else edged up to £25 at current prices).

In my view this suggests that in agonising over whether people are prepared to pay three or four quid for the information they desire, you are addressing yourself to the wrong end of the question. In short, are you trying to make a profit or to provide a social service? Cynical though it may sound, it is hard enough to make a profit and survive, so any thoughts of pricing down to rock bottom aren't worth serious consideration. The only people who can do that and survive are those who move vast amounts of essential commodities – namely Tesco's. And in marketing esoteric information, I submit that one is closer to the vendor of an "infallible" betting system or a Tarot reading than of cut-price groceries.

Well I trust that all this may have given you food for thought, whether palatable or not is another matter I suppose. As regards the Helios name, as far as I know you are quite at liberty to use it. And do feel free to come back and ask any supplementary questions. Although from what I have said you will gather that I would not wish to come in as a participating author. However, my experience and advice, for what it is worth, is always available free – although worth every penny of fifty quid an hour!

56. To Ray Rue   *13ᵗʰ August 1992*

Dear Ray,

I was very pleased to receive your letter, on several counts. Not least because you were of very real help to me in your report on *The Rose Cross and the Goddess*, as a result of which I think that the book in its new incarnation as *Evoking the Goddess* is very considerably improved. And I hope that as such, it will prove helpful and illuminating to a lot more people. If so, then your perceptive comments will have played no small part in the process.

The book was originally a bit half-baked I now feel, being basically a collection of essays and lecture material on a more or less common theme. And although it seems obvious now, I don't think I would have found my way to improving it without the benefit of having your suggestions.

It's rather odd, in that at the end of last year I had an astrological birth chart drawn up with prognostications for 1992. The first time I have ever bothered with such a thing. I prefer to handle things as they come, from day to day, without the complication of esoteric charts. But I had one drawn up for my daughter as a new year gift, her circumstances at the time being in some turmoil, and as there was a bargain offer of "two for the price of one" decided I might as well have my own transits looked at too, at no extra charge.

I was somewhat intrigued, not to say amused, to find the comment for March – "An Older Man or Teacher shows you the Way Forward". This did not mean much to me at the time, but having reached the age of 62, and not generally seeking the company of elder gurus anyway, it did not seem a very likely eventuality – even if perhaps welcome if it happened. Imagine my surprise when I got Leslie's letter containing your report, out of the blue, which had the effect, I have to say, of a great enlightenment. "Wow – Of course!!" I said, on reading your comments, and immediately sat down and did what was necessary and which seems to have well satisfied Destiny Books. This included five practical workings which ran through in my head almost consecutively over the space of a couple of days – and which left me feeling very considerably spaced out. I have since worked them with a group and find them to be more powerful and coherent as an integrated system than I realised at the time I wrote them out.

So, I don't know whether in terms of years you qualify as an "Older Man" but you certainly fit the bill as "Teacher" who "shows the Way Forward". Thank you very much.

It thus came as an additional pleasant surprise to find that you are also responsible for the very evocative image on the new cover for the book, which in fact now graces my study wall. And above all this that you should have been so smitten with *Experience of the Inner Worlds*.

As you well realise, and as has been made plain to me on more than one occasion, what it contains is not exactly popular on the general esoteric scene. However, what has to be said, has to be said – and I am sure that the truth is a "universal solvent" that will eventually find its way through the most impervious of mental and emotional barriers. Let us hope that the decision makers at Destiny Books do not prefer to wash their hands of the situation. Anyway, I am sure you have done your best, and I could not have wished for a more responsive reviewer to the challenge the book contains. It is in any case a challenge that is not going to go away – but there is plenty of time, to say nothing of the rest of eternity – whether or not my book is a major vehicle for it.

In some respects it has justified its publication in that my small personal group, which is capable of some quite powerful stuff, have all been trained on it. And as you have found for yourself, the exercises work.

What very few people know is that originally those exercises came through the channel of an orthodox minister of religion whose path in life crossed mine at a crucial moment for both of us – one of those inner plane set ups with which I imagine you must yourself be familiar. This was the Reverend Canon Anthony Duncan who, somewhat to his discomfort, is a natural psychic as well as mystic, and was rather embarrassed to find himself in receipt of it. I was sufficiently impressed to publish it for him, and at the same time secured his agreement for me to write *Experience of the Inner Worlds* around the symbolism contained in it.

I will send you a copy of this original – it's called *Lord of the Dance* – along with a copy of *The Magical World of the Inklings*, which, if you have not come across it, may I think contain some thought provoking elements for you.

Interesting what you say about the "Haniel" figure. From current impressions and experience I think that the angelic world is getting closer and closer. This is perhaps a part of what Alice Bailey refers to as the Externalisation of the Hierarchy, but I fancy that there are more hierarchies than most New Age people, let alone the general public, realise; and that some very strange and surprising things may herald their presence in the next decade or two.

I have been doing quite a lot of research over the past two or three years into the angelic domain, which of course is responsible for most of the chemical patterning of physical substance, besides the dynamics of plant and animal species, and even the destiny of nations – to say nothing of the basic physical laws of temperature, pressure and so on, upon which the whole material level of consciousness depends. And although there is no doubt something can be gained from the traditional angelic figures and species to be found in Qabalistic exegesis on the one hand, or the Christian pattern of "The Celestial Hierarchies" (based originally on Greek paganism via Aristotle), what strikes me most of all is the considerable paucity of knowledge.

The most perceptive approach to the angelic in modern times has, I think, been conducted in some of the novels of Charles Williams, and also, somewhat in disguise, by Tolkien (for justification of which, please refer to the Inklings book).

However, my own pet thesis is "by their works shall ye know them", and so it should be possible to get a closer acquaintance with the nature of many of them by appropriate meditation and contemplation of crystal, plant and animal forms. Although I should say that this is not entirely original on my part, for this kind of approach has been advocated by Rudolf Steiner (and earlier by Goethe) but a problem seems to be that this channel tends to get silted up with some pretty impenetrable Teutonic translations and sectarian thought processes.

As to your thoughts about adding a kind of angelic addendum to a Tarot set, I hesitate to interfere with anyone else's intuitive perceptions which may differ quite validly from mine. However, as you have asked me, I have to say that I think I would rather see the Tarot left largely as it is, but to think in terms of a separate Angelic system entirely. (The subject is certainly more than large enough to justify such an approach.) One might, and I write entirely off the top of my head, think in terms of suits of angelic sub-creators based on substance (very alchemical), botanic (flower and plant devas), animal (very powerful totemic images), human heroic paradigms (without getting too racialist).

Although all of this may be a reflection of some quite strong stuff coming through to me at the moment about "Star Lords" – and I have been constrained – not to say nagged – to make myself a set of cards based upon the 48 traditional constellations of Ptolemy. (Everyone makes such a fuss of the 12 zodiacal signs, with hardly any regard for the 36 others, associated with the Milky Way, and some very potent bits of Greek mythology. And for the sake of sanity and bearing in mind the shortness of our mortal span, I am confining myself to Greek star lore for the present at least.)

All this is closely related to the mythical and legendary theme of the Voyage West, in some way. This goes back in star myth to Perseus but also has its topical slant with the Columbus quincentenary, apart from Tolkien applications (also the centenary of his birth). It raises also for we denizens of the Isles of Albion some quite powerful historical/legendary archetypal forces, such as for instance Sir Walter Ralegh who lost his head through failing to find Eldorado in what was to become British Guyana, and who did much to found the original colony in Virginia. Also of course the Elizabethan magus Dr John Dee whose quest with Adrian Gilbert for a North West passage to the East almost brought him half Canada as personal real estate. All of which has something to do with the Americas and their destiny in world history in the broadest sense.

Whether or not the Holy Grail is to be found on your shores (and persistent quasi Cathar voyager contacts keep hinting at something having been brought over and hidden), there has been a spate of contacts lately coming my way from Vermont, of which your letter was the latest. At the beginning of next month I have another of your state compatriots coming to see me – Helene Shik, of Purple Mountain Healing Center, down in Putney. She first came to my attention when I was last in New York, as she had had a strong nudge that she should come to a weekend workshop I was doing, an impression to act which seemed also connected with the late Dion Fortune, to whose teaching and influence I am much indebted. I have been in desultory correspondence with her since then but I was somewhat taken aback a couple of weeks ago when, along with her news that she was coming over here, she sent me the clipping of an interview she had given to a local journal, called *Earth Star*, all about Cathars – which of course chimed in with this inner Cathar contact that has been powering through to two or three of us over here since the beginning of June. She is also on her way to Rennes-le-Château, so it will be interesting to see what comes of all this.

I have to say that I tend to be somewhat sceptical about much New Age to-ing and fro-ing. Some of the wilder claims and theories also, I am sure you will agree, do not help the cause very much. And in this general ambience I am inclined to include Shirley Maclaine, who last came to my attention during the Harmonic Convergence event of a few years back, when she took off for Lake Baikal to do her bit for the cosmos. However, she is an attractive enough personality and I did try to read one or two of her books a while back, but was very much put off by what seemed to be to be an unreadable mixture of show-biz and New Age gush.

However, a couple of nights back, I just could not sleep. I remained wide awake when I went to bed at midnight. Got up in desperation at one o'clock and did some reading and writing and drawing. Ate some corn flakes. Eventually, still wide awake at 2.45, I switched on the TV for want of something better to do. What should be starting but Shirley Maclaine's film of her first involvement in esoteric interests "Out on a Limb"! I found it extremely watchable. Wandered down to the public library next day and found on the shelves *It's All in the Playing*, which is her book about making the film. So I am beginning to wonder if there is not some rather strong hint here that I should not be quite so esoterically snobbish. And after all, she has got millions thinking in more or less the right direction. Whereas, how many paltry thousands have the books of Gareth Knight ever got to? And then most of the time preaching to the converted.

Anyway, enough of this. You ask about tapes, and I enclose a list of bits and pieces, though I think the books I'm sending may be of more value to you. However, if there's anything you'd like to listen to, let me know, and please allow me to make a gift of them.

57. To Morag Cameron   *6th December 1992*

Dear Morag,
Many thanks for your letter. Funnily enough you had been in my thoughts lately, but perhaps that was the result of your thinking about writing to me!

I'm glad to hear that you have been down to Drumelzier and the Altar Stone along the side of the valley, which certainly seems to have been eventful, if not quite in the way one would have wished.

If I were you I would not put too much store by theories of 'warnings' or inner opposition of various kinds. Such are very rare, and whether the case or not, the general inner atmosphere is only rendered worse or fouled up by one's own emotive speculations. Remember the example given by Dion Fortune of the magical apprentice who made a protective circle about himself and then filled it up with all kinds of demons of his own imagining!

What is more likely the case is akin to the fairy tale of the Prince going to rescue and awake the Sleeping Beauty in her enchanted castle in the middle of a gigantic briar bush. If you push yourself through a long untended thorn bush then you are likely to get pricked and scratched by the very momentum of your own movement forward. So a certain amount of discomfort can be put down to your own progress. And the condition of the inner dynamics of Merlindale would, to my mind, be rather of the nature of a long untended thorn bush with something very beautiful that needs awakening inside.

I would discount any thoughts of positively evil opposition. Even the heavy guys do not have the remit to squash us like flies. They can only operate by playing upon our own fears or fantasies, and general manifestations of mis-emotion, that generally make it so difficult to get a group together and keep it going without a lot of squabbling. In other words, we have to open the door to them – they cannot burst their way in – or set up physical disasters.

However, I do recall that it is fairly easy to have a bit of an argument or attack of general tetchiness on a visit to Merlindale. One forgets about this afterwards, with the memory of the inner grandeur of the place. But I would put this down to the 'thorn bush' principle, not especially to any Christian/pagan confrontation.

Where one does have this inner Christian/pagan confluence (Cerne Abbas in Dorsetshire is a similar case in point) there is a rare inner beauty and peace and calmness that remains in the memory. It is a place for the full manifestation of the spirit. This can make things a little discomforting for the unregenerate bits of oneself, which react like squalling and mischievous kids. With this in mind, it might thus be better to conduct any rituals off-site, rather than on-site; and as I mentioned in my previous letter, this is my preferred method of working in any case.

Similarly I would not set too much store by the rearrangement of rocks where the waters meet. Schoolboys would seem to me the most likely explanation. Occult political separatists, if such exist, would need to be pretty thick to think that they can overcome the laws of fluid dynamics and gravity to change the course of the Powsail without very heavy duty earth moving equipment. And even then I doubt if the result would cause much constitutional change of opinion at Westminster. What interests me though is your mention of the circular depression in a large rock at the base of a little cairn, which had not been noticed by me on my visits to the place.

Your experience with the wand, whatever the physical explanation, seems to me to have been quite symbolically deep and valid for you, and to focus on to the underlying importance of the place. And the fact that a small group seems to be forming now may well indicate that, however inadequate you feel, you may have started a required ball rolling.

I sympathise with your feelings about perhaps being a bit out of your depth and nervous of lack of experience, but these are very sensible healthy reactions, and if you have got this far by your own efforts I am sure you will make out all right. We all feel much the same way when it comes to working with these major dynamics but I suggest you can take comfort from the fact that you would not have been allowed to make contact with them if you were not capable of useful service, and we are all watched over and protected in this work. I will be happy to give what advice and support I can should you need it. As a general guide though, you might find it helpful to go to R. J. Stewart's little book *The Way of Merlin*, published by Aquarian Press, adapting its exercises and principles to local circumstances.

58. To Annie Wilson   *6ᵗʰ December 1992*

Dear Annie,

Thank you for your letter out of the blue.

Your long sojourn in France interests me, if only for the fact that I have over the past few months developed a consuming interest in France, to the point of studying the language to A-Level as a prerequisite to enrolling with the University of London to take a degree in French – which at the age of 62 seems going over the top a bit! However, it should serve to keep me off the streets and presumably may have some esoteric purpose.

Certainly my wife and I have been impelled to take a few trips to Belgium and France over the last couple of years. This seems to be something to do with an inner bridge of very long standing between the isles of Albion and the rest of the continental shelf. (All this seems to be at a far deeper and long standing level than any latter day concerns with a channel tunnel or the EEC, although one supposes that these will have some relevance as a drop in the ancient cauldron). What I mean is that we were very conscious whilst standing at the ancient port of Harfleur of the embarkation of William the Norman to conquer England, and then the reverse flow in 1944 for the liberation of Europe. And we seem to have spent more time than we might otherwise have wished for, traversing battle grounds and beaches where much blood has been spilled. All sounds a bit heavy and gruesome perhaps, but there is a great feeling of peace and purpose about it all, as Helene Shik may have mentioned; she seems to be quite intuitively tuned in to it all.

Again there is another dynamic that seems to flow down the Rhine, from the mouth of the Thames (and once conjoined in the same prehistoric river) and thence to the Danube and the Black Sea. The old river route I suppose whence the Celts came from, to end up in the far West.

Of course being in the East of England puts one closer to the dynamics of this kind of inner bridge building, whatever it may signify.

I can sympathise with anyone's reluctance to want to live in East Anglia, especially after the warm inner comfort of the West country. There is a marked inner difference between the two. One is, after all, moving out of the area of "greater Wessex" into the lands of the Dane-law. However, once you get used to it, the bleak flat landscape has an inner dynamic of great beauty and power that can hold its own with any of the more popular and esoterically fashionable Celtic lore. I think for instance of Sutton Hoo, the site of the Saxon king Redwald, who was by no means an ancient lager lout, but part of a surprisingly high civilisation (read Layamon's Saxon version of the Arthuriad, the first to introduce elves and mourning queens). Redwald was broad minded enough to have a dual purpose Christian and pagan shrine – a man very much after my own heart – there really need be no conflict between the two. Added to which it is interesting to note that the Elizabethan magus John Dee did a bit of excavating at Sutton Hoo, but missed the treasure by just a few yards. It was eventually discovered thanks to communication via a spiritualist medium in 1939.

However, I am not set on writing an esoteric travel brochure for the East of England. Merely I think pointing out my own fairly recent realisation of what ought to be obvious, that the whole of fair Albion has its inner importance and esoteric significance.

I spent a lot of time a couple of years back having my nose rubbed into the importance of London, and there are various pointers to this via some modern novelists, who I think are probably more clairvoyant than they, or most of their readers, realise. I think of Peter Ackroyd in particular with his evocative and somewhat dark *Hawksmoor*. Despite its somewhat negative elements it led me to realise the importance of Wren as a would be rebuilder of a New Jerusalem in the city laid waste by fire and pestilence. Odd that he should be an astronomer rather than an architect by original profession. And his link with the ancient powers of stars and sea remain in stone at the Royal Naval Hospital and the Royal Observatory at that ancient seat of royalty, Greenwich, from which the measurement of the world takes its zero marker.

Another novelist of wider application than Ackroyd is Andrew Sinclair, with his Albion trilogy *Gog, Magog*, and *King Ludd*. He has, also, I have just heard, written a book on the Holy Grail, which is published in New York by Crown publishers, but is not available over here, to my chagrin, as it seems to lead on from an interesting book that Helene gave me called *Holy Grail Across the Atlantic*. This is all to do with some of the dispersed Templars having ended up in Scotland, from whence they made a trans-Atlantic trip under the aegis of the Earl of Orkney, one Henry Sinclair, taking something of importance to North America and Canada.

All of which brings me rambling back to the French connection with which I suppose you may have had enough of by now, having lived there for some years. As I said at the beginning, I'm not sure where this is leading me. I do not feel any great impulsion to follow the well worn track to Rennes-le-Château, Mont Segur and the rest. My interest is broader than that, and may have some reincarnational connection, perhaps Templar, perhaps as recent as the First World War. Or even an early fascination with Maurice Chevalier in his heyday in the early thirties. (My favourite film star next to Shirley Temple, until Errol Flynn arrived on the scene as Robin Hood in 1938!) I tried to watch that film recently on TV and found it impossible. How could one be so impressed with such crap? Even at eight! But then it spoke to something deep, as I suppose did Maurice Chevalier. It did not occur to me though that for French translations of my books I should take the name Chevalier – Knight seems to cause considerable problems to the French, and I have even been billed as K. Nihgt.

Well it takes all sorts to make a world I suppose. I come down to Stroud some half dozen times a year, so if you are still in situ in the new year, we could perhaps meet for a chat.

59. To Lance Slaughter   *7ᵗʰ June 1993*

Dear Lance,

Thank you for your letter, and I am glad to hear that you have found some of my books useful. I enclose a number of information sheets that may interest you. These include the *How to Read the Tarot* taped course, which is the only one that I advertise publicly. But as you are plainly more deeply into the esoteric scene, and more or less on the Dion Fortune wavelength, I also enclose details of a few tapes that I make available on a more selective basis. And as an *aide memoire* I have put in details of how to obtain most of my books in the USA through normal booktrade channels.

In reply to your questions, I do not know that the Society of the Inner Light would be a great deal of help to you, not because of any doctrinal problems, but because physical attendance is really necessary to get much out of the way it works. An organisation that is geared up to teaching at a distance is the Servants of the Light (founded by W. E. Butler with a little assistance from myself many years ago). Butler was a former member of Dion Fortune's group and knew her personally. The group does have some kind of USA supervisory network and its current Director of Studies, Dolores Ashcroft-Nowicki, seems to be on a permanent world tour laying on workshops and lectures for those affiliated.

In the USA there seems to be some reasonably worthwhile effort to keep the Golden Dawn tradition going, under the aegis of Chic and Sandra Tabatha Cicero, who have just asked me to contribute to a *Golden Dawn Journal*. They have also written a book on the practicalities of ritual.

Your second question sent me back to look at what I wrote back in 1961/2 or whenever it was. If given the chance to revise the book I might change the tone of the remarks. Thirty years on one is less inclined to pontificate on complex and controversial subjects – and there is not anything more complex or controversial than human sexuality in whatever form it is expressed.

However, the *Practical Guide* was largely based on "received" communications by various mediators or mediums in the Society of the Inner Light, and what I wrote was pretty well verbatim (with the exception of D. H. Lawrence, which was my own bit, keen as I was in those days to show off my literary interests). I have to say that later communications on the subject emphasised this position, to the extent that the SIL instituted a vetting process on all intending and, as far as I know, existing members, to exclude homosexuals from membership.

When one of the communicators was questioned for confirmation of this line the reply was to the effect that "the nature of the act" should be sufficient to make its evil obvious. The communicator would seem to have anal intercourse in mind, although no reference was made to such behaviour in a heterosexual context, but this would presumably equally apply.

I was by this time no longer a member of the society so I am not aware of any more detailed comment on the matter. The reason I left (in 1965) was because at the time the group seemed in my view, in trying to come to terms with the Christian dynamic in occultism, in danger of becoming a mystical rather than a magical group, with Roman Catholic inclinations. It has since, I think from informal contacts I have made with members, now swung back from this more extreme orientation.

My own conclusions on this matter should be obvious to you from *Experience of the Inner Worlds*. From this you will gather that I think the Christian dynamic very important in magic, but it is quite difficult finding the right balance. The traditional Dion Fortune line was a balance of the three paths of Hermetic magic, devotional mysticism, and the dynamism of the nature contacts. Her own Christian orientation, although brought up a Christian Scientist, was more toward the Liberal Catholic, and she was at one time head of the Christian Mystic Lodge of the Theosophical Society, but thought rather more highly of Jesus Christ than as a "minor master" as taught in the more orientally biased wing of the Theosophical Society.

In retrospect it would be possible to lump the SIL's stand on homosexuality as part and parcel of its approach to Roman Catholic theological and moral precepts. And with such precepts, in their life enhancing aspects I tend to agree, at any rate in principle. (Living up to them is another matter – and trying to force others to live up to them something yet again – whether it is in the domain of contraception, abortion or euthanasia).

However, occult fraternities, if they are on their contacts, should be "the antennae of the race". (Ezra Pound's remark *re* poets – I have not sloughed off the literary parallels yet!) And in this regard I know that the SIL were years ahead of the outside world in a concern for the duty of humanity to the natural world, to Gaea (under the name of "planetary being") which has now become a package of blindingly obvious concerns to even the most materialist of governments. I just wonder if the sudden alarm bells about homosexual practices came from foreseeing the consequences of the AIDS catastrophe. Not that I think the disease a punishment inflicted by a grey beard moralist in the sky, but the anus being a one-way device as far as my limited knowledge of human biology goes, its use as a sexual toy could well be an infringement of cosmic design that brings its own consequences, like many other human abuses of the natural order.

Hope this is of some help. As a simple practising magician I rather regret the role of arbiter on public or private morals that is sometimes thrust upon one, but in this case, in writing as I did, I suppose I asked for it. As for books on the subject, I really cannot advise. I think sexual as indeed any other morality very much an individual responsibility – although there are of course limits where the weak and the innocent have to be protected by force of law. I suppose you are really looking for a text on moral philosophy or moral theology. Both are really outside my competence.

60. To Frann Leach   *15th July 1993*

Dear Ms Leach,

Thank you very much for your interesting letter. I am glad to hear that there are still a few copies of *The Treasure House of Images* around. After Aquarian Press was taken over by international publishers Harper-Collins it was put out of print on the grounds that it was not selling fast enough. This is one of the problems I fear when small specialist publishers are taken over by large organisations who depend upon mass markets.

However, I am glad to say that it has nonetheless been re-issued by a small American publisher (Destiny Books) under the title *Tarot and Magic* and continues to find a discerning public over there even if their distribution over here is not too good. I did however, buy up a couple of hundred copies to supply to anyone who is interested.

Emily Peach's *Workbook* has its merits but its very basic step by step treatment can be something of an irritant, as you have evidently found.

I am glad that you found the Figure 29 layout to be particularly helpful, because as it happens it later very much blossomed for me and led to me writing a course in which I took a couple of hundred people through. This became rather too labour intensive for my taste however, so I gave up giving lessons and packaged it up as a book, including questions and answers thrown up by working with students, under the title *The Magical World of the Tarot*. At the same time I produced a parallel version in audio tape form which I sell direct, through adverts in *Prediction*.

The line I take (which is based on my own experience) is that given the chance, and if approached in the right way, the Tarot will do most of the teaching. In other words once you have made the contact you really do not have need of books on the subject. This seems particularly the case with this four-fold pattern, which (in accordance with principles of Jungian psychology) is a very self balancing figure.

I find it very encouraging therefore that you have found your own way along these lines and that you have your own modifications and interpretation of the system – which all goes to show that the Tarot can be 'bespoke tailored' to the individual needs and outlook of whoever is using it.

The insights that you have had make it an interesting system that has I think a resonance with the four-fold pattern of buddhas and their dakinis around a centre that is found in Tibetan Mahayana Buddhism. Almost a pattern for a western version of the Tibetan Book of the Dead.

I made a cross reference to this system in another book of mine called *The Rose Cross and the Goddess*. This was also published by Aquarian and has met the same fate as *The Treasure House of Images*, although it is to be re-issued shortly in expanded form in the USA by Destiny Books as *Evoking the Goddess*.

There is just one modification to your plan that I would respectfully suggest you consider. That is the attribution of "oppressive or military rule" to the Emperor. This appears to be the only instance in your system of attributions of a negatively biased reading. I would suggest that the Emperor be regarded as representative of the *detail* of rulership or organisation, which does not necessarily have to be oppressive or macho in its application. Thus the Emperor becomes the external or executive expression of the principle of wise rule embodied by the Empress.

In this context I found, when I was running the course, that one or two women students felt the Emperor to be a threatening or oppressive kind of image. (This surprised me because I had expected all problems of this nature to be found in relation to more apparent 'malefics' such as Death or the Devil). It seemed therefore, that the Emperor can act as a focus for any bad experiences of male chauvinism of one kind or another, or with the father, or with authority in general, and that this obscured the good and positive side of the image.

I found however that this boorish or threatening ambience of the Emperor could be readily overcome by having the student take on, or be accompanied by, the figure of Strength. Having been confronted with the girl controlling the lion, the Emperor came back into line.

I hope you may find these comments of relevance and helpful.

61. To Simon Buxton   *17ᵗʰ August 1993*

Dear Simon,

Thanks very much for your card. And I have just heard from Debbie, who was away for a few days, that the later article will be going forward for publication in *Ophir* in September as planned, no problem.

I quite like the atmosphere of *Ophir* and presumably of the small group The Order of the Lamp for which it would seem to serve as an Outer Court. Has something of the rather cosy atmosphere of the earlier Inner Light as it comes across through some of the earlier papers and the *Inner Light* magazine. However, the Inner Light, as I myself, have gone on to rather less cosy heights and power levels, though I say this without any intention to patronise or "put down" Debbie's efforts, which are all part of the greater plan of hierarchical strategy, I am sure, to provide appropriate niches and areas of work for all who are genuinely upon the Path. It is just that some are at different heights, and upon different faces, of the Mountain of Abiegnus than others.

Which brings me to your queries about the SIL in earlier days as I recall them, and CC's role in particular.

In my day, (which extended from starting the Study Course in October 1953 to initiation into the 1ˢᵗ Degree in October '54, and then progress through the Lesser Mysteries to initiation into the Greater Mysteries in June 1959), there were three LM degrees, which formed a general process of training in which the 1ˢᵗ Degree was principally theoretical and finding one's feet in the Fraternity so to speak; the second got on to more technical matters of magic; and the third had a more mystical intention in the sense of forging the contacts through which power could flow through the magical structures built in the second degree. At least that was the methodological theory as I later came to see it, although going through it at the time was not nearly so clear cut. There was a certain "woolliness" surrounding it all. For instance although there were papers dealing with subjects as magically specific as "the magic mirror" and the "rod of power" (in the sense of tools of consciousness, giving clairvoyant ability and magical direction) there was much that was implied but not really followed through in practical instruction. Similarly, a knowledge paper on "Elemental Shrines", although issued, was somewhat frowned upon by CC, although what it said would be regarded as pretty well common knowledge these days.

Those of us who were keen enough, such as Alan Adams and myself, to so arrange our outer lives that we were close enough to HQ to be round there frequently, picked up a great deal by "osmosis". Certainly there was a lot of power around, both in 3QT and 38SR, what with Margaret Lumley Brown around the place, as also Anne Fox, as she then was. And in course of time I made a niche for myself as librarian and typer-up of recorded scripts, whilst AA specialised into becoming a generally invaluable Ceremonarius, in charge of temple equipment, symbols and such. And being readily available, as LM initiates we both received a unique education and experience in sitting in as ritual officers, eventually in all three degrees, as well as attending the weekly Wednesday evening meetings, which although ostensibly just "readings" from the CD and what not, could be pretty powerful events. So what with this and a well stocked library, and the chance to be flies on the wall while senior members occasionally gossiped, we both had a pretty good esoteric training. Whether things were so effective for members who travelled up from the country at most once a month is another matter, although there were plenty of papers issued for members to meditate upon. And whatever I may say in a slightly facetious way about initiation by duplicating machine, there is no doubt a certain power in many of the papers which could be picked up by any who worked conscientiously and regularly with them. And much of the more powerful ones did happen to come via "trance address".

As I have just remarked to Debbie, there is probably a continuous spectrum when one talks about trance, ranging from one end where there is complete passivity and unconsciousness on the part of the recipient, through lighter degrees of trance, toward a mind-to-mind contact that is hardly discernible from ordinary meditation or day dreaming or writing books for that matter. The important factors are of course, whether or not there is another mind on the other end (that is, an objective being, not just a figment of the subjective conscious of the medium/mediator) and the other is the integrity of the latter, which includes not only having a well stocked mind but also the ability not to interfere in the communicator's messages, either through pre-conceived ideas or other assorted prejudices or inhibitions, conscious or unconscious. On this score most "channellers" appear to be sadly wanting. And from my own experience it is a very delicate skill, not far removed from tight-rope walking.

The backbone of the training of Lesser Mystery initiates had, from the earliest days it appeared, been their attendance at the four Quarterly meetings, and especially the Equinox meetings, and of these the Vernal Equinox had the equivalent of a three line whip put upon it. Here, the assembled Fraternity would be packed in, (not too comfortably), while the medium in the centre came through with a "trance address". And throughout all my LM days this was Margaret Lumley Brown, although how much entranced she was would be difficult to say. She was anyway so clairvoyant, by natural gift and by training, that I am not sure that it made much difference, and I am sure it varied in intensity according to circumstance and immediate temple need. Anyhow, the importance of these meetings was held to rest in the opportunity it afforded for a direct contact between members and the Chancellor (or Supreme Magus as I think he was called in earlier days). And it was this, as much as anything that was said, which was regarded, on inner plane authority, to be important. If attendance was not possible then meditation upon the substance of the address was reckoned the next best thing, and it was always a matter of priority to get this typed up and duplicated and issued to members as soon as maybe. In later days a tape recorder was used, but for most of the 1950s it was taken down in shorthand by a "scribe" – which I fancy was generally Miss Westwater. In days of yore, of course, a function carried out, to the best of his ability, by AVO.

So much for the Lesser Mysteries. The Greater Mysteries were rather a different kettle of fish. There was an introductory period as "dedicant", corresponding to the "Threshold Course" prior to entering the Lesser Mysteries, and then one might be admitted. Here things were much more on a basis of personal initiative and responsibility. There was one regular rite, upon which much store was put, the Grail Ritual, which had been originally composed by CC. Apart from that, meetings consisted of members doing their own thing. Each, as they felt inclined, writing and performing their own rituals, assisted by other members. It is upon this pattern that I latterly formed my own group (a task which took me twenty years) and which still performs and indeed has gone on a bit from there. Whether towards what constituted the Inner Greater Mysteries in those days I do not know. I never made it that far, although AA did. Before I got to that level CC had cut the whole Fraternity down to one Degree.

So what led CC to take this action, which is what all the above is building up to, for I think it needs to be stressed just what was abandoned.

I have to say, that to some extent I saw the need for some kind of radical action. There had grown up a rather cavilling critical attitude towards other members' work. I can recall the rather callow attitude of both myself and AA in taking some malicious and self righteous pleasure in talking about writing or reading "a stinking report" on some or other event or occasion. And one senior member was drummed out for making what were deemed to be snidish comments about the integrity of other senior members in a report. The ins and outs of this are not important, but the general ambience that bred it all certainly was. And I think the root of the trouble went a long way back, to the assumption that Greater Mystery initiates were a race apart – superior beings. This certainly was not, and is not true, but the assumption, derived from simplistic Theosophical type teachings, certainly led to some assuming that they were perfect, or not far off from it.

I think it was to lance this boil that the justification for lopping things down to one degree has its justification and force. Although of course much depends upon what is going to be allowed to grow up again from the patch that one has so weeded. In my view it appeared to be precious little, which is why I subsequently left (in 1965) but I live in hope that I might eventually have been proved wrong, at any rate in the longer term.

Two things seemed to precipitate this move. One was the contact that Anne Fox claimed to have received, direct with the "Master Jesus". I am not sure about the validity of this, as one or two addresses from this source seemed to have a penchant for the language of scientology. Both Anne Fox and Rosina Mann had become deeply immersed in this field. Anne indeed still is, I believe, and Rosina had cleared off to America soon after I joined the Society, and became quite close to Ron Hubbard himself.

What was valid was the need to come to terms with the Christian needs and dynamic of the western world (to say the least of it) and disentangle the Western Mysteries from a weedy growth of half-baked oriental and monist ideas. This I have sought to do in my own way as recorded in *Experience of the Inner Worlds* and elsewhere, and my association with Anthony Duncan.

This contact, which meant a great deal to AF, and also to CC, resulted in her moving in to the basement flat at Steele's Road, and she did much of this work with the assistance of Robert Greig. This was an unlikely kind of combination. RG was almost an archetypal Officer of the Southern Gate, an ex-colonial officer of the best kind, a father figure in the best sense of the word, dedicated, loyal, kind. However, one thing evidently led to another and he too moved into the basement flat, and eventually of course they got married. This was not until after, however, a very embarrassing interlude when the first Mrs Greig, who lived just down the road on Haverstock Hill, was understandably extremely upset about what this weird cult was doing to break up her marriage.

You can imagine what heart burnings this caused to CC. For how could a contact with the Master of the Masters, the very Christ, come about in association with, or as a consequence of, an adulterous relationship?

It was at this time that Rosina appeared back on the scene. At first, to my eyes she seemed particularly out of touch and inept, but whatever else she is, she is a brilliant practical psychologist, and it was not long before she had the full confidence of CC. And from thence one thing led to another. The whole graded system was disbanded. Anne and Robert married and moved off to Greenstead. (I fancy Robert resigned from the SIL and became for a time closely involved with the Lucis Trust in an administrative capacity.) Margaret Lumley Brown was increasingly marginalised, and Rosina took over as the centre piece at the Quarterly meetings, and bringing through most of the new teaching papers.

You can make your own judgment on these. They are certainly not without value, but to my mind they come from a different kind of source than that which I associate with the old DF contacts. In the end, what with this teaching being phrased in convoluted and jargon-like language, and the general drift of the group seeming to be not a rebuilding of the old structures, but as a kind of semi-enclosed religious sect, I felt that time had come for me to go. An act which did not come without a great deal of heart searching, but my own way was gradually coming to be made clear, and from this led Helios, the SOL and all the rest.

Despite what might seem implied from the above, I hold all the parties involved in the greatest respect – but in the final analysis, their ways are not my ways – and where DF and her contacts fit in to it all is not for me to judge. No doubt all will come out in the wash with the passage of years when one can make more objective assessments.

As to what CC may have destroyed or otherwise suppressed, I was never present at any formal clear-out but from what he has said in semi-public at the Wednesday meetings I have a good general idea. It was his contention that DF's failed marriage had led her to cause some of the communications to be biased against the marriage state. And he seemed particularly bitter that at a crucial stage in his life he had given up the prospect of marriage because it was held and taught within the Fraternity that one had to be single to be wholly dedicated to the Mysteries. And if this is the case then I think that he probably did right. It raises of course more general questions as to how far the responsibility of a spiritual director goes, or a warden of a fraternity, in deciding what is "kosher" and what is not. As we know, no communication is infallible. But who should wield the Imprimatur and Nihil Obstat, that is the question – or should one let it all hang out? Or at least leave things on record so that those of a later generation can form their own conclusions?

Anyway, that's enough of me for a bit. I'll be glad of any information you come up with on the outer Carstairs. It could be a help to my inner work. Your commissioning me to work upon these Letters over the past couple of years has led to some unexpected results, as I said on the phone. And seems to have opened a tap that is running at a spate of 800+ words a day. 20,000 words so far, since starting on 24th July. What happens to this, who is to be judge of it, how much published, privately circulated, burned up – who knows?

At least the flame still burns that was lit in 1922/3 or whenever it was. And I doubt if I am the only faucet.

62. To David Spangler   *23rd January 1994*

Dear David,

Thank you very much for your kind letter. Nice to know my work gets to parts far flung from Braintree and is used and appreciated. John Matthews also speaks of you with affection and respect.

I appreciate too your acting upon an inner plane initiative. Even if such actions do not immediately appear to lead to anywhere or to do anything dramatically significant, it seems important from an inner plane point of view that some of their wishes are acted upon physically in some way. It seems to be a kind of talismanic action which is important. Rather like supplying an earth to an electrical appliance, or even making the last vital but unspectacular connection of a lightning conductor.

However, things seem to be stirring into activity on the inner in many unexpected ways and coincidentally (ha!) I have received in the same week of your letter a couple of transatlantic phone calls seeking my services, one way and another, so something seems to be coming up to the boil. Added to which I have done a film interview for a couple of Brooklyn girls and had two American editions of my books come out at the end of the year. One of these should please the Judaeo-Christians and the other the pagans, so as long as folk read the right books and not those meant for the other side of the esoteric tracks I should be OK. However, in another way of looking at it, maybe they *would* do better to read the "wrong" books. Nothing like broadening the mind as well as trying to extend it upwards and downwards into vertical superiority, which I suppose may be what constitutes the false divide between the feuding parties.

The two directions of work you mention strike resonances with my own experience, particularly what you say of immigrant and colonial impulses. I found this particularly striking when I came across to New York for the first time in 1988. This was a period when I had largely unexpectedly started getting very strong contacts from urban dynamics in England, most specifically London. I spent days just tramping the streets of the city picking up on it, and found contact with powerful psychic strata going right back to Roman and pre-Roman times, but more especially in the fifteenth, sixteenth and seventeenth century periods. This starts with magi such as Dr John Dee and goes through adventurers like Drake and Ralegh up to the work of Sir Christopher Wren after the restoration of the monarchy and the Great Fire of 1666. Maybe John Matthews has mentioned some of this, as he was quite useful filling in bits and pieces from his contacts at the time. One or two of whom were particularly excited at my New York trip, and sure enough when I got there the most important psychic task (more so I think than any workshops, which were simply the excuse for getting me there!) was treading some of the old Dutch colonial town south of Wall Street, which was itself of course the site of the old colonial palisade. And particularly powerful was the churchyard there with the graves of some of the early colonists. It seemed important to link consciously in my mind the treading of equivalent streets in each city. Don't ask me why.

However, one could speculate upon various dynamics. In the light of history, the opening up of America to the old world has had profound effects. Some good, some bad, but we must presume for the most part (by a small majority maybe) good. It is interesting that someone like Dee should have been so involved with encouraging transatlantic navigation, and it is probably down to him that the language of North America has turned out to be English – for better or for worse – but again don't ask me why. So I think what this leads to is that important though the indigenous Amerindian wisdom and example may be at the present time in having a mellowing effect upon immigrant values dominated by commercialism and technology, in the last analysis it is the peopling of America with a mélange of emigrants from the old world that has the most important bearing upon the future of the world. And maybe it is going to take another hundred years or so (or am I being optimistic?) for this great conglomerate nation to find its soul.

Of course there is also a possible earlier stratum, maybe a seeding phase, responsible for the rather strange legends of the Grail or some other such object having come across with remnants of the Templars, as maybe John has speculated with you.

The second project you mention also rings bells, and it is one that I have tentatively explored, and where John has had some difficulty in appreciating what I am up to. I have about half a book written on the subject, called *Stars, Crystals and Heroes* and it is largely taking modern science head on and finding a mystical dynamic in some of its discoveries. I do not think I am alone in this by any manner of means, there have been books around for some time of the ilk of *The Tao of Physics* etc., and the early Theosophists had a go at clairvoyantly researched chemistry, with mixed results. More near the mark though I think are some of the Rudolf Steiner people such as Ernst Lehrs in *Man or Matter*.

My own approach has been somewhat more magical. At one level the magical dynamics that can be constructed from the harmonics of the Periodic Table; and at the other end a look at the esoteric significance of discoveries of modern astronomy as to the function of stars in creating the elements in the first place. This gives one a great angelically constructed loom, the electron microscopic at one end, and the radio telescopic at the other, with observing mankind as the harmonic mean in the middle.

And in another way it all seems patently obvious. If the adage "by their fruits shall ye know them" holds true, one of the most obvious routes to understanding the angelic hierarchies is by analysis and comparison of some of the bits of sub-creation for which they are responsible. This goes all the way from the laws of physics (Lords of Flame) through the properties of chemical elements (Lords of Form) and the life sciences (Lords of Mind) to the multifarious Principalities and Powers behind plant and animal species and races and nations of men.

Or in other words, why be content with building a magical view of the universe upon the traditional Ptolemaic structure. How about a bit of post Einstein practical metaphysics? We've got the science, whether we like it or not, so why not use it? I'm jolly sure Dee would have! Anyway, enough of my rambling. But feel free to reciprocate.

63. To Simon Buxton   *23rd January 1994*

Dear Simon,

Thanks very much for your long letter and I enclose a few copies of the Holy Grail week[1] programme. I should say that I have already sent a copy to David Williams and to "the Librarian" at the SIL for luck. I will discreetly bear in mind your warning about John and his shamanic drum, although I have to confess to beating Drake's drum at a previous Hawkwood, to say nothing of Arthur's horn a year or two before that! However, we will try to keep the party respectable this time and noise pollution free. I have something of this in my own group with Michael Waldron, who is prone to wander through the woods with tabor and tin whistle. The best quasi musical thing I did at Hawkwood though was at one of the very early ones, when at the close I hyped them all up about esoteric harmonics and sat down at the grand piano to an expectant hush to give a rendering of "Lulu's Back in Town". (Might be appropriate as a theme tune if we are ever contemplating a revival of "Sea Priestess" dynamics!).

I was interested to read your reactions to coming across a Dion Fortune book for the first time, because it seems exactly the same reaction experienced by me. Once having made that initial contact there was only one possible road in life.

[1] Five day workshop at Hawkwood conducted by GK and John Matthews.

64. To Notis Michalitsis   *27th March 1994*

Dear Notis,

It was a very pleasant surprise to receive your long letter and also the two bottles of your most EXCELLENT wine. I was, alas, not able to understand the content of the booklets that you sent with your letter, but if your teaching is anywhere near the quality of your wine then I am very impressed indeed. We have drunk one bottle and are saving the other for a special occasion. The decorative box in which the bottles came is also very attractive and will become a household ornament to remind us of you all.

Thank you too for the photograph of the little film star. I was puzzled when I first looked at it, before I read your letter, because he reminded me of somebody I was sure I knew, but I could not think who it could be. When I read the letter or course, all was revealed, and I realise that I recognised in little John the features of *two* good friends. And with such an array of wise and good godfathers and godmothers he is a lucky lad indeed.

... ... The development of Iamvlichos sounds very encouraging and it seems to me that you are putting down very sound roots for the future of the Mysteries in Greece in the years to come. This is in no small part a result of the exceptional dedication of all your group, over a number of years, in often very testing circumstances, and it seems to me that you are all of you, the core of your group, hand picked in heaven, so to speak, coming into incarnation with an important destiny at an important place and an important point in time.

The difficult and in many ways depressing phase which you have been going through reflects, I think, broader issues. Whenever new phases begin to manifest there is a sharp reaction from old forces and also considerable sense of disorganisation and even chaos. I think the thing to do in all of this is to meditate upon the forces of Daath, whose virtue is Confidence in the Future which in itself represents forces changing to a new level of reality. Certainly very great changes indeed are upon us, which are being reflected in the international situation in many ways, and much will twist and turn I am sure until the new forces of light and growth spring forth in the new millennium.

All this turmoil, of conflicting vortices, of the action of mighty Principalities and Powers behind human endeavours, will manifest in strange and many ways, one of which I suggest is this series of slanders against the Mysteries in general which you have been experiencing. Obviously you need to keep your heads down for a bit while the chill and bitter wind blows but this will pass, and I am also convinced that you are all under protection. Let me know at any time if you feel I can help you in any way.

There are very powerful tides running on the inner at this time, in my own work, although I think this is part of a more general picture. A great deal of power was released coinciding with the publication last Autumn of the Dion Fortune War Letters, under the title of *The Magical Battle of Britain*, which I edited. This very practical instruction by Dion Fortune to her group in 1939-42 had waited over fifty years for its release to the world and it seems had built up quite a head of steam during this period. I do not recall if I sent you a copy, but if not I will be happy to do so now, although I will not send you anything until such time as you tell me it is not likely to make difficulties for you. Also tell me to which address to send any books.

I also had a couple of new editions published in America in October. One was of *Experience of the Inner Worlds* which is a text I published myself some twenty years ago and upon which my own inner group is trained. The other was a new edition of *The Rose Cross and the Goddess* with the addition of some practical path workings, under the title *Evoking the Goddess*. Let me know if you would like copies of either of these.

America is the most promising place for publishing at the present, partly because they have a large population which can sustain works of minority interest. The acquisition of a number of small British publishers by large corporations only interested in mass market rubbish has not been good for the provision of books of quality. Thus I, and others like me, such as John & Caitlín Matthews, or Bob Stewart, find our existing books being put out of print in England because they do not sell in sufficient quantity, but being taken up and republished in America by American publishers.

I retired from full time work at the beginning of this year, and had assumed that I might increase my public lecture work, particularly in the United States, but I find now that I am not so keen to spend my last years doing this kind of thing. My interests lie more towards Europe than to the Americas, and I am currently studying French at London University, as some of my books are published in France and I have a small but dedicated following there. In the United States my reputation is almost legendary it would seem, at any rate in places, but I do not find working with Americans too rewarding. You can generate a lot of interest but the attention span of the average aspirant seems to be about three weeks before they are off looking for some other way of wisdom.

My own group, which not many people know about, but which some of you have met, is the focus of my esoteric interest, the growing point of things, and that is where I think my present duty lies, rather than in spreading the word more generally. I have, after all, done plenty of that in my time.

I have however, made an exception with a week long course on the Holy Grail, which starts tomorrow, and I enclose a programme for your interest. I also enclose a couple of small value banknotes which I just discovered in my desk. They are no use to me as I cannot change them at the bank, so perhaps they are of some very small use to you. I hope this will not give rise to rumours about you being sustained by massive amounts of international funding by wicked Qabalists!

65. To Steve Dwares   *20ᵗʰ July 1994*

Dear Steve,

Many thanks for your letter. I'm sorry to say that *The Secret Tradition in Arthurian Legend* has just gone out of print over here, so unless there is any residual stock in odd bookstores it will not be available until such time as I can interest another publisher. Such books sell in relatively modest quantities over a long period, but big accountancy-led companies like Harper Collins find them difficult to handle. All their energy and interest goes into the type of material that will sell in large quantities even if over a very short period.

So the current trend is that most, if not all of my books will undergo a republication by relatively small specialist American publishers.

... ... Apart from this I'm trying to write a major 8-10,000 word article for each of the six-monthly editions of *The Golden Dawn Journal* which Llewellyn have just started to produce. The first, just out, was on the theme of Divination. The next, due December, is on Qabalah, And the one to follow that, which I'm just wrestling with at the moment, is on Hermetic Arts (whatever they are!) My purpose in contributing to this venture is to try to knock a bit of practical experience and common sense into an area which, although welcome to be revived, may, I fear, possibly get bogged down in slavish theoretical adherence to the symbolic complexities of the Golden Dawn founding fathers.

This writing sums up the main drive of any public work that I currently have in mind. I do not retain too much interest in public lecturing and workshops as they no longer seem to represent the most efficient use of my time and energy. I get all the advanced magic I can handle with my own group, which meets at Hawkwood six or seven times a year, and so public work, which involves either taking risks with a largely unknown clientele or turning down the power to safer but less interesting and effective levels. Not that I am not open to taking up an invitation, such as the recent Grail week, if it seems the right thing to do. The nudge has to come from the inner though, preferably with 'signs' preceding by way of fortuitous coincidences or circumstances. Anyway, if any more turn up in the future rest assured that I will let you know. The success of the Hawkwood Grail week, on many levels, led me to wonder if we might be called upon to have some kind of follow-up, but up to now the call has not arrived, so it may have been intended as a 'one-off' – or possibly 'two off' as John Matthews was doing a kind of repeat of it at a Benedictine monastery in Massachusetts not long after, when my own group was coincidentally meeting again at Hawkwood.

One is never quite sure what the purpose of these events may be, as the shots are called from the inner planes. However, they are no light work for those who carry the main burden of them, and I cite an example, for your instruction. You may recall the girl from my group who made quite a mark with her involvement, not just with her singing, but carrying the archetype of Dindrane. This is not an easy archetype to carry and John and I were a little uneasy about it, indeed I was somewhat irascible with someone present who found it the subject of a joke. However she took it all in her stride and afterwards remarked that it had all been surprisingly easy. However she has since had to revise her opinion, as shortly after the occasion she was delighted to find herself pregnant, only to have a miscarriage on Mid-summer's day.

So if anyone finds me on occasion a bit reserved or preoccupied in the course of these events, that is one of the reasons why. Play can get a bit tough in the major league. This rather reminds me of the parody of a line or two from Kipling's *If* – "If you can keep your head when all about are losing theirs – You probably haven't understood the situation."

We also had someone blow up and leave in distress, fulminating upon the 'hostility' and 'lack of sympathy' of John and myself. But that was a fairly straightforward situation, a quite healthy example of the scapegoat formula in action, when someone cannot cope, for whatever particular reason, leaves, carrying the similar problems of the group as a whole. Indeed in any magical or mystical working of any power, some considerable effects are made upon the patterns in the 'astral light' (for want of a better word) and this will affect all present in some emotional way or other. Included in this emotional effect is projecting images, or impressions, upon others present, particularly the leaders – which may be positive or negative. Hence possibly another reason for your colleague's comment on my perceived demeanour, although, as I say, it might well have been an accurate observation, according to time and circumstance.

I'm interested in what you have to say about Warren Kenton's workshop, and on reflection I guess it figures. I've never attended anything of his myself. I had always tended to write off Warren as a mildly philosophical theoretician, but revised my ideas upon meeting him, when I realised that he does have power (however he chooses to use it, or not) and I have found useful instruction, or at any rate confirmation of my own discoveries, in some of his written work. It is quite useful to have some of one's Gentile magical Qabalah supplemented by someone closer to the Judaic mystical tradition.

66. To Jim Kaelin *6th February 1995*

Dear Jim,
Thanks for your letter passed on by Steve. I am pleased to learn that you have been actively interested in what I had to say in *Experience of the Inner Worlds* for so long. I had not realised that it was known at all in the United States. It

was published over here in 1975 I think but it is not easy for titles brought out by small publishers to make much penetration on a world wide basis. Now that Weiser has brought out a US reprint it seems to have caused a little flurry of renewed interest.

The Golden Dawn Journal seems a very worthwhile project to me, and I hope that it proves successful enough for Llewellyn to keep it going. It would certainly be very difficult, if not impossible, to make a go of a multi-author volume like this in England. Chic and Tabatha will be over here lecturing later in the year, when we hope to be able to meet up. The standard of contributions is very pleasing and I look forward to reading your own. The Nordic pantheon has a very special place in the Western mysteries that I think is not generally realised, and when it is realised it can be all too easily perverted. However, in its essence it has a very great purity, all to do I think with being at the top of the world (literally) and thus closely connected with the axis of the Earth's turning and the Circumpolar stars. It is a very complex and intriguing subject, and I do not know that anyone has done more than scratch the surface, especially with regard to the mysteries of the constellations of Draco and the Great and Little Bears and the Precession of Polar Stars, and the closely associated Perseus/Andromeda mythology.

I have done a bit of work along these lines in the past and hope one day to publish some of it, either in opportunities such as are afforded by the *GD Journal* or in book, or failing that, privately circulated form. One problem we have over here particularly is that what sounded like a good thing, Harper Collins moving into the esoteric publishing scene, has proved something of a disaster. The small specialist publishers who were prepared to issue more advanced minority interest material have been swallowed up and destroyed, and in their place is this great maw of a publicity machine that can only cope with books for beginners, the same pap for babes endlessly warmed up and recycled. Anyhow this is a problem that I am turning my mind to these days, and although I have no desire to get involved in starting a small publishing house again, as I did with Helios, with the advances and universality of word processor technology it should be possible before too long to get some kind of worthwhile information exchange going. Not that I have anything I can usefully enclose with this, here and now!

I will keep in mind what you say about intelligent and informed interest on the East Coast. As Steve has told you, my perception of priorities does not impel me to do too much lecturing or workshop work these days, however if and when I do get back to it, I would be inclined toward being a guest of a functioning group or circle of informed acquaintances rather than an Open Center kind of job where one has to spend one's time with a miscellaneous collection of people whose only common denominator is that they have stumped up the entrance fee, and often for quite the wrong reasons. I'm sure you know the scene!

67. To Phillip Newman   *7ᵗʰ February 1995*

Dear Phillip,

Thank you for your letter postmarked 1.20.95 which comes as a result of your reading my book *Tarot & Magic* I believe.

The descriptions of Tarot archetypes that you mention seem to come, if my memory serves me right, from the work of an American, C. C. Zain, who has written a whole series of books, not all on Tarot, through an organisation called the Brotherhood of Light. Although there have been a number of other decks I believe using the same Egyptian style symbolism. This derives from a Frenchman called R. Falconnier who produced a book on the subject in 1896 inspired by Egyptian paintings and sculptures in the Louvre Museum in Paris. This original book was called *Les xxii Lames Hermetiques du Tarot Divinatoire*. I have never seen a copy and I do not imagine it is very easy to come by, even in France.

For practical work upon the archetypes, although not in the Egyptian style, I would recommend my own book, *The Magical World of the Tarot*, or *The Tarot* by Paul Case. Case founded an organisation for the study of the Tarot which is based I think in LA. It is quite well known, and is called B.O.T.A. or Builders of the Adytum, and has branches world wide, giving correspondence courses and the like.

Most modern commentators, including Case, are much influenced by a book called *Key to the Tarot* by A. E. Waite, published in 1910 but still readily available. And if you want to read just about everything that has ever been written about Tarot design there is the three volume *Encyclopaedia of Tarot* by Stuart Kaplan. This is of course quite expensive but worth borrowing if you have the library facilities to do so. He probably has the largest collection of Tarot decks in the world, and his encyclopaedia illustrates just about every deck that has appeared since 1450, with discussion about various variant designs and ideas.

Again for a very user friendly step by step into working with Tarot archetypes I would recommend the books of Mary Greer. These are published in the USA. The first of these was called *Tarot for Yourself* but she has followed up with others, whose titles I am not sure of.

The most popular book with students on divination, that gets down to basics in a very practical way, is *Easy Tarot Guide* by Marcia Masino, published by a small American publisher called ACS Publications.

I hope this covers most of what you wanted to know.

68. To Cinnabar Productions   *8ᵗʰ February 1995*

Dear Tracy and Joan,

Thank you for your letter of January 25ᵗʰ. I will be happy to be interviewed again when you are next over here, but let me know as soon as possible in advance what your dates of arrival are likely to be.

It is interesting to note that serious historians are beginning to take account of the 'irrational' side of their subject matter, and your maintenance of an approach along these lines would seem to me to make the whole project worthwhile.

Being aged only between 9 and 16 during the war years I can offer no personal experience of what might have gone on, and my own contribution to the subject can only be somewhat at second hand as the editor of Dion Fortune's war letters in the book you have. As will be obvious from the book there seems no case for thinking that Dion Fortune was part of any 'official' initiative on the part of government circles, but it is interesting to note the synchronicities between various of her group's realisations and chosen meditation subjects and public messages to the nation from official figures. Was this just picking up on the group mind of a nation at war, or was the source a specific 'psychic broadcasting' of ideas? And if so, what was the source? Inner plane or outer plane? A lot of interesting debate for anyone prepared to take the subject seriously.

Your timing seems propitious as there is a 50 year rule that allows for the release of hitherto confidential and secret documents from government archives – which of course now takes us up to the end of the war. I enclose a couple of press cuttings taken today. They are not directly relevant to what you are looking for, but there may well be material available now that does have a bearing on your research. Not that I can help you much in this myself, but rather it might be worth getting any serious historians you have involved to take a look at what is now being made available.

Apart from that my only suggestion is to try to find anyone who took part in Dion Fortune's war time meditation group. But there will not be many left alive. There is one old lady who contacted me recently on another matter, and I will sound her out to see if she has anything useful to say. And I imagine you will have made or will be making your own approaches to the Society of the Inner Light.

Anyway, best wishes for your project.

69. To Donald Tyson *19th February 1995*

Dear Donald,

Was interested to receive a letter from you. Coincidentally I had been looking though Volume 2 of the *GD Journal* – could well have been on Tuesday, when you wrote or were working on No. 3, but I won't drive coincidence to staggers by the minutiae of speculation or false memory syndrome. Anyway, in the course of this, my attention focused on your article with which I have to say I was very impressed, not to say enlightened. It underpinned with some serious scholarly evidence what I had been trying to point out, (with some trepidation), in my own article, that the Tree of Life system of correspondences is not nearly so cased in concrete as many Golden Dawners and others seem to think. So we have a meeting of minds on that score.

I had thought that my browsing through *GD2* (I had not found time to read any of it before) had been occasioned by my completion of my contribution to *GD4* but in the light of the subject matter in your letter, I fancy that it could have been occasioned by someone on the inner doing the reverse of what you describe as putting a flag up above the surface of the waters and waving it. In this case I suppose, pushing one down into the turgid depths which you and I as incarnate beings currently inhabit.

It has become increasingly evident to me recently that the whole business of magic is intimately concerned with concourse with spirits between one plane of consciousness and another. Well this has always been fairly evident in practice but one is tempted to play it down, certainly to outsiders, and even to insiders and oneself, in the light of the implications raised by this. Not least the large embarrassment factor occasioned by the mass of false witness that is churned out by various "channellers" and assorted nuts – although I am not so sure that this is not a protection, and a useful smokescreen for the very small percentage of genuine contacts. After all it is perhaps better to be scorned as an associate of a self deluded lunatic fringe, than to be taken too seriously as one who is in contact with spirits from the vasty deep. I mean if the CIA took it as seriously as they might take contact with agents of a foreign power one would be under very oppressive surveillance I am sure.

However, on the other hand, it also seems to me that such contact is a great deal more common than is realised. Indeed almost commonplace. That whenever the imagination is involved in certain levels of flight then there is intellectual or emotional intercourse between the planes. This can come not only by means of imaginative fiction or lifting the spirits in various ways through the arts but in odd hunches and impulses that come to every man and his mate. In other words the imagination is a recipient of levels of perception beyond the physical, which are taken for granted or ignored.

This is no more than the realisation of the commonly held idea that everyone has a guardian angel to watch over them, or even in the catholic doctrine of the communion of saints. However, it can work the other way around, as in the case of violent mobs or political and religious fanatics, or those easily led into criminality or various excesses. The mechanics of this I have gone some way to describe in the *GD3* article you have just read. Although I should perhaps add that the bulk of that article, not just the bit in italics, comes from an inner communicator and not from me.

However, the gist of your letter concerns a more conscious, deep and long lasting contact than the general concourse of spirits that, figuratively speaking, are all about us. This seems very much the province of the adept. As I have a twenty-four year start over you in terms of current physical life, an account of some of my own experience along the way may help save you some unnecessary detours or heart searching.

During my own training in the Society of the Inner Light (1953-65) inner contacts were regarded as very much a specialisation. I think this was a natural development from Dion Fortune having originally started the group and been the sole source of teaching in this way – originally in full trance mediumship back in 1922/3. Over the years this gradually extended to include a small band of others, some officially recognised, some not, and trance mediumship gave way to a more conscious mind-to-mind link, although "trance" is a continuum which has many gradations.

Anyway, by the time I came along there was quite a sizeable mass of material of this nature, and it was my aim in *A Practical Guide to Qabalistic Symbolism* to get as much of this material out into the public domain as possible. So I cannot take credit for much of the wisdom contained in that book. I was, however, pushed more onto my own resources in the second volume, and in doing that I found the beginnings of specific inner guidance beginning to come through, in that I would be intuitively directed to the particular books in the library to which I needed to refer.

Most of my books after that were largely "me" although my life generally seemed to be guided along required lines that led to the forming of Helios and its various off-shoots. I began to realise however that the distinction between my own writing (rearranged intellectual furniture), and ideas being dropped into my head as I wrote, was becoming increasingly thin.

There is almost a measurable process in this. In the early days one might receive in meditation a very strong contact which seemed in effect to slam some kind of information cassette into the back of one's neck, from which one could then "read off" as if it contained one's own ideas. This led towards a process whereby writing became more of a continuous meditation. Lectures similarly, so that one was still thinking in terms of one's own ideas but being rather agreeably surprised at the power and wisdom one occasionally came up with. This kind of thing is of course usually ascribed to tapping the subconscious mind, and there is no doubt a large part of this at work, but then it all depends how you define your psychological terms. For myself, I tend to shy off them these days, as limiting and misdirected in conception; however they can have a limited use in trying to explain what one does, in five minutes, to journalists and other outsiders.

A noticeable sea change began with my book *Rose Cross & the Goddess*, (recently reissued by Destiny as *Evoking the Goddess*), the parts of the first section of which almost wrote themselves on what I can only describe as a strong "Merlin" contact, which came in very strongly and then gradually faded. Oddly enough, the last part of the last section of that book also came in "on contact" although from another (but probably related) source via my wife.

But "taking dictation" as it were came in quite obviously into my later Tarot books. The second part of what is now called *Tarot & Magic* came in very strongly as an extended series of visions, although originally seemed intended as a children's story. (Possibly by me or my contacts being unduly influenced by the success of C. S. Lewis in this genre). In the end, for this book, I cut out the kids and their dialogue and published it as a straight path working for students who could not rely upon their own imaginations.

I then got bounced by "The Fool" and, although I am not quite sure what came first, the chicken or the egg, evolved a self instructional method of approaching Tarot whereby one evoked the Fool as an instructional entity, and then by extension his alter ego as Magician, and functional expressions as the other Trumps. This seemed at the time a very important development, a means of teaching magic to a wider public, and I put out a course for three or four years, which eventually was issued as a book *The Magical World of the Tarot*. I think this remains, in potential, one of the most important things I have done, but I needed to move on from it. Being a full time teacher of elementary magic to Tarot students is not something I needed to be saddled with, there were more important fish to fry.

A great release of power seemed to come about after I was asked by the Society of the Inner Light to edit Dion Fortune's war letters, issued as *Dion Fortune's Magical Battle of Britain*. Apart from whatever intrinsic value they may have as history or leaves from an occultist's case book, they somehow restimulated contacts that Dion Fortune made, initially in 1922/3, to start coming though me.

Like you, I was very dubious about my abilities at this kind of thing. And in the end I had to be almost tricked into it. One of the three contacts involved kept on nudging me to try writing a novel. I have in my view little talent for writing a novel, and less inclination, given the problems of getting fiction published, so I kept pushing this mad idea to the back of my mind, until in the end I agreed to spend a little time at any rate, giving it a whirl.

This started off just by visualising Carstairs, the author of the transcript you like, being a character whom the fictional "I" met in a bar, and then him taking me, in visualisation interspersed with light conversation, into a room, where, blow me down, were the other two characters that had contacted Dion Fortune. And being face to face with them, sitting in a room, the only thing I could then do to continue the "novel" was to write down what they said.

This turned out to be 80,000 words of stuff churned out between July and October of 1993. They then more or less said that that was enough to be getting on with, and that more would come after I had found means of using what they had given me. Some of this material I am in process of putting into the public domain, via the *GD Journal* and such like, although the bulk of it is pretty specific stuff, a complex system of magical imagery, that is more suitable for a working group than for general public dissemination. I have therefore been issuing this in instalments to the GK Group, to whom it will serve as a sheet anchor and fly wheel, (or vortex if you like), in giving the group an independent identity in its own right, spanning the planes. Although any general observations that can be publicly stated from these specifics will be put out as and when opportunity arises.

Some of this relates to the role of "historical characters" that tend to turn up from time to time in magical working. And to the role of a certain group of dedicated inner plane adepti who manipulate them almost as astral holograms in the national interest, or in other works that go rather beyond one's limited incarnate understanding. I don't know how much of this I will be able to incorporate in a book of magical images I am writing at the moment for possible publication by Llewellyn next year. The more one goes on the more one realises that the terms "occult" and "esoteric" are essential limiting factors in one's work. That as one progresses, so there are fewer and fewer people able to understand what one is on about, or to make sensible use of it. I suppose this happens to some extent in any human art or science but in a demi-mondaine subject such as magic it becomes more oppressively felt.

But things have moved on in other directions of communication since then, and toward what one can only call the world of "faery". Here we come up against the old traditions of magicians mating with elementals, which seem very persistent. One thinks for example of that strange old book *Le Comte de Gabalis* by the Abbé de Villars, or the Reverend Robert Kirk and his involvement with the faery realms, to say nothing of more ancient traditions of Merlin and Nimué etc. Obviously there is a certain attraction in this subject for all kinds of spurious eroticism and so I fancy it may be a matter best left to magicians in their declining years, when young men's fancies are no longer such a dominating element in one's emotional needs or body chemistry.

70. To Mark Whitehead *2nd September 1995*

Dear Mark,

Many thanks for your letter of 20th August. I trust that your meeting with Mike Harris has gone well and that he has not disgraced himself in any way with the citizens of New Mexico, and I am also very pleased to hear that you may be able to make it to Hawkwood in October along with Rab and Bernie. I will be happy to meet up for any extra-curricular festivity although the weekend before I shall most probably be in Paris for a get together with one of the Martinist groups there.

Esoterically this is quite a low key venture but with a lot of fraternal camaraderie. I first attended it by coincidence a couple of years ago, being in the right place at the right time, and it is nice to be invited back. It consists of a banquet after visiting the grave of Dr Gerard Encausse ("Papus") in Père Lachaise cemetery in the morning. Père Lachaise is something to behold in its own right, a veritable city of the illustrious dead, from Oscar Wilde and Edith Piaf to Frederic Chopin and Jim Morrison not to mention Voltaire, and Aberlard and Heloise; at some point the French conceived the idea of digging up the famous and laying them to rest here. Although the most moving are the great memorials to resistance fighters and concentration camp victims, and it was at the wall at the bottom of the hill where the remnants of the commune of 1871 met their come-uppance.

They are good enough to sit me next to someone who has good command of English, my French being still somewhat limping, and last time this happened to be a professor from the Sorbonne, Antoine Faivre, who amongst other things holds the chair of "the History of Esoteric and Mystical Currents in Modern and Contemporary Europe." He spends a fair bit of time in the States and I have since taken a look at a couple of his books published by the State University of New York Press, *Access to Western Esotericism* and *The Golden Fleece and Alchemy*. It's nice to know that the world of academe is starting to take us a bit more seriously, but on the evidence so far there is still a long long way for most of them to go. As Persig said in *Zen and the Art of Motorcycle Maintenance*, modern universities are 'temples of reason' and that in one sense is their fundamental limitation. So it seems that the nearest they can get to us is by way of History of what we do, or else treating us as exotic objects for study in the department of Anthropology. Joscelyn Godwin, as musicologist, seems to be the closest to getting anywhere near a hands-on approach, but I witnessed him getting pretty heavily savaged at a conference some years back when he made a few slighting remarks about Rudolf Steiner, so it is still very much like trench warfare, with not much encouragement for anyone on either side to put their head too far over the edge of the parapet.

There is also, taking up points you made in your letter, a great disparity between how different nationalities approach the subject, and so I incline more and more to the opinion that one can only feed in general ideas across frontiers and let whoever is sympathetic among the natives do the necessary translation or transformation of the information for their own tribe. Although in this regard I am currently in the somewhat ironic situation of having my books put out of print here only to be taken up and republished in America. I have just heard that Weisers are going to publish *The Secret Tradition in Arthurian Legend* and *The Magical World of the Tarot* in 1996. Although this is not so much a case of "a prophet being without honour in his own country" as the vagaries of the publishing trade, pretty half witted at the best of times but not helped by the ministrations of eagle eyed devotees of 'market forces'. Thank God, for all his faults, Don Weiser seems to be able to survive as a publisher of the old school.

71. To Magis Books (Tom Clarke)   *4th October 1995*

Dear Magis Books,
I write to you at the suggestion of Chris Seers of Greensleeves, enclosing a specimen complimentary copy of *The Rose Cross and the Goddess* written under my pen name of Gareth Knight.

This has been out of print for a couple of years now, as a result of Harper Collins policy with regard to Aquarian Press titles that sell less than a zillion copies a week. It has in fact since been republished in the USA by Destiny Books in a revised and expanded edition under the title of *Evoking the Goddess*, but although they have world rights, few copies seem to penetrate the UK book trade.

Anyway, I have a little stock of 400 copies of the enclosed in my attic. Would you be interested to take a quantity off me for £1.00 each plus carriage or £300 for the lot? Original price new was £5.95.

72. To Bernie Buedden   *8th October 1995*

Dear Bernie,
I was interested in your remarks about the naivety of newly made adepts. I think this very true, with the somewhat daunting prospect that until one finally reaches home base all one's activities are a bit off the wall in some way. I was contemplating only recently what immense energy and self-importance

I had put into *New Dimensions* and all that, when now I would not lift a finger to launch another occult magazine. Similarly, when circumstances in the publishing industry seem to be crying out for another Helios Books I could raise no current enthusiasm, despite my skills and experience in the field, to do anything about it. Much the same kind of attitude occurs in regard to big public powerhouse workshops such as those I got involved in at Hawkwood during the 1980s. I do very little workshop or lecturing these days.

However, it all seems to be an essential part of personal progress. And it is not as if I have given up all these activities and attitudes and assumptions that spawned them, in order to do nothing. In fact I was never busier. The Hawkwood public workshops have given place to the private workshops of my group, which now may be opening up to a more public (but group oriented) phase. My past publishing and writing activities have been replaced by opening up personal inner plane communications and producing these, and more specialised kinds of articles than the general public wants, for the relatively small circle of the group. Of course twenty years further along the time track I may be in the position of wondering why I bothered to do all this – but then twenty years from hence I shall probably be viewing things from a different perspective anyway – if not in a state of general decrepitude I do not care to contemplate.

Similarly I do not think it at all possible that one can make any judgements upon the activities or personal circumstances of others. As you say, at one time it all seemed quite logical and even inevitable that a small group of you should be centred in New York to forward the work of the group. In retrospect and current circumstances this seems quite a simplistic and naïve assumption and your moves to pursue your own perspectives outside the cosmopolitan hot house of NYC seems a much more positive, expansive and promising scenario. I must say, by the way, that I am much moved by the way that you are all renewing contacts by coming back to Hawkwood at the end of this month. And David and possibly Chuck too. David in fact came over for the Grail week that I put on with John Matthews the Easter before last, and seems to be developing along his own lines well.

73. To Mark Whitehead   *24th November 1995*

Thanks for yours of 17th. I had Tony Duncan on the phone last night, highly delighted to have received a bundle of contracts from you and he seemed well pleased with their terms, so I would not take any old buck from his agent if she tries to prove herself a clever cookie. Even the token amount of the advances is OK by him as anything of any magnitude is likely to cause complications with the Byzantine pension arrangements of the Church of England under which he has to live the rest of his life.

He tells me that you are interested to take on *The Christ, Psychotherapy and Magic*, which he also welcomes. I had half promised to dangle it in front of Don Weiser but I will back off from doing this now, and frankly I do not think that there was really much chance of Weiser's taking it on.

As to my own little works, we seem to have a slight misunderstanding here. I did not mean to imply that we should have no contract between us. I think it is important in your interest as well as mine and our heirs and successors that there should be a memorandum of what we agree to. What I meant was that I was not much bothered about the sums of money or percentages involved. I do not want any advances, and as to royalties I would be content with say five percent of sum received (i.e. 'net'). This for English language rights as Harper Collins have retained administration of foreign language rights.

… … Thanks for the mention of Tony Duncan's little booklet on *The Psychic Disturbance of Places*. I took the opportunity to ask him for a copy when he was on the phone last night. He had almost forgotten about it. Apparently it was something he knocked up for the fellow clergy of his diocese when he was approaching retirement, and he reckons only about 24 copies were ever produced.

Glad to hear that you find the Abbey papers of help. The Abbey appears to be a pretty powerful, almost universal, archetype upon the inner planes, so I make no great claims to originality; but what we have there is a personal application as far as our group is concerned and of course extensions from the group such as yourselves. The impress of the Chancellor seems very strong upon them, which is what I think makes them particularly valuable to us. Glad to hear that Bernie is up and running well.

74. To the Revd Canon Anthony Duncan   *28ᵗʰ November 1995*

Dear Tony,

Many thanks for the little packet of poems under the title of *The Spheres*. I'm impressed, and in more ways than one. On the one hand by the felicitous mode of expression, and on the other, by the deep resonances of that which you express.

It impels me to send you a little something by way of return. I am not sure what you will make of it but I think it may ring a few bells. It is the core material on which my current group is imaginatively (or magically) structured. Thus you should consider yourself highly privileged in being vouchsafed a copy of it without having to have gone through awesome rites of passage, assorted initiations, and oaths of secrecy with one trouser leg stuck in your sock. But I am sure I can trust in your discretion. Don't leave it out on the coffee table when the secretary of the PCC calls – or are you beyond all such organisational hassles now?

Anyway, it is not more than you deserve, in having, as a young curate, taken an apprentice to magic through confirmation classes. Call it your karma if you like. And when it comes to 'communications' I hardly think that Mr Douglas Warren[1] is in a position to throw the first stone. Let it be said however, that I only consented to be on the receiving end of such communications with extreme reluctance – which as you say in your little Hammer of the Spooks (for which many thanks) – is a pretty safe guide in these matters.

Actually it is a rather amusing story really, if not a psychiatric case study, in how I was 'tricked' into it in the first place. I thought I was writing a novel, only it turned out to be the imaginative preliminaries to being got into an upper room with these three fellas, who then proceeded to start dictating as if to the manner born. All this training on my part to end up as a stenographer! But as one of them is reputed to be a saint of the church on the side, I supposed they cannot be all bad.

But as with all such things, the proof of the pudding is in the eating. So I leave it to you to get on with it. The general structure is that of a certain abbey of your acquaintance, but is not an exact replica. A sketch map is included for reference, that of the tower is of course in side elevation. And you will find the pages all in reverse order. There is no symbolic significance in this – at least none is intended – it is simply that I cannot be bothered to re-collate them from the order they came off the printer.

As I said, thank you for letting me have a sight of your little paper on the disturbance of places. It served as a useful reminder to various principles in these matters. Subject to the risk of the totally unexpected, which can be a factor in these cases, given the natural urge, as you say, in some quarters, for concealment, I am not expecting too much further bother from what the chaos brigade left behind. The mess the cat left having been cleared up off the carpet, so to speak, and with sensible rules of hygiene things should soon get back to normality.

An odd thing is that in at least a couple of quite respectable academic quarters recently, I have heard the OTO being referred to as misunderstood gentlemen. This they are not. Their approach is for the most part intellectual but has some rather unsavoury trimmings. One has of course seen this kind of thing described before, by C. S. Lewis in his science fiction. Although I hesitate to think the OTO (an old Crowley playpen, standing for Ordo Templi Orientalis or some such) are anywhere near as powerful or intrusive as the fictional NICE, or have the ambition to be so. 'Chaos theory' is rather trendy scientific cant at the moment which some part of the fringe of the esoteric, understandably, finds attractive – but anything of the chaotic would, I think, by its very nature, tend to self destruct.

On a more positive note, I was reading through *The Mind of Christ* recently. One thing that struck me was how terminology can be so important to understanding. For instance, if *The Mind of Christ* were entitled *The Aura of Christ* (in the sense that those of like mind, in esoteric terms, share the same aura) it might go like a bomb in esoteric circles – 'Mind' seeming rather chill and intellectual. But then of course it would probably put off a lot of more orthodox readers. Perhaps we should think of these things in terms of translation rights as a new element for publishers' contracts. "Psycho babble edition" being listed alongside things like Large Print editions for the chronically short sighted.

Anyway, I look forward to seeing your package of manuscripts seeing the light of day in published form, as they thoroughly deserve to be, along with the old favourites *Lord of the Dance* and *The Christ, Psychotherapy and Magic* which I had not yet found an appropriate time and opportunity or favourable configuration of the planets to lobby Don Weiser with.

[1] Originally proposed as a pen-name for Duncan on *Sword in the Sun*.

75. To the Revd Canon Anthony Duncan   *10ᵗʰ December 1995*

Dear Tony,

Many thanks for your comments on the Abbey papers. I feel pretty positive about them myself but it is good to have referred back to base for a navigational fix, so to speak, and to receive confirmation that I am still more or less on course.

As to their deserving a wide audience, I think that may be so, but the time is not yet. For the time being they seem to serve a more useful and functional purpose in being written for the few. I hope that does not sound too precious or closeted. Rather is it I think (and hope!) 'esoteric' in the true and proper sense of the word. That is they serve as a body of knowledge for the relatively few numbers of people who are sufficiently in tune with what I have to say as to be in sympathy with them, and give them a focus for the work to go on after I have shuffled from this mortal coil. 'Focus' being understood very much in its original sense as a 'hearth fire' – private or communal.

It may seem to be adding pretentiousness to preciosity in concerning myself with writing for 'posterity' rather than the current common herd, (who ain't much interested anyway), but let me say that I consider myself very much the junior partner in the production of this material. Who the chaps at the back of it are, I would not care to make too many claims. They have functional personalities within my own head that serve very well to get the business done but as one of them remarked to Dion Fortune: "What we are you cannot realise and it is a waste of time to try to do so, but you can imagine us ... ... and we can contact you through your imagination, and although your mental picture is not real or actual, the results of it are real and actual." So really they might have fluffy wings and dalmatics for all I know.

Fundamentally it is the content that is the crux of the matter. Although I have to say that the more I work with these fellas the more do I feel a part of something that is of the holy, the humanly warm and the true and the good. So at least half the purpose of writing up and circulating this stuff is that those who find a sympathetic chord with it will be brought into that same ambience. In esoteric chat this might be called being merged into their 'aura', individually or collectively, but in a sense that is not very far from your own meaning in talking about the 'mind' of Christ in your book of the same name. (And what dancing master really wrote that I would like to ask!)

Anyway, what nudged me into sending off this little lot to you was the receipt of your latest bunch of poems, because in *Spheres* and its evocation of halls and chapels and personages met, there seemed to be a distinct resonance with the abbey stuff. Mind you, yours is more abstract and individually tuned (the natural way of the mystic I suppose), as compared to my more plodding architectonic approach, but both seem to be part of the 'Interior Castle' or 'City of God' which others have entered and described with rather more distinction than ourselves, but I imagine witness has to be given to suit all ages as long as all ages continue to roll.

Apart from all this I am continuing to write 'my own' stuff, even if publishers don't seem to be too interested these days. Never having written anything in the past that has not been commissioned beforehand I find this an interesting experience, and a purifying one as well, as regards intentions and motive. By writing just what I think it is important to write for a few close friends, I fancy I can turn out something rather more significant than writing with one eye on some imagined 'market'. And again, time scale is not important.

The work in hand at the moment is a series of articles, or chapters, on various archetypes chucked up in my magical experience over the years, which oddly enough, (or perhaps not so oddly actually), coincide with many of the images and subjects that captured the interest of the once popular poet Alfred Noyes. Hardly ever read now, and academically derided, he was, from about 1905 to 1925 phenomenally popular. And popular because he had a gift for tapping into the British and indeed the American group soul – the images from the crypt in the order of things.

Mind you, he would have been horrified to be associated with anything 'magical', being a very conventional old stick, which is rather odd for someone who had a very 'magical' type of mind. That is, psychically open to that range of the inner side of things that gives the human race its ideals and aspirations – or cynicisms and corruptions if one is looking at the other side of the fence. So he could uplift and inspire a lot of people. Mind you, although technically competent in many ways, he wrote too much, and was a bit sloppy with it at times. And some of his anti-modernist literary criticism was a bit silly, but by and large he worked a power of good.

Anyway, writing 'my own' stuff as well as the 'received' stuff is a useful exercise in making a differentiation between 'me' and 'them' and retaining my own personal integrity. A matter which they are very meticulous in trying to observe, I have to say. I think their material is rather better, but they do tend to dictate at such a rate, and sometimes in gobbets of ideas, that it is difficult to get it down grammatically and coherently. It is rather like taking dictation in a foreign language and having to translate it at the same time as you go. About 500 words an hour is my usual going rate, but in a recent extended session of dictation I had to whack down about 4500 words in three hours.

Anyway, I must say I was rather taken with an Evangelical phrase you quoted: "I claim everything for Christ." Very apt for a lot of what I do, even if misunderstood. And might even be handy to inscribe across my insurance policy if the Fundies ever come round to firebomb my dwelling. Although they seem to reserve their fire of the Holy Spirit for psychic shops. (Not that some of the merchandise in such emporia do not thoroughly deserve it!)

But having survived the 75 car pile up on the M1 this morning, unscathed in person or property, I put my faith in the fact that somebody 'up there' still loves me. Or at any rate is giving me a further period of probation.

76. To Alan Adams   *10ᵗʰ January 1996*

Dear Alan,

Many thanks for your response to my card. Yes, why don't we exchange a few notes as to where we are on the Ladder of Perfection? Tempus is fugiting and I have suspicions that we are beginning to be looked upon as "grand old men" of the contemporary Western Mysteries. At least I have just realised that I am now about the age that Israel Regardie and W.E.Butler were, when I first contacted them with some kind of awe, in my immediately post-Inner Light activities, back in the mid sixties.

Anyway I seem to have achieved my ambition of reconstructing the kind of group such as I remember of the OGM at 3 Queensborough Terrace. Unlike you, I never managed to scramble up to IGM level before it all fell apart, but the remembrance of what it was all like seemed worth getting together again. Along with an accommodation of the Christian mystical tradition without becoming an off-beat religious sect, such as seemed to me to be the way the SIL was going when I felt I had had enough, about 1965.

From 1973 I started gathering students together with this goal in mind and since about 1981 have pretty well succeeded in getting there, with a group that is GM only – any LM training being done on an individual basis on the traditional master/apprenticeship basis.

We do not own any bricks and mortar as we have found a spiritual home that suits our purpose at Hawkwood College, in Stroud, the place where I made some kind of mark some years ago by conducting weekends where I gradually introduced more and more pathworking and then ritual until these began to get powerful enough to be difficult to handle without some restriction of membership. So I more or less packed in the public work and went in for private meetings about six times a year. We meet up for about 24 hours, from Saturday to Sunday lunchtime, and whoever feels like it lays on a ritual or other kind of working, and so we get through about three or four quite strong workings during the time. The interesting thing is that although there is no prior consultation, the work always turns out to have a common theme, which is pretty convincing evidence of inner plane running of things, or at the very least of a strong telepathic framework between members of the group.

A couple of years ago though, things moved up a couple of notches on the power levels, coincident with my being asked to edit Dion Fortune's War Letters, which were published under the title *Dion Fortune's Magical Battle of Britain* subsidised by the SIL. This formalised renewing of links, however much at arms length, brought a most unexpected influx of empowerment for me. I found myself the recipient, at first very much against my will and better judgment, of a great raft of communications from the three principal IPA associated with the SIL in the past: TM, MS and DC.

I have learned to live with this, and the flow still continues, and seems to be building up a body of information papers, rather like the raft of stuff that was a mainstay and powerful flywheel for the SIL (a lot of which of course CC was good enough to allow me to publish in my *Practical Guide to Qabalistic Symbolism* and *The Secret Tradition in Arthurian Legend*). It is not really for me to pass judgment upon the quality of this material but at least it seems more in the style of the communication one used to know before Rosina took over the SIL. It seems to do the trick for the group, and my old Helios and SIL colleague John Hall, to whom I vouchsafed a set recently, remarked that to him reading them felt like a "coming home".

As for the SIL, I have very little 'official' information. The Director is now David Williams, who I remember being an Outer Court Supervisor for, and who tells me that I took the Western Gate at his 1st Degree Initiation. But I have only had a somewhat tenuous business relationship with him as a result of doing the editing for the DF letters book. Rosina has apparently been put out to grass, and that last of the old guard of administrators, John Makin, was put out of capacity by a stroke a year or two back. They play, as ever, their cards pretty close to their chests, although they have ventured into a little bit of publishing, with a new edition of *The Cosmic Doctrine* apart from the Letters.

So that, in part, answers your question as to what I am writing, although it is rather in the stenographic mode. However, I am encouraged also to write something on my own account (as a prophylactic measure against being swamped by the consciousness of communicators, if nothing else). But what I am writing now is more for the circle of my own initiates than for the general public. This may sound a bit 'precious' but publishing in esoteric subjects is in something of the doldrums at the present, as a consequence of most of the small specialist publishers being taken over by multinational corporations, whose main interest is in fast selling titles with a broad market base, of which mine certainly are not. However, all is not lost, for there are small niche publishers in the USA who are keen enough to take over old titles – (sometimes changing the title) – so in the last couple of years *The Rose Cross and the Goddess* and *The Treasure House of Images* although out of print here, have been issued in the States as *Evoking the Goddess* and *Tarot and Magic*, and *A History of White Magic* as *Magic and the Western Mind*. Last year *Experience of the Inner Worlds* made the trans-Atlantic transition, to be followed this year by *The Secret Tradition in Arthurian Legend* and *The Magical World of the Tarot*.

And I have to say that writing for a small group of like minded initiates brings something of a release to trying to cater for an amorphous 'general market', goaded by politically correct script editors or mentally teen-aged marketing managers, which is the general ambience of things editorially these days. And of course most of DF's writing was, in the first instance, for the readers of the *Inner Light Magazine*.

If I were thirty, maybe even twenty, years younger, I would go back to 'niche' publishing myself, because the technology now makes this kind of thing a lot less risky and capital consuming than in old Helios days. But fortunately it seems that I don't have to, as one of the overseas members of my group, (we do have a handful of distant out-riders), has just started up just such a venture, called Sun Chalice Books, in Albuquerque, New Mexico.

Anyway what I am writing now is as close to an autobiography as I am likely to get, although autobiography is completely the wrong word, rather a kind of occultist's case book – something after Dr Taverner[1] I suppose, although I cannot hold a candle to that gentleman's melodramatic abilities. However, someone has to say what relatively high powered white magic is all about, and this seems to be the best way of doing it.

The other is more in the nature of symbolic historical fiction (I think) or it could be some kind of flashback either of my own or other people's memories. It all revolves around the Crusader Kingdoms of Jerusalem in the 12th/13th centuries and such is the pull that I have taken up serious study of French. Am currently reading Chrétien de Troyes in the original and taking a BA in French at the University of London as an external student, and tripping across to various sites in France that seem to have a connection.

This is also helped by, and is helping, (as ever, the Masters seem quite keen and capable of killing several birds with one stone), my having something of an input into French occult circles. Some of my books have been translated into French and I am at last now capable of lecturing with a degree of facility in the language.

However, whether in French or in English, I have rather gone off public jobs these days, apart from the occasional lecture. Doing 'workshops' for disparate groups of individuals whether in Bath, Avon or Lower Manhattan takes too much energy for too little results. Although being a guest for an already existing study or meditation group can have its rewards – at least there is some semblance of a group mind already in place without having to build from scratch.

Well, all that is quite enough to be going on with I think. Perhaps you will let me know what you are doing to usher in the new age. I got some idea from odd coded descriptions in Tanya Luhrmann's *Persuasions of the Witches' Craft* (ridiculous title) and assume you may have got a bead on some of my activities from the same source. But it is not the same as straight from the horse's mouth.

[1] Protagonist of Dion Fortune's book of sensational stories *The Secrets of Dr Taverner.*

77. To Simon Buxton   *29th February 1996*

Dear Simon,

Thank you for the photocopy of *Aphorisms of Creation*. Like you, I am not too sure of the validity of Nick Farrel's commercial assumptions so I do not intend to invest too much time and effort on what may very well end in tears. However, if the project seems editorially interesting I do not mind taking a gamble.

As I said before, Moriarty's work does not particularly enthuse me and indeed I gave away copies of his books that I previously had, as I felt that I could find a better use for the cupboard space. However, it will be an interesting exercise to read through the *Aphorisms* with Dion Fortune's *Cosmic Doctrine* in mind, and see if anything gels that might make the basis of an interesting commentary.

As regards your proposal about a joint Kenton/Knight do, I did have quite positive feelings about such a proposal when last you raised it, and this led to Warren and me meeting at his house, where we got on very well indeed. However, I got the feeling that he rather prefers to keep magic at public arm's length, and I can't say I blame him – even if basically we are in very much the same business! However, since then I have been having to review my own goals and aspirations and allocation of my time, and I am not really prepared to take a week out of my life for any residential workshop work of this nature. I feel my efforts should be concentrated on getting to grips with more specialist work, largely within the confines of my group, rather than expending effort on general educational work to the wider public.

As to the 1997 May conference – again I find events of this nature terminally boring, although if in London or some similar accessible place where escape to the real world is not too far away, I would quite enjoy the opportunity to chat with some of the other guests. Bugger the workings and the talks though. And on that score if I were to participate I would rather do so on the basis of a short platform talk rather than any kind of practical work, which generally has to be watered down to a degree of soporific blandness if catering for all comers on a semi-public basis.

Regarding SIL rituals, it is now some thirty years since I was a member, so I doubt if anything recently performed had much to do with what was going on then. However, I returned all papers to the Society, like a good boy (and photocopiers were not universal in those days!) nor were any rituals allowed out of the house at that time. I regret I cannot help you on this one.

Sorry that much of the contents of this letter are on the negative side, but I lead a very active and positive life really! It's just that things do become more 'occult' and 'esoteric' as one grows older. As to the Quest conference, (which came out of positive reaction to the *Magical Battle of Britain* actually), I have already been propositioned for lunch but I imagine that things will be sufficiently informal for anyone to join in, so will welcome a chat if you are around.

78. To David Williams *24ᵗʰ May 1996*

Dear David,

What ways do I find *The Cosmic Doctrine* to be a 'flawed masterpiece'? Well there's a short answer to that and also a long one, perhaps several long ones!

The short answer, I think, has its roots in paragraph 3 of page 16 of *Introduction II* in the current edition, and in particular the sentence: "A well-stocked mind tends to combine its contents into organised complexes, and then the complexes form units which have to be stimulated as a whole and can only function according to their own nature and *cannot be recombined to express new ideas.*" (my italics).

My point being that I think that DF, possibly implicitly encouraged by CTL, had tacit assumptions that she was embarked upon a work of wide ranging cosmic theosophical metaphysics whereas I fancy the real intention might have been more specific and focused, that is to say the mechanisms of the transmission of energies from one plane of existence to another. This assumption may also have been encouraged by her former teacher Theodore Moriarty's approach to things. (In reading his work, particularly *Aphorisms of Creation,* one is immediately struck by terms that reappear in *The Cosmic Doctrine* – Lords of Flame, Form & Mind, for instance, – and also his wide metaphysical teaching intentions, which, however, to my mind are little more than warmed up and rehashed elementary theosophy. Although in fairness one has only the uncorrected notes of those who attended his lectures, and he must have been a bit more capable than he appears, to have so impressed DF in her early years).

So I think gobbets of half-digested Moriarty tend to push the communicator(s) off course a bit. In my own limited experience of taking communications, I have found this to be the most subtle and difficult of distractions to avoid. The communicator is happily picking over the contents of one's subconscious mind when he picks up some morsel which disconcertingly turns out to be latched on to a great string or complex of associated ideas and so the whole lot comes through as 'communication'. This kind of thing can be got over in the end, partly by intelligent and spiritually informed editing and also by further sustained experience of the parties involved working together. (The communicator possibly learns the hard way which treacherous bits of the subconscious to avoid.) If you are lucky the communication simply turns out to be a bit more prolix and circuitous than it need have been. In the *CD* as a whole I think it tends to put a slightly off centre slant upon the general direction of the work.

Easy to criticise of course, particularly after seventy years of hindsight, so I hasten to add that I still regard it basically as a masterpiece. And this because of the intuitive and spiritual attraction it has, rather like myth or legend, or an old mystery tradition *ludibrium*. There must be something in it to have caused me to have read it more, I am sure, than a hundred times over the years, to say nothing of intense study of particular parts. So it can't be all bad! But when you get down to detailed analysis of some of the comings and goings of the swarms and the joining up together of complex atoms there is a considerable grinding of the gears discernible, which suggests that all is not received quite as it was intended. However, the adage "to train the mind rather than to inform it" provides enough mental lubrication to keep things from seizing up altogether.

Something of the same misunderstanding of direction happened with the communications that Yeats received, via his wife, at about the same time, which he later published as *A Vision*. He spent much time working over it assuming it to be a work of cosmic historio-philosophy, to be told by the communicators that their main intention was to provide images for his poetry. Which indeed it did and no mistake. There are more ways to kill a cat than cosmically lecture it to death.

79. To Randall Prickett   *11th July 1996*

Dear Randall,
Glad you liked my contribution to *GD Journal II*. I also have an article in *No. III* which is largely of an inner plane origin although I have not gone out of my way to say so – don't want to encourage indiscriminate "channelling", there is so much junk being passed off via that route. And it is the quality of the text that counts, not who is supposed to have dictated it. Nothing then until the Alchemical edition, when I have contributed some relatively far out stuff on the intelligences behind the chemical elements.

Otherwise Llewellyn have rather cooled off me. Perhaps because *Magic and the Western Mind* (their version of *A History of White Magic*) is not a best seller, but I think largely because they are fairly heftily inflicted with the neo-pagan virus which makes me *persona non grata* in certain circles. I offered them the rights on *The Secret Tradition in Arthurian Legend* and *The Magical World of the Tarot*, which they declined, and probably that was for the best as they have now been taken on by Weisers, who recently reissued my text of Christian Qabalistic magic *Experience of the Inner Worlds*.

May I recommend *Patterns of Magical Christianity* to you, by Nicholas Whitehead? He is a young (by my standards) Canadian who lives in New Mexico and has worked with me in the past. His book is on much the same lines as *Experience of the Inner Worlds*, and uses much the same sequence of symbolism (which in any case derives from *The Lord of the Dance* by Anthony

Duncan – a bit of high power channelling that I originally published some twenty five years ago).

He has started up his own small publishing company devoted largely to Christian based magic and as well as his own book is reissuing a couple of my neglected oldies *The Practice of Ritual Magic* and *Occult Exercises and Practices* to be followed up with a companion new one on *Magical Images and the Magical Imagination*. Also *The Lord of the Dance* and a number of other titles by Anthony Duncan (a highly clairvoyant and mystical Anglican clergyman, now retired, that James Hall may remember meeting at my house in Tewkesbury). He has also just sent me some tapes called *The Christian Mysteries*, part of a correspondence course, which are very well done indeed.

I don't have much to say about your symbolic suggestions and queries. You seem to be on much the right lines, and it is really for you to decide on angelic names and such rather than have me dump my assumptions upon you. I have had a letter from James Hall in the past few days, and will be replying to him as soon as I've printed off this one to you.

80. To Dr James Hall 12th August 1996

Dear James,

Thank you for yours of 2nd. I have already responded to letters from Randall and Jim and don't have anything more to add that is likely to be of use. If they have what it takes to start a new group then they ought to be able to find the necessary guidance from within themselves without involving you and me in a long distance vicarious course in esoteric driving instruction.

The Eastern Esoteric Tradition has never taken up too much of my attention, the Western is quite demanding enough without trying to complicate the issue. I might have once toyed with the idea of a grand synthesis but do not these days think it to be very realistic an aspiration. What was it Kipling wrote? *"East is East and West is West and never the twain shall meet"*. People usually cut off the quotation at this point but it does go on to say: *"Till Earth and Sky stand presently at God's great Judgment Seat"*, which while it gives some hope to syncretists I concede, may seem rather a long wait. But as more immediate answer to your question I think the wisdom lies in the following two lines: *"But there is neither East nor West, Border, nor Breed, nor Birth,/When two strong men stand face to face, though they come from the ends of the earth!"*

And although, as I recall, all this was preliminary to some kind of spectacular punch up, the moral I feel lies not with the Schwarzeneggers and Sumo wrestlers of this world but with each one meeting the highest calling of their own particular localised integrity. I suppose in the end this comes down to esoteric federalists and esoteric militia men – which is perhaps the expression of one of the fundamental polarities of human existence.

Which I suppose leads us naturally into Qabalah. I do not know if Alan Adams and I are in current agreement on this philosophy as we have not exchanged opinions on the subject for the past 30 years and more – we are laconic folk, we British. But as we cut our teeth in the same occult cradle I presume we are not too far apart in basic assumptions about the machinery of the universe, whatever we may have bolted on by way of personal modifications along the way. I have not read Scholem's *Origins of Kaballah* but if it is the same Scholem as who wrote *Major Trends in Jewish Mysticism* then he can hardly be quarrelled with as one of the leading academic experts upon the subject world wide. But then you have to take into account that Jewish Qabalism is a very different thing from the "pick and mix" bag of tricks that Gentile occultists and hermetic philosophers have come up with, by raiding the Jewish tradition since the Renaissance, starting with Pico della Mirandola. In his *Major Trends* ... Scholem called Crowley's version of Qabalah (and by implication all Golden Dawn derivatives) "highly coloured nonsense". It isn't that, (or if it is I have just wasted a life), but it does indicate the great gulf that exists between Jewish mysticism and post-Renaissance magical philosophy. Tony Duncan's *The Christ, Psychotherapy & Magic* puts the issues into easily comprehensible terms.

Thanks for using the word "henotheism" – just the one I was looking for in a new book I'm writing.

I am not on e-mail or fax. I was going to say "I regret to say..." but on reflection I am not. I incline toward the life of a recluse these days, and would have the phone cut off if it were not for Roma and the kids. Not that I do not welcome communication from old friends such as yourself but I grow increasingly conscious of "time's winged chariot" whilst I still have a lot more stuff to write down for the benefit of an unsuspecting but I trust deserving posterity. Have four books on the go at the moment, and am doing a BA in French at the University of London so that I can read up on Francophone sources. So retirement from full time work is turning out to be quite busy.

So this also gives the reply to your little note of a couple of weeks back. A grand esoteric free-for-all might be welcome to some – but not for me. Is there a Jungian archetype for the lone Magus locked up in his attic writing more and more obscure words of wisdom so that in the end only he can understand them? Don't think I have quite reached that stage yet, although I become aware that perhaps the greatest truths can only be presented in terms of fiction. Hence the Rosicrucian penchant for 'ludibria' of which I think Apuleius' *Golden Ass* to be an early example. I suppose this is maybe a rather long winded western form of Zen koan. But now we are back to Kipling again...

81. To Dan Staroff *1ˢᵗ January 1997*

Dear Dan Staroff,

Thank you for your letter and specimen Tarot artwork which arrived a couple of days ago, and which I am returning enclosed herewith.

I am impressed with your standard of draftsmanship and artistic sense, and your designs remind me very much, and I must say compare favourably, with Lady Frieda Harris' work on *The Book of Thoth* for Aleister Crowley, only in your case without some of the Mega Therion's symbolic and philosophical idiosyncrasies.

It would seem that Betty Lundsted is similarly impressed in order for her to suggest some kind of collaboration between us and to take the trouble to forward your proposal to me. However, I regret to say that I do not think this is a feasible option.

This is largely because in the light of some thirty years experience since the *Practical Guide* was published, I have moved somewhat away from the rather rigid symbolic formulations that appear in that book towards a very much more flexible approach, something of which I have published in my more recent *Tarot & Magic* (Destiny Books 1993) and *The Magical World of the Tarot* just re-issued by Weisers. In these I have publicly gone on record encouraging people to formulate the detail of their own Tarot images as the best way to learn the magical ropes, and also to make them as simple as possible so as to give the opportunity for specific ancillary imagery to build up round them as occasion demands. It follows from this that I can hardly lend my name to a very complex and detailed set of designs such as you propose and their quite rigid adherence to the Golden Dawn system.

I should say that there already exists a deck of *Gareth Knight Tarot* which I worked on with a Dutch artist way back in 1962 and which were originally intended to appear alongside *The Practical Guide*, although for various reasons (largely financial) they did not actually see the light of day until 1985 when Stuart Kaplan of U.S. Games Systems took an interest in publishing them.

Anyway you could do worse than approach Stuart Kaplan with your proposal. He is probably the leading collector in the world of Tarot decks, and has authored a three volume encyclopaedia on the subject, as you may already know, besides being the president of U.S. Games Systems Inc. I think your work of sufficient quality, artistically and esoterically, possibly to interest him even without the backing of a "big name".

One word of warning though, as I imagine you are a design professional, do not expect to make a fortune, or even a living, out of Tarot cards for the Qabalistically sophisticated. Unit sales are likely to be in the hundreds rather than the thousands which does not leave you with much reward on a five percent royalty.

Should Stuart Kaplan not be interested you could think about an approach to Chic and Tabatha Cicero who edit the *Golden Dawn Journal* and who have written one or two books on the subject, with Israel Regardie's blessing. They would seem to have their finger on the pulse of what would be your main market and might be able to give you a helping hand.

Of course I suppose it is always possible that Weisers might be interested to take the plunge if a suitable collaborator could be found, and I am sorry that I am not able to put myself forward in this position. Anyway, thank you for thinking of me and the confirmation that some of my scribblings, even the apprentice work, continue to be of use.

82. To David Williams   *12th June 1997*

Dear David,

I enclose article as promised for the next Journal, 'Wells of Vision', and hope you will find it acceptable.

Also enclosed is a photocopy of a poster shortly going up around the Cheltenham area vis-à-vis a play that Rebecca has written. Although we do not talk about such things outside a small discrete and trusted circle the play is largely *about* our friend Carstairs and to a large extent *written* by him.

We attended a rehearsed reading of it recently that was put on as a try out and it was very funny, very sad and also packing quite an 'inner' punch. Anyway it was sufficiently successful to attract no less than two companies wanting to put it on, and Rebecca has also been asked by the Gloucestershire Red Cross to write a musical play based on the records of local military hospitals during the 1st World War.

All this seems to be very much part of an 'inner' push to keep the memories of that of 1914-18 (and indeed other wars) alive. One or two chapters in *An Introduction to Ritual Magic* related to the same theme.

I have received a single advance copy of the book and am quite pleased with the standard of production. I shall not be receiving others though until I return from holiday after next weekend. Rebecca, Roma and I are going to Ypres and environs from 14th to 21st which on the face of it seems likely to be something of a busman's holiday, at any rate for Rebecca.

You are very welcome to get up a coach party of Inner Lighters to come and see the play in September, but should that not be a practicality I enclose a script for your interest and files.

Am hoping to be sending you and Tom MSS of *The Circuit of Force* by the end of the month, but it is going to be a bit tight for time, as an enormous amount of research has had to go into it. However, I do take deadlines seriously.

83. To Mark Whitehead   *1ˢᵗ November 1997*

Dear Mark,

First of all, many thanks for your statement of sales and most welcome cheque. It is good to see the books doing so well, and I think that, apart from any distribution arrangements you may have, the excellent book designs you have come up with will have played a large part. I look forward very much to seeing MIMI in all her glory in due course.

I was much interested in the book reviews and I must say it was a refreshing change to find a reviewer who seemed actually to have read the books concerned. I think he has rather too strong a penchant for the word "derided" and I trust that none of my works, or Tony Duncan's, gives the impression of "deriding" anybody – it is possible surely to take a firm standpoint of opinion without necessarily flinging derision over anyone who does not agree. However, there has ever been a slightly paranoid tendency in many folk upon the esoteric scene.

Apart from the publishing side of things I was most encouraged to see the progress you are making with getting the message across, not only in interviews, but in getting people doing some actual work. Your description of the Dallas set-up, "still in the Victorian Age – all covert and somewhat fearful" was priceless, and from what I have been able to judge from past correspondence, only too accurate. Mind you, that was the ambience in which I learned my trade, and also Alan Adams, who was my associate in the Society of the Inner Light as we made our way up the grades in the late 1950s. Alan was always very much of a traditionalist and has evidently put his mark upon groups he has helped to set up, both in Dallas and London. There may still be a place for this approach, it marks a particular stage and standard in the evolution of the tradition, although I am more than pleased to find you making such a success in following along the lines of my own more free wheeling and laid back methodology. More importantly, it is a great thrill to see the kind of results you are achieving, particularly when thinking back to the small beginnings between Tony Duncan and myself in Tewkesbury back in 1964/5. Mind you, it has taken thirty odd years to get this far, but I feel that it may very well start to snowball.

My own efforts are very much in an easterly direction at present. Not very far easterly, just across the English channel. It is something of a different ambience as the French people I am working with take the Christian side of things for granted, they just need beefing up on the practical possibilities. I have just come back from a weekend in Paris coincident with the French language publication of *The Secret Tradition in Arthurian Legend*.

Apart from that I have the very rewarding task of carrying on the work of revamping some of Dion Fortune's bits and pieces, the first of which you have seen. Am expecting the page proofs of *The Circuit of Force* any day now and am halfway through writing my half of *The Principles of Hermetic Philosophy* with *Spiritualism in the Light of Occult Science* to follow early in the new year – which I am quite looking forward to as an opportunity to get to grips with various problems ancient and modern about inner plane communications. On the subject of which another very exciting roller coaster ride has been Rebecca's unexpected level of ability at all things magical, and her contact Carstairs' ability to make things happen. I only hope that, tender of age as she is, she manages to fulfil what seems to be a pretty impressive and demanding potential.

84. To David Williams   *26ᵗʰ November 1997*

Dear David,
I have pleasure in enclosing finished typescript, including rough drafts of illustrations, of *Principles of Hermetic Philosophy* which I hope will meet with your approval.

I enclose three copies of the David Carstairs scripts,[1] which I promised to send some time ago, but events have been more than hectic on the Rebecca front. Immediately after the play was produced she was into the business of selling her flat, buying a house, and on Saturday is getting married. This will be to the young man who played David Carstairs' batman but I don't know if this has any symbolic significance.

As if this were not enough there now promises to be a professional London run of the play, starting February 9ᵗʰ at the Grace Theatre in Battersea. Not exactly Shaftesbury Avenue but a step in the right direction I suppose.

Anyway I am off to Cheltenham for the weekend to fulfil my paternal role as best I may and will return on Sunday to get stuck into the delights of *Spiritualism in the Light of Occult Science*. One thing about this series of books is that it gives me the opportunity to dig back in to a number of areas of belief that one has taken for granted for years, dust them off and have a new look at them. I am quite looking forward to getting to grips with the issues of inner plane communication of various sorts over the past couple of hundred years with a view to discerning where we should go from here.

[1] Written inner plane communications from David Carstairs, taken by Rebecca.

85. To Billi Roberti   *27th November 1997*

Dear Billi,
Thank you very much for persuading your sister Susan to write to me about her meditational experience with the Chapels of Remembrance.[1] My daughter and I were very much encouraged by it, as it shows that the work is not only powerful but being pushed through from the inner on a world wide basis.

It has all led to some quite remarkable experiences for us, following visits to Belgium and France over the past two years, and I think I can do no better, by way of a thank you, than to send you a preview of an article I have written for the next issue of the *Inner Light Journal*, which describes in some detail some of the dynamics of this work.

It was very good of Dolores to speak in positive terms about my work but I would hesitate to spread the impression that we rush about the astral somewhat after the fashion of Batman and Robin. However, magic is a powerful technique and has resonances that seem to be able to ring bells far afield.

[1] Rebecca's ritual for relief of war victims, described in *An Introduction to Ritual Magic* by Dion Fortune and Gareth Knight (Thoth Publications 1997).

86. To David Williams   *22nd December 1997*

Dear David,
Many thanks for all the material recently received. An article is enclosed for the next magazine which I hope will meet with approval and prove entertaining and instructive for readers.

This as you will see, is on Margaret Lumley Brown, or at any rate some of the outer aspects of her. As with most occultists of high inner rank the whole truth can never be told because few people would understand. This I suppose is the real reason why the subject is called 'esoteric' – for the few. It has little to do with barriers of secrecy, which to my mind can cause greater ills than those they try to prevent.

As to ideas for a new book, what you have sent me suggests two possible avenues to me: one on Margaret Lumley Brown and the other on Esoteric Therapeutics.

Book on Margaret Lumley Brown. As you will see from the article I have quite a lot of material of hers in the form of articles that have been published in magazines in the past, from the *Occult Review* to *New Dimensions*, and also the short book *Both Sides of the Door*. Supplementing these with relevant snippets judiciously chosen from her esoteric diaries I could weave a coherent kind of fabric out of it all. Thus most of it would be by MLB herself, (in or out of trance), but with linking commentary by me. [1]

Esoteric Therapeutics. I would prefer to call any resultant book *Principles of Esoteric Healing* I think, and to credit it entirely to Dion Fortune, as I am convinced that it is pretty well entirely through her mediumship. A first shot at the prelims is enclosed which shows the kind of thing I have in mind.[2]

Ted Gellately may have been given the job of trying to sort it out a bit with a view to circulation, if not publication, but I do not see anything original by him in any of this. I knew him moderately well and did badger him from time to time to put some of his wide experience of esoteric and orthodox medicine into writing. Such a proposal did not seem to interest him though.

We are thus safe in assuming, I think, that it is all Dion Fortune's work. The material on the Ghost was around by May 1940, for it was published in the magazine then; and the bit of stuff from Vaughan, which I have seen previously in manuscript when I was librarian, dates I am pretty sure from about 1934. There are also verbatim reports of trance interviews, the earliest 1921 and the latest 1942. Although EG joined the Society young, and figures as A. of S.M. in MLB's diaries as early as 1946, this puts him pretty firmly out of court as an originator.

If my preliminary calculations are right (which depends on how much duplication I have yet to find) it should make up into a full size book without any input from me – which is just as well for I have little of my own to add to the subject. However, it does need a thorough editing job, rephrasing some of the infelicities of expression, and putting it all into some kind of logical order.

Finally I much appreciate your sending me the supplementary material on the M.R.'s remarks on Dion Fortune. I don't know if personal files of lapsed members have been kept, in which case you will be able to read up that this little episode was sparked by my being 'bounced' by the said entity shortly before. Not quite in the league of MLB's experiences but quite hair raising enough at the time.

I had a long message from the Chancellor and was given a couple of weeks free processing by Anne, and no great problems have been experienced since.

Quite a good story could be made out of this long running saga but not I think suitable for general publication. It is odd how all this apparently far ranging star and ancient civilisation stuff has at the same time such a claustrophobic side to it. I have done some ancillary work on the matter from time to time since, in order to resolve some of the outstanding problems of what, by its very nature, is a kind of hall of distorting mirrors, which is the kind of complication you get when Higher Selves start jumping into each other's Personalities.

[1] Subsequently published as *Pythoness, the Life and Work of Margaret Lumley Brown.*
[2] Subsequently published as *Principles of Esoteric Healing* by Dion Fortune.

87. To Professor Sir Michael Dummett   *15th January 1998*

Dear Professor Dummett,
Thank you for your letter of 12th. Yes, I know of you from your big Duckworth book from which I gained much pleasure and profit, and I have asked my local library to bring me a sight of your latest.

You seem to be contemplating quite a challenge in the sequel to it. However, despite the plethora of books and packs since the nineteen sixties, a very large proportion seem to take in Arthur Edward Waite's old washing.

I would be happy to meet some time. London is most convenient for me, as it is an hour by train, although I am at a loss to suggest a suitable venue. Alternatively I can run across to see you by car one day, although I do not much care for Oxford's horrendous parking facilities.

Anyway, as regards date and time I am very flexible, I have a number of writing commitments which keep me busy, but being retired from the world or work I can come and go as I please. Perhaps you would care to ring me with your preferred options.

Please give my regards to Tanya Luhrmann if she is in your immediate circle of acquaintance.

88. To Professor Ronald Hutton   *17th February 1998*

Dear Professor Hutton,
Thank you for your letter of 13th. Glad to be of service in a good cause. The stamps present no problem, as a correspondence chess player, every little helps in this direction.

Interesting what you say about Crowley's diary entry in early '45. It ties in with suggestions that DF was, or felt herself, under some kind of occult attack (possibly from sources favourable to Indian independence who identified her in some way with support for the British raj). I have heard verbal speculation about this and it has some documentary support from fragments of her esoteric diaries that I have seen. If in such a situation, who better to consult than the old monster? He was indubitably one of the most knowledgeable practical magicians around, and had shown himself well disposed to her by sending her a complimentary copy of his *Book of Thoth*. This, I should emphasise is mere speculation on my part. I have never encouraged such kinds of theory in public, as it is helpful to no-one, whether true or not. One also has to take into account the onset of leukaemia which struck her down in January 1946. Not that this is necessarily the result of any psychic attack but that her general concern with such may have been a symptom of the oncoming disease.

I do not see much disagreement between us over the watershed in the early/mid 30s. To my mind it is still *The Mystical Qabalah* which is the important work, during the writing of which, in instalments for her magazine from about 1931 on, it seems to me she very much found herself, and there is a marked change from the somewhat naïve pre-1930 bright learner to the mature teacher. We have to bear in mind in all of this that book publication follows about a year or so after the actual writing. The *MQ* was published in book form in 1935. *The Winged Bull* was published very soon afterwards, possibly the same year, and forms part of a trilogy in which she specifically says that the aim is to illustrate in practical terms the theory taught in the *MQ*. She then went on to write *The Goat-foot God* which was published a year later, in 1936. There was then a hiccup in the publishing sequence, and it seems to me that the publishers found that the novels did not sell too well and so declined to publish the third, *The Sea Priestess*. She published this with her own money in 1938. At the same time she writes some articles in her magazine spelling out to the dim public what they are obviously missing, analysing some of the symbolism.

I would not disagree with you about *Moon Magic* being started very soon after *The Sea Priestess*, which indeed would place its commencement possibly as early as 1937. However, the book would not gel in the writing of it, and she later records that she started and re-started it half a dozen times before hitting upon the idea of writing it in the first person singular, when it took on a considerable power somewhat like giving expression to a secondary personality. It was unfinished at the time of her death, and the last two chapters were added by another hand, a very good one, I have to say, in my opinion. Whether inspired or entranced is open to conjecture. There is no evidence to my knowledge that places the actual writing of the various attempts at *MM* in time. I have tended to assume them spread out over time during the war period, but on reflection it may well have been that she did all this re-writing just before the war, and then the outbreak of war brought other priorities so that it was abandoned incomplete in 1939.

What *is* specifically in the war time period is the weekly war letters 1939 to 1942. Followed by monthly letters from 1942 on. These latter contained 'Principles of Hermetic Philosophy' (April 1943 to March 1944), and 'Esoteric Principles of Astrology' (November 1942 to February 1943) which I have edited and will be publishing together under the former title. 'The Circuit of

Force' dates from February 1939 to August 1940 as articles in the *Inner Light* magazine, which folded through paper rationing with this last number. This is also in production under my editorship from Thoth Publications.

I agree that there is a strong pagan element evident in 1937/8 in the *Inner Light* magazine, and this reflected work and thought in the Society at the time, although at the same time it should be remembered that the Guild of the Master Jesus was still going strong, even if some members (e.g. Colonel Seymour) did not think much of it. It seemed to me that Dion Fortune and others were deeply influenced by Jane Harrison's classic *Prolegomena on Greek Religion* at this time, and seem recently to have discovered it although it had been around since 1903. The war time writings of DF are generally Hermetically philosophic in tone but with a bit more open handedness in practical details vis-à-vis circulation of light in the aura, etc. Stuff which is largely common knowledge nowadays but in the pre-war period there was considerable paranoia about occult secrecy and the need for it – even amongst open minded pioneers like Dion Fortune and Israel Regardie.

The important point I would like to emphasise is the three-fold strand of Christian/Elemental/Hermetic which was central to Dion Fortune's work and thought. It is necessary to emphasise this because there are many who, enamoured of one or other of these three strands, try to read their own specific preference into phases of her life. No doubt there are times when one or the other becomes more predominant in on-going work, ask any practising occultist about this cyclic feature of practical work, but I would not like to see you giving too much credence to one party or the other in any special pleading.

She started off with very much a psychological slant, which gradually drew her towards hermetic studies and practical spiritualistic techniques on the quiet. She then was brought up short with a Christian impact. (This happens from time to time throughout the whole of the modern esoteric movement in the west and is worth a PhD thesis from someone.) After this she grabbed or fashioned the three fold strand which to my mind characterises her life's work.

89. Dr Terryl Kinder   *23rd February 1998*

Dear Terryl,

First of all, thank you very much for the magnificent book, which is not only a joy to the eye and a feast for the brain but admirable exercise for my French. Roma and I are toying with the idea of a motor trip around parts of France in the coming year so if this comes to fruition I hope we can take the opportunity to meet up and take a look round some of your domain. I am getting quite heavily into Eleanor of Aquitaine at the moment and feel the need to get around to Fontevrault by way of a good round trip, coming down through Flanders and Champagne towards Vezelay and then cutting across to Poitou and Anjou and back up through Normandy. Am very keen to visit Fontevrault although I suspect it may have been touristically sanitised pretty drastically by now.

At any rate it will make a change from the 1914-18 Western Front which we have spent the last two years visiting with Rebecca. Her play[1] about Carstairs has transferred to a London 'fringe' theatre, where it is playing throughout February in a professional production. Am pleased to say she had a very good review from one of the leading critics, Michael Billington of *The Guardian* who wrote "The standard first world war play is still R.C. Sherriff's *Journey's End* but Rebecca, a 29-year-old from Cheltenham, knocks it into a cocked hat... ... a more than promising debut". As a result she has had two agents looking to take her onto their books, which is the main aim of the game at the moment.

By way of some small return for your magnificent tome I enclose my own latest publication, *Magical Images and the Magical Imagination* which you may find of some help in getting to grips with the rationale of the abbey complex. I regret I cannot take you on another grand tour of the building but if instead of going round on another quick trip you concentrate on one or two specific locations and see what you get or "who" you can contact you should in time start to get some practical results – though do not be discouraged if you do not find the same facility as Rebecca, who does seem to have something of an unusual gift for the game. Result of a mis-spent childhood secretly reading her father's books under the bed clothes it would seem, or maybe it's in the genes.

[1] *This Wretched Splendour* by Rebecca Wilby, subsequently published by Skylight Press.

90. To Professor Sir Michael Dummett   *4th May 1998*

Dear Michael,
Glad to hear you and your wife had a good time on Lake Como. At the moment my wife has deserted me to go on a trip to Prague, which leaves me time to make a few comments and corrections as requested. I have written numbers on the script to which the following notes refer. If you have any supplementary questions or you would like me to check through again any rewrite feel free to come back to me.

... ... Trust all this will be of help. I have read *A Wicked Pack of Cards* since we met, and am filled with admiration at your meticulous devotion to this self imposed task. If I make one comment, it is that I am not sure that any conspiracy theory would be an accurate assessment of the motives of the occult fraternity in making false claims about the history of the Tarot or indeed of the esoteric movement in general. There is such a thing as natural ignorance and naïvety based upon it.

Speaking for myself, the system works as a framework for various kinds of imaginative work of an occult nature. It is a natural assumption (which you and your colleagues may well prove false) that it was designed to be such. If you do so I personally will not find it to be the end of the world, simply because it manifestly works. It may well be that any association of stock images from the general cultural store would do as well – a kind of grand psychological Rorschach ink blot test, I suppose. That is to say, given enough complication, then the mind may start to project its own structures, or structures of a higher form of perception, within it.

As I say, the system works. So, for me, the history of its coming together is largely an irrelevance. (My most distinguished critic, Kathleen Raine, considers me to be the "most pragmatic" of magicians. I was not sure what she meant, until considering the matter in this context.) Where you and your works will upset a lot of occult aficionados is when they have the history of the system bound up as part and parcel of their belief system. Thus if you destroy their historical assumptions you will seem to be destroying their cherished spiritual beliefs – rather like fundamentalist Christians faced with textual Biblical criticism.

For myself I very much welcome the fact that some professional scholarship is being applied to the esoteric field these days, as in my opinion the truth never hurt anybody. But then I always was a bit of a naïve optimist.

91. To Debbie Rice   *6th May 1998*

Dear Debbie,

Many thanks for your letter. I don't know, but everybody seems to be in the wars at the moment. We have just been burgled, the poor old cat is under the vet, Roma has been having minor ups and downs in health, and a coach company have been doing their best to ruin a week's holiday for her, whilst daughter Rebecca and her husband are both suddenly out of work. Oh, and the drainage system in our back garden is on the point of collapse.

However, others seem to be getting things even worse, so we are just counting our blessings. The flu epidemic which floored me twice at Christmas and early in the New Year did even worse for poor Alan Adams, who never recovered from it and died in March. I found this quite a shock as he and I were close friends and contemporaries in the SIL, and more or less raced each other up the grades in the 1950s. I was also best man at his wedding, to another SIL initiate, Mary Popper, as she then was.

I was quite gobsmacked at the funeral when in walked their daughter Juliette, who is the exact spitting image of her mother as I remembered her from forty years ago! Put me in quite a time warp for a minute or two.

With regard to the SIL I trust that all the reported changes prove to be beneficial. By another odd time warp I was invited back to visit the house just a few days after Alan's funeral, and met the company now in charge. David Williams, the current Warden, and I are old acquaintances, as we were associated in one or two little publishing ventures in old Helios days, and he was a contributor to the old *New Dimensions* magazine I used to run. Apparently, although I had not remembered it, I was also in western office at his initiation.

Anyway, it was quite something to be invited back to look around, after 34 years wandering in outer darkness. I was quite impressed with the feel of the place and what they are trying to do, and to cut a long story short, have just been re-admitted to the Society (without having to do the study course or work my way through the Lesser Mysteries I am glad to say) as a direct entrant to the newly opened OGM. So we will see where we go from here!

I am enclosing an article which I hope you will find suitable for *Ophir*. As luck would have it I am just in the process of typing up the best of my old articles from the past thirty odd years with a view to their being published in a collected edition in America. This will not see the light of day until about the year 2000 so in the meantime I think it very worthwhile if some of the stuff gets another airing in *Ophir*. This first one is an elaboration of the talk I gave at the first of Bob Stewart's 'Merlin' conferences, in London.

And by all means help yourself to anything you fancy out of old *Quadriga*s. Anyway, all power to you in all you do, and the best of luck to go with it. It's not a bad old planet as long as you don't weaken!

92. To Warren Kenton   *3rd August 1998*

Dear Warren,

Thank you for your note about the Kabbalah Society conference, in which I will be pleased to participate on the terms you outline. Qabalah (never mind the spelling!) as taught and understood from Robert Fludd via Athanasius Kircher, Eliphas Levi, Papus up to the alumni of the Golden Dawn will be fine by me, which I assume can include its latter day students such as Paul

Case, Israel Regardie and Dion Fortune. (I suppose Crowley calls for a brief mention, not least because he is mentioned by Scholem in his magnum opus – but I understand and concur with the purpose of the conference to concentrate upon the philosophical and spiritual aspects of the subject rather than any highly coloured applications.)

I append below the first shot at a biographical programme note for me. If you would like it amplified, elaborated or recast in any way, let me know.

Gareth Knight learned his Qabalah from the school of Dion Fortune, author of "The Mystical Qabalah" (1935) and latter day representative of the Golden Dawn tradition, and has since contributed his own authorship to the subject in "A Practical Guide to Qabalistic Symbolism" (1965). He is well known internationally as a lecturer upon this and related subjects, particularly in Paris where he lectures in French, generally as a guest of one of the Martinist Orders. A publisher of academic textbooks by profession, he is now retired and whatever time is not given to reading or writing devotes to music and chess, both of which he plays badly but with romantic enthusiasm.

93. To Mike Harris

3ʳᵈ October 1998

Dear Mike,

Many thanks for the further thoughts on group re-organisation. I have in the meantime been giving some more thought and intuitive meditation to the matter and am rather coming to the conclusion that we should be looking at change in the running of the group rather than in trying to bolster up the existing system.

All groups change in their perspectives as indeed the recent 25-year history of the group goes to demonstrate. If a group is to survive as a worthwhile and vibrant entity it has constantly to temper its aims and ideals against the quality and quantity of its membership, and the outer world circumstances with which it has to cope – all elements which are also subject to change.

We have gone through various phases since the group was founded in 1973 as a close reading of the history will reveal. The driving force behind much of its life has been my vision of trying to reproduce what I had found best in the Greater Mystery degrees of the Society of the Inner Light after that group, in my opinion, had fallen away from the way I felt they ought to go.

To begin with, with our three Lesser Mystery Degrees, complete with magazine for the Outer Court, we tracked along the way that the SIL had developed in the decades before the war. Once we got to the stage where we could operate a Greater Mystery Lodge such as I envisaged, a corps of

Adepti meeting to perform their own work, we let the Lesser Mysteries drop away, for better or for worse, although I must say I do not regret having done so, even if our recruitment of new members has barely kept us quorate, a situation which we have alleviated recently by inviting visitors.

Once having created this group of aspiring Adepti it was not my wish to hang on to leadership indefinitely, and it seemed to me an interesting experiment to try what might be regarded as a Round Table Formula of circulating headship that functioned also as a training role in esoteric leadership. Over more than a decade this has worked very well, by and large, but there would seem to be a limit as to how long we can play this game.

There is plainly now a dearth of new recruits for such a post and even recycling former Magi begins to have a tired air about it. As is fairly obvious, organisational ability and commitment do not necessarily go hand in hand with magical ability, and we are probably lucky not to have had any major disasters, even if my eyes have been turned in supplication to the heavens at times. It is also arguable that unacceptable burdens have been sometimes placed on those who have been asked to perform the function, and felt obliged to do so, whether from moral obligation or ambition.

I am therefore quite happy to concede that we have reached a time when the old system should be abrogated. The sixty four thousand dollar question then, of course, is what do we put in its place?

As an optimistic pragmatist I am not too concerned with trying to draw up a detailed constitution to try to cope with every possible eventuality. As for 'practical problems' – I think these can rarely be accurately foreseen and best left to whoever has his-her-their hand on the tiller to deal with as they arrive.

For my part I am happy to accept a system whereby anyone who is willing to take on the job may do so, provided there is a consensus that they are competent to do so, and that they have a sense of spiritual vocation that is not a vehicle for ego problems in disguise. There are also two elements to this – one is that organisational competence and commitment is important; the other that with the levels of power being worked with nowadays they need to be particularly psychologically mature and magically experienced.

94. To Joan Baran   *24th January 1999*

Dear Joan,
Many thanks for your letter, I regret to say that I have not caught up with *Nazis: The Occult Conspiracy* but then there is an awful lot I have not caught up with these days as I am kept very busy. I rejoined the Society of the Inner Light last year, which seemed to be a mutually advantageous thing to do, after

having gone our separate ways for close on 33 years. Quite an experience, leaving as an 'enfant terrible' and going back as a 'grand old man'. It has given me the run of the Dion Fortune archive and so I am busy rummaging through and bringing to light various bits and pieces which are being published with some commentary by me.

My daughter Rebecca, who knows about these things, has just fitted me up with a bibliographic web site so you should be able to look up the latest news. I am not, however, on the internet myself.

I had not realised that you were at my Arthurian workshop at New York Open Center some years ago. Open Center are getting quite ambitious in casting their conferences wide and I spoke at one in Wales last year on the Holy Grail, and am booked to give a talk at one on Qabalah at the Ashmolean Museum, Oxford in May[1]. They tend however to use rather out of the way places for other of their events, which does not attract me too much. A one night stand is OK but I do not relish being cooped up for several days on a remote site, the captive of an audience of esoteric junkies.

Someone sent me a Schwaller de Lubicz book but I cannot say it did a lot for me. Ancient Egypt and star magic seem to be very much in the air at the present though, and the latest hot potato by all accounts is *The Star Mirror* by Mark Vidler published over here by HarperCollins.

[1] Actually organised by The Kabballah Society, New York.

95. To Dr Andrew Walker   *24th January 1999*

Dear Dr Walker,

Someone recently drew my attention to your article on C. S. Lewis in the 27th November 1998 issue of the *Church Times*.

I write to thank you for your generous reference to my book *The Magical World of the Inklings*. As a kind of cross disciplinary work, if indeed of any recognised discipline, it has not exactly been a runaway best seller, but I look upon it with affection as one of the best I have done, and which I most enjoyed doing. I suppose you cannot have fun and make money at the same time – although I hesitate to pursue any metaphysical extensions from that.

The *Church Times* was, I must say, the last organ where I could have expected any accolade, but it is nonetheless welcome for that. I was also somewhat amazed to find an American academic, earlier this year, referring to the book on familiar, even respectful terms.

I do not think my views likely to have been too welcome to many admirers of Lewis, or particularly of Charles Williams, who wish to corral them into orthodoxy. But Williams was a member of A.E. Waite's magical society for many years, and he and the Steinerite Owen Barfield plainly had an enormous influence on Lewis. When I first read Lewis I was convinced that he must be an undercover occultist, and it was only by reading through all the rest of his works that I realised that this was not the case.

I have to say that in all of this I found Lewis' Christian apologetics an enormous help in sorting my own ideas out, and so I think you are absolutely right in your last two paragraphs in assessing Lewis as a potential guide for an unchurched generation towards the door of the church. But it is likely to be a pretty recalcitrant flock.

Thanks again for your encouragement.

96. To R.A. Gilbert   *21st May 1999*

Dear Bob,

Many thanks for your letter and enclosures today. I much appreciate your taking such trouble. In conjunction with various transcripts of trance mediumship undertaken by DF when Maiya was present, the bits and pieces help put together a more complete picture of the influence of Maiya Tranchell Hayes upon DF. There is a sequence of these trances in the early days in 1922/3 and a further sequence in 1940/2.

If MTH felt that DF had wasted her talents by this kind of activity then it did not apparently stop her from joining in some of it, and in the early events seeming to take quite a supervisory role, when there was just herself present with VMF as medium, and a scribe (probably C.T. Loveday). The first of these are on 11th January, 8th February, 15th February 1921 where those present are recorded as V.M.F. and Mrs. C-W.

These include the first contacts with an inner communicator called the Master of Medicine, which however did not get into full swing until 1927 after DF had married Dr Penry Evans. Having a qualified medical man present obviously helped along this kind of communication, and they evidently had hopes of forming a kind of esoteric healing side to their activities. Some of the material was privately circulated from time to time to those sufficiently qualified and unlikely to abuse it. I have finally collected it together, apart from clinical material unsuitable for the public domain, to be published as *Principles of Esoteric Healing* in the USA within the next year.

MTH does not appear after 1923 until a rather cryptic series of sessions commencing August 1940, under great secrecy, not revealed even to the most senior members of the Inner Light for almost a year. Initials of magical names only are used, which put me off the scent for a bit, but the inner contact is referred to as "Shemesh", which I believe was the name of a similar being favoured by the Felkins when founding the Stella Matutina. The gist of these meetings is that MTH has been left high and dry as the only surviving member of her Order but that in the meantime DF had unwittingly, in building up the SIL, provided just the requirements for the continuation of that work. The two of them appear to work together like mad for a year or two which evidently produced a raft of material known as the Arthurian Formula which I subsequently incorporated into *The Secret Tradition in Arthurian Legend*.

Then in 1942 there comes the phase where DF turns her mind to rebuilding the SIL for the postwar period, relaunches a study course for new members, and also makes overtures to the spiritualist movement with a view to a kind of 'united front' for the new age. C.R. Cammell, newly appointed editor of *Light*, was pulled into this initiative, and so I was interested to read in the material you sent me, that Cammell also happened to be very thick with MTH; therefore she may well have acted as some kind of go-between.

This whole thing eventually fizzled out it would seem, but I am publishing some of the correspondence and the articles DF wrote (at first anonymously) for *Light* in *Spiritualism & Occultism*, an expanded edition, with commentary, of DF's *Spiritualism in the Light of Occult Science* – to be published by Thoth Publications as part of the series of Dion Fortune/Gareth Knight texts that we have under way.

Then in 1942 we see MTH listed as being present at a short series of experimental trances by DF with invited medical men (no doubt as substitutes for her estranged husband). The first of these had rather a sceptical medical man present asking 'test' questions, which rather put a damper on proceedings, and it is interesting to see MTH taking the lead in drawing the conversation into less confrontational waters. Again I am publishing much of this in *Principles of Esoteric Healing*.

It would then appear, from remarks in the material you sent, that DF predeceased MTH but whether they parted company before that I do not know. However, it is arguable that MTH's input may well have affected the esoteric organisational structure of the SIL in the immediate post-war years, until the great reform of 1960/1 when it almost converted into a religious sect for a generation.

Thank you too for the copies of DF/FIR correspondence which are quite a joy. I published some of Regardie's stuff when I set up Helios's publishing arm back in the 60s and later met him in London at a wing-ding organised by Carr Collins, and we got on very well.

I am only an hour's train ride out of London so would be happy to meet up there at any convenient time. I also appear in Bristol from time to time as my son lives there but I generally get too embroiled in domestic socialising to think of much else on our fleeting visits.

Chic Cicero sent me a copy of your Dartington conference programme, which looks like being a good do. I am sorry I could not grace the speakers list myself but these days I don't enjoy such events very much, so only appear for the necessary hour or two at events that are no more than a hundred miles distance from home. That just about takes in Oxford where I am due to speak Sunday week at Warren Kenton's Kabballah event at the Ashmolean. I got shanghai'd by John Matthews into a Holy Grail job at Lampeter last August and cursed every mile of the journey there and back. I had mistakenly thought it to be the near side of Cardiff!

Bob Stewart phoned me yesterday to say he had changed his address, to a place called Nevada City, but I expect you also are informed of that. Josephine has found a publisher for her novel it seems and I must say their web-site looks very impressive.

I regret to say that John Hall died on April 29th. He apparently lost a lot of weight around Christmas time and started going downhill, possibly with a recurrence of the leukaemia he had previously suffered from. He was 81/82 so I suppose had a good innings. But it seems like the end of an era. He was a good friend, and we taught each other what little we knew about bookselling.

97. To Mike Harris   *10th June 1999*

Dear Mike,

Having finally emerged from a maelstrom of various commitments, from lecturing the great and good at Oxford to entertaining my granddaughter over half term, I can get down to responding to your last letter and enclosures. I did read the latter a couple of times soon after I got them so they have been mulling around in the back of my mind and not simply lying inert in the in-tray.

Rebuilding the Tabernacle. I am not as familiar with this line of country as you might think, although I have been vaguely aware of it in the background from odd comments made by people who have made some kind of serious effort to come to terms with recent bible scholarship without getting too enmeshed in the wilder money spinning theories of the Holy Blood and Holey Bucket variety.

I have rather tended to take the easy way out and follow the popular Christian mythos, more or less off the Xmas cards, for at least it is magically effective and particularly if one can attain that "willing suspension of disbelief" to regard it, along with C.S. Lewis, as a myth which came true in historical reality – angels, shepherds, miracles, the lot.

However, effective though this might be in magical terms, and as a comfort to the believing general populace, there is, I am aware, rather more to it than this. It is myth come true – but in a rather more complex manner than the fairy tale version.

This puts one in something of a cleft stick I find. On the one hand one enjoys denouncing some academic bishop like he of Durham who incurred the Lord's displeasure to the extent of blasting York cathedral with fire and lightning, whilst at the same time conceding that the good bishop was probably right. Nonetheless my real quarrel with him would be that he ought to choose whether he wants to be a shepherd of souls or an academic and not be one whilst posing as the other.

My private view of just what did go on in Jerusalem at the beginning of our era is to reckon that probably Rudolf Steiner has got closest to it, but I am not too sure that I understand him. Therefore I do not generally raise the matter in conversation.

I do know that there is an almighty powerful magical/mystical dynamic surrounding Jerusalem, Glastonbury and Joseph of Arimathea. I did a working at Hawkwood a while back, the script of which unfortunately seems to be lost, in which I took the part of Joseph of Arimathea, and bare foot and with a Jewish skull cap I recall pouring water and wine at the root of a representation of the holy thorn in a reconstruction of Glastonbury abbey. All remembrance of the event has escaped me except to recall that it was bloody powerful and with a mystical dynamic that one does not normally come across – the kind of feeling you get in reading the more high flying of the Grail romances.

It also seems back of this persistent background obsession I have to concern myself with the Kingdom of Jerusalem of the Crusaders and the 12th century cauldron of troubadours and Arthurian tales from the Celtic – of which *The Secret Tradition in Arthurian Legend* was but a preliminary skirmish. In passing you may be interested to learn that in my most recent sifting through the SIL archives I have discovered that the initiative for all this stems from 1940/2 when DF reforged contact with Maiya Tranchell-Hayes, her old Golden Dawn mentor, who had helped her original contacts at Glastonbury in 1921/3. Thus the SIL had a re-injection of the GD egregore, which was in need of being engrafted onto younger stock as Maiya T-H was the last surviving member of her GD Temple.

All this was frightfully hush-hush at the time and not even senior members of the SIL were told about it at first. It was then developed by MLB after DF's death. Then worked with at the cutting edge of the SIL's Greater Mystery work through the 1950s until the lid blew off the kettle in 1961, (which I am now engaged in fitting back on). It then remained dormant until the Hawkwood Arthurian event of 1981 and subsequent publishing of much of the material in my Arthurian book with various practical off-shoots, from the Matthews developing their Hallowquest version to recent spreading of the published material into the USA and French and Italian.

Those ripples having spread far and wide it would seem to me likely to be time for another large pebble to be dropped into the centre of the pond – which is maybe what all this current Glastonbury/Joseph/Jerusalem stuff is all about.

The Inner Fire – or It Ain't Arf 'Ot Mum! I am not quite sure as to the best destination for this but it is high time that something was written in plain terms. It is obviously what DF was obliquely, and sometimes not so obliquely, referring to or hinting at in much of her works. The closest she eventually came is what I have hauled together in *The Circuit of Force* which even so is a bit pathetic when you consider that it has taken more than fifty years to get it into print, and it still ponces around the periphery.

Israel Regardie seems to have come closest to anyone in spelling out the detail of practical occultism in *The Middle Pillar*, *The Art of True Healing* etc., but still leaves a lot unsaid.

Mind you, much that is churned out by the likes of xxxxx xxxxx gets close to psycho-porn – with little left to the imagination, but in much of this it is either wanker's pabulum or esoteric frills for those who are jaded with more commonplace erotic thrills.

Motive of course is all, in all of this. And when physical sex walks in the door then the magic flies out of the window. Nonetheless the sexual cop-out can be a useful safety valve if the magic gets too hot.

All of this leads to certain dilemmas. As the troubadours were ever fond of singing, it is difficult to work up a polar charge with one's lawfully wedded, because familiarity leads to a different kind of love than that which feeds off mystery and distance and unattainability which is very much a part of the magical as well as romantic dynamic. Hence the charge associated with faery women and even Mary Magdalene and the Virgin Mary.

Where trouble occurs in practice is when innocent parties, like spouses and children, get their lives ruined and put through a mill that is not of their making if things get out of hand. In this respect I suppose there is something to be said for the conception of a Mystery Group being an enclosed order of those without any familial or social connections. However, in these days, when we seek to externalise the Mysteries, things are not so easily surrounded by a *cordon sanitaire*.

Of course general moral conventions are not what they were. As a cartoon in the paper today has it, with a vicar giving encouraging advice to the pending royal bride – "It's only an oath before God in a church – it's really no big thing!"

98. To Alan Richardson *27ᵗʰ June 1999*

Dear Alan,

Thanks for your letter. Not so much cheeky as you suggest, rather, I feel, more in the synchronistic line of things. It was just a week ago that I got the OK to embark on a biography of Dion Fortune with access to all the SIL archives. I rejoined the Society about a year ago, I should say, and the climate is less chill than it has been at times in the past.

With the material I have at my disposal, and my own predilections anyway, it will be more of an interior biography, provisionally entitled *The Magical Life of Dion Fortune*. I do not therefore see it necessarily knocking your own off the shelf. However, if you have any old documentation knocking about in a bottom drawer that might be of use to me in filling out the general picture I would be much obliged for a sight of it.

The kind of thing that exercises me at the moment are records showing that her mother and father were present at some of her private séances. They apparently had retired to Glastonbury in the early twenties, and were also associated with Letchworth, which has lots of ramifications to do with Alice Buckton at Chalice Well, Letchworth Garden City, Christian Socialism and what not – including interest in the soya bean, which may well have had something to do with Penry Evans' continued involvement with food products that are hinted at here and there in the 30s.

She also was doing occult work with Bligh Bond in attendance in 1921, as well as Maiya Curtis-Webb, who turns up again between 1940 and 1942 working very closely with her on various projects as Maiya Tranchell-Hayes. Anything on this lady's life would be interesting to know, particularly which husband ran which mental home and when.

Anyway, to turn to your own immediate concerns, *The Inner Guide to the Megaliths*. Are your researches confined to the British Isles? I ask because some of the most vivid experiences I have had concerned the megalithic remains in Malta. If you are restricting things to closer to home I've had some interesting associations with Avebury, Wayland's Smithy and environs, also the place in Pembrokeshire where the Stonehenge blue stones allegedly came from. The problem is where to stop. And do you include things like hill figures (Uffington or Cerne Abbas) in your trawl?

You could do worse than send a copy of your leaflet, with a covering note, to my esoteric colleague Mike Harris, who could probably fill a book for you on Snowdonia and Anglesey.

Regarding pitiful sales of books, it is the fate of us all, although it depends how you define pitiful. When I was a publisher at Longman's, I and the other 50+ commissioning editors used to have to go through the sales and stock records every year and dump everything that was not generating more than a certain cash target (warehouse space costs money!). That is how multinational companies work. No room for high ideals or sentimentality – everything depends on the bottom line on the balance sheet.

It was something of a disaster when HarperCollins moved in and took over Thorsons, who had in turn been hoovering up all the little companies in the years before. Far from being a blessing and circulating our books throughout the universe, in came the big-shot's accountants and ruled that the modestly selling works of authors like Gareth Knight, R.J. Stewart, John and Caitlín Matthews, Dolores Ashcroft-Nowicki, were best remaindered or pulped.

However, it has meant another turn of the cycle, and particularly with the information aids of the internet and modern word-processor and print technology, the small niche publisher can find a place in the scheme of things once again. Hence I was never busier – writing books for little publishers. Sales of course are not enough to live on, let alone retire on, but I should care with a Longman's pension!

I think middle of the road specialists like Llewellyn and Weisers will still carry on, as long as they in turn are not gobbled up by some greedy multi-national. Although I think that the "returns on assets used" merchants have realised that taking over tiddlers can be more of a liability than an asset.

Anyway if you want to meet up some time and chew over possibilities or weep into a glass over the iniquities of publishers I'll be happy to accommodate you.

99. To Wendy Berg   *5th January 2000*

Dear Wendy,

Many thanks for your letter and the enclosures. I think these represent a promising start and if you go on in the fashion that you have started then you should not go far wrong. There is always a certain element of doubt as to the validity of what one is getting but I think this the sign of the better type of medium or mediator. MLB and DF for that matter always maintained a certain scepticism about the validity of their communications (as indeed I do myself), and I think this a healthy sign of integrity and psychological balance. It is those who believe implicitly in the infallibility of what they get who are likely to be the ones to lead themselves (and credulous others) astray. Of course, the flip side of this is that one should not allow self-doubt or destructive scepticism to get the upper hand, for that will just cause the system to freeze up. Belief and faith are essential – at any rate at the time of making contact and communicating. Plenty of time for scepticism and evaluation later on, for the acid test of any communication is its content, not in the alleged authority or from whom it is assumed to emanate. Given good quality of material, it is of secondary importance whether it comes from a Master, or your own subconscious or superconscious. But I expect you know all this, although it does no harm to have it confirmed by someone else with experience.

Signs following communications that seem to be genuine are, as you say, a feeling that something has happened, rather as in a ritual, although after slightly another manner. Also of course the speed and ease of effort. As someone who has written and still writes a lot off my own bat this is very noticeable. When it is 'me' I have to slog and sweat away through several drafts to discover what I want to say and how to say it. With 'communications' they come through fast and without anything like the effort. Sometimes so fast that the written text is almost unreadable scribble and has to be typed up immediately afterwards while I still have a fairly fresh recollection of what was said.

There are various types of communication though, sometimes coming through in blocks of ideas (which is the faster stuff) and sometimes quite slowly and deliberately word by word, when one can use one's best handwriting.

One is also using a creative process very similar to one's 'own' writing, and although I did not start consciously to get specific 'communications' until 1993, there was a kind of overlapping period when parts of some of my books were definitely overshadowed in some way even though I assumed it was me who was doing the writing. This happened to some extent even in the early days of writing the *PGQS* I think, only then it could work by having a hunch to go and look at a particular library book for necessary hints and inspiration. More latterly, the opening part of *Rose Cross and the Goddess* for example, came in on what seemed to be a strong Merlin contact.

It was not until the Abbey Papers though that I began to get stuff coming in that was mostly communication – although in reading back over the stuff I detect a certain prolixity in the earlier papers, and gobbets of dubbed in subconscious material, or unconscious or semi-unconscious padding, that are absent from later material. So one does improve at this game, and of course occasionally have 'off' days, as, presumably, do the communicators! Or like short-wave radio sometimes the conditions of reception are objectively not good through astral atmospherics or interference.

One added feature that I have experienced since rejoining the SIL is that one may occasionally be grabbed by the scruff of the neck and communicated at, willy nilly, even woken up and dictated to at four o'clock in the morning when something of importance needs to be said. Not too often I am glad to say, but this kind of thing certainly helps on the faith side of things.

Normally I work at around midnight for routine communications – which I find easiest for this kind of thing. Of course I have the luxury of being retired so I can lie in a bit the next day if need be.

If stuck, asking a question is a good way to get the ball rolling. Particularly if you write it down. Also, as you have found, they seem to enjoy one fiddling about with symbols and candles – and I also find lightly dinging on a bell quite a good opener.

100. To Simon Buxton   *10ᵗʰ February 2000*

Dear Simon,
Many thanks for taking the trouble to send me the photocopies from Hutton's latest book, but I am glad to say that it is back in print and I now have a copy, along with a couple of his other books. I am astounded by his application and erudition. I'm glad I was able to help him a bit on his DF section, which he is good enough to acknowledge in the footnotes. The trouble with the SIL having been so aloof in the past is that speculation has tended to take the place of fact, and so even someone like Hutton has to rely on rather inaccurate secondary sources such as Alan Richardson's books with their slant towards Christine Campbell Thompson's prejudices. I feel a bit sorry for poor old Chris Creasy who is now branded "a mystical Christian of narrow minded piety" by a major historian. I knew him. It just was not so. As hard evidence, it was he who selected the contents of *Applied Magic* and *Aspects of Occultism* for publication in 1962, with their Isis worship and all – expurgated from later editions by a hand that might better qualify for those epithets.

101. Professor Ronald Hutton   *20ᵗʰ March 2000*

Dear Professor Hutton,
You may recall that we corresponded early in 1998 when you were checking out facts about Dion Fortune at John Matthews' suggestion. I have now read (and bought and paid for!) *The Triumph of the Moon* which is obviously a major work in its field, and offer you my congratulations, and thanks for your kind acknowledgement of my small assistance.

It seems incumbent upon me however to take up one or two points of disagreement between us, which I have done in the enclosed article, which will appear in the Summer issue of the *Inner Light Journal*. Since we corresponded I have had the good fortune to have been commissioned to write a new biography of Dion Fortune, with access to the Society of the Inner Light archives. This will be published by Thoth Publications, Loughborough within the next few months, as *Dion Fortune and the Inner Light*. Had my researches been conducted a little earlier I would have been able to make a more convincing case for my view of things than was apparent to you from the more limited sources at your disposal.

An item from her published work has just struck my eye however, on having read through *Sane Occultism* once again in order to write an Introduction for a new American edition. Originally published as articles in *The Occult Review* in the mid 1920s, she states even then quite unequivocally: *"The fully initiated adept should have the three-fold contacts of mystic devotion, occult wisdom, and the primitive nature forces."*

Nevertheless, I expect we shall continue to receive earnest enquiries from trans-Atlantic neo-pagans asking for details of which 'coven' she belonged to!! But that is no fault of yours. Rather one of the penalties of fame allied to a less than perfect appreciation of public relations by her immediate successors.

102. To Alan Richardson   *20th March 2000*

Dear Alan,

As this directly concerns you as one of the main sources Ronald Hutton used for his section on Dion Fortune in his recent book *The Triumph of the Moon* I am enclosing a copy of my letter to him today along with my forthcoming article in *The Inner Light Journal*.

I am no great fan of public controversies but feel that, within the limited sources at my disposal, I have to put on record just where I think Hutton has been getting it wrong.

In the forthcoming biography I have not drawn attention to differences of interpretation between your books and mine – let those who choose to read them come to their own conclusions. Obviously there will be a number of differences if only for the reason that you were somewhat limited in your available sources – not helped by the polite but somewhat aloof attitude of the Society of the Inner Light at the time.

It seems to me CCT may have had it in for W.K. Creasy a little bit, although from internal records at the time it appears that it was he who was the victim of somewhat malicious gossip in the early war years when he was working closely with DF. The riot act had to be read to wagging tongues within the house. I wonder if something of this stems from CTC and WKC having been initiated on the same day in 1934, with he rising to become

Deputy Warden and she somewhat sidelined along with Colonel Seymour after about 1938.

However that is not a speculation I intend to air in public, although I feel I need to put in a good word for poor old Creasy, whom I knew well, when I was a stripling of 35 and he was an old hand of 70 – which is what I am now!

I look forward to reading your next magnum opus.

103. To Professor Ronald Hutton   *29ᵗʰ March 2000*

Dear Ronald Hutton,

Thank you very much for your letter of response to my article, and especially for your words of instruction upon the arcane laws of engagement for the parfit gentil knights of academe. This will come in particularly handy, as I have enrolled myself upon a distance learning MA at Sheffield Hallam in September, on a history related course, "Imperialism and Culture". Bearing your remarks in mind I trust will save a certain amount of exasperation on my tutor's part, to say nothing of improving my own likely performance.

This butts onto the uncertain and treacherous frontier between the occult and the academic which I find to be an area of great fascination and one which needs careful charting. The point being that in the deeper waters of occultism one finds oneself coming up against 'historical' archetypes, which, like the assumed antiquity of the modern wiccan's beliefs, have a considerable power. (I prefer not to psychologise this away in Jungian terms of collective unconscious, and so on, but to regard it as having a certain objective reality at its own level, rather beyond the confines of one's own skull, even if the imagination is the organ of perception concerned.)

The point is that Lewis Carroll wrote a profound esoteric truth in the words of the Bellman in *The Hunting of the Snark*, which were, "If I say something three times it's true!" Rather like the thought experiment of Schrodinger's cat in sub-atomic physics, if the consequences of this do not disturb and shock, then one has not understood the problem. It is by no means as flippant or cynical a remark as it may at first seem.

It goes partway to explain Dion Fortune's blithe disregard of historical accuracy in locating the origins of the Winged Bull. To those who make the act of faith of believing what she says, in an esoteric context, it makes little difference if its actual origin was Nineveh, Babylon, Atlantis or the Old Kent Road – if it is given a noumenous context within the mind it will trigger certain other very vivid reactions. Thus as far as the occultist is concerned it is what is plausible and evocative rather than what is factually verifiably that opens the gates of higher consciousness or expanded awareness.

(I do not offer this as an excuse for her, by the way, as I agree that she might have been expected to do her homework a little better – not that my own work is free from the odd howler or two!)

It follows that an academic who approaches the occult is in for a considerable culture shock, in certain respects. This works both ways, for I am sure you have given quite a shock to many neo-pagans by kicking the struts away from certain elements of their belief. Once they get over the shock however, they should come to realise that it does not really matter all that much that the foundations of their belief system are more modern than ancient. Even so I imagine you will have come up against a certain amount of resentment about your heaving rocks of brute fact in the metaphysical glass house. Nonetheless most pagans of my acquaintance seem to retain a soft spot for you – which augurs fairly well for the future I think.

I had a very interesting exchange with Michael Dummett, Professor of Logic (of all things!) at Oxford, who as a keen bridge player developed an interest in the history of playing cards, and decided to write a long book about it, which drew him into the subject of Tarot cards. The more he got into this the more horrified he became at the morass of conjecture and misinformation in which the occult side of it all was steeped. At first he threw up the whole project in disgust, and decided to close the subject in the early 19th century in his book *The Game of Tarot* (Duckworth 1980). Nonetheless, he felt a desire to rise to the challenge, and with the help of a couple of colleagues, a professional historian (Thierry Depaulis) and a museum curator (Ronald Decker) took on the 19th century in *A Wicked Pack of Cards* (St. Martins Press 1996). He came in touch with me when they decided that despite exciting some howls of pain, not to say execration, from certain quarters, they would like to tackle the 20th century. We met, and I think to our mutual surprise, got on extremely well with one another, when I was able to convince him, (unless he dissembled well), that all who lived in this strange demi-monde of occultism were not necessarily cracked or duplicitous, and that it was possible to be reasonably intelligent and of good faith even if seeming at odds with received academic wisdom.

To my mind Robert Persig dealt with this problem rather well in his celebrated *Zen and the Art of Motorcycle Maintenance*, which rather closer to home Tanya Luhrmann set out to answer, as you probably know, in her *Persuasions of the Witches' Craft*, with a great deal of laudable field work in my experience. I figure to some extent in this tome although I am not sure that I am very accurately classed as a witch, and was somewhat surprised when this PhD thesis which I had helped to vet for this personable young student suddenly turned up as a published book. Anyway, she got her doctorate, which I suppose is the main thing, and I think she came very close to understanding what we queer folk were all about; although when she gets into heavy anthropological overdrive she might as well be writing in Greek as far as I am concerned, so I am not quite sure where she ultimately stands.

Anyway, I for one certainly welcome the serious academic interest that is beginning to be shown in the occult side of things, even if it is in the 'safer' areas of history rather than the metaphysical or philosophical quicksands. I cannot say that I have been entirely impressed with some of the work that has come out of New York or even the Sorbonne, but I have found lucid conversation possible with for example Joscelyn Godwin and Antoine Faivre.

The $64,000 question as far as I am concerned though concerns what is commonly called the Whig approach to history. Occultism is steeped in it, it seems to me, in a very profound way, in terms of Theosophically derived assumptions of the history of the evolution of consciousness. On a somewhat less than cosmic scale though, what interests me particularly, is the validity (or not) of that kind of history which felt its duty to offer paradigms of conduct – great and famous men and women, some of whom became very powerful legends like Drake, to say nothing of the semi-legendary Arthurian heroes. I suppose this easily drifts into rather ominous kinds of state propaganda in our own times, but to my mind Plantagenet apologists such as Geoffrey of Monmouth were performing a role of some importance that goes rather beyond the academic historian's perfectly understandable assumption that they were early P.R. men or ignorant primitives.

I suppose much of this is all old hat to you, so forgive me if I have galloped up and down too long on a hobby horse.

To return to the detail of immediate concerns, I sympathise with your reservations about Dion Fortune, and plainly she was a bit of a burden to some of her close associates (aren't we all?) and although Israel Regardie always insisted to me that the Great Beast[1] was a somewhat misunderstood gentleman (and even a great poet!!) I can't say that I find some of his followers very fragrant personalities, and by and large think I would prefer the company of brusque, breezy and possibly sometimes overbearing Miss Firth/ Mrs Evans to that of the old monster, who did treat some of his followers and friends quite appallingly.

If you should, in the future, still be game enough to pursue your studies of Dion Fortune, you would need to make a formal approach to the Warden, the Society of the Inner Light, 38 Steele's Road, London NW3 4RG if you wished to be allowed into the hallowed precincts, for whatever purpose. However, most of what is available from old articles from the *Inner Light Magazine* or her Weekly or Monthly letters from 1939 to 1944 has now been published or is in the process of publication.

[1] Aleister Crowley.

104. To Janine Chapman *14th May 2000*

Dear Janine Chapman,

It was a pleasant surprise to receive your letter of April 30th addressed via the Society of the Inner Light, although so much time has elapsed since I wrote to you originally, in August last year care of Weisers, that I have now completed the book. So it will have to stand now, for better or worse, without benefit of consulting your material. Thanks for the offer anyway.

You are very welcome to a spare copy of the DF 'wedding photograph' which I enclose herewith.

Dion Fortune and the Inner Light will be published by Thoth Publications over here in a few weeks time, and I will send you a signed complimentary copy as a small token of my appreciation for the pleasure that your own "Quest" gave me, to say nothing of the very interesting new information it contained. This has enabled us to home in on the Studley archives and discover some new photographs of Dion Fortune when she was a student there, which will also appear in the book.

I am so glad that my letter way back in 1973 was of some help to you in your original project.

105. To Kathleen Raine *18th January 2001*

Dear Kathleen,

What a nice surprise to receive your letter! And quite coincidental too as Roma and I were just off to London to visit the Blake exhibition at the Tate. Anyway, we are now back from that and much impressed with what we saw. I was particularly struck by the hundred original plates of Jerusalem that are normally kept at Yale, and still have a crick in my neck and slight eye strain from close reading of them – alas not all, there is a limit to physical endurance – but I have most of Blake's work in black and white reproduction at home and its sends me back to that with renewed enthusiasm. It is funny how a face to face experience with the originals makes such a strong direct impact – no doubt something to do with the talismanic power of the imagination in addition to the vibrancy of the colour.

I am glad to know you liked my book on Dion Fortune, which in some ways is I feel one of the best things I have done. It was not easy, apart from the detailed grind of writing about someone else's life (with which I am sure you are very familiar) and all the facts to check (and even so I got the date of her death wrong by 48 hours, as a guardian of her grave at Glastonbury has hastened to tell me) it was quite a powerful emotional experience. Almost like a revisit to the Judgment Hall of Osiris, or Mount Purgatory, along with her. After it was done it also felt as if I was free of quite a heavy burden, or released from some long standing commitment. At the tender age of 23 when I first came across her writing, it was *The Esoteric Orders and their Work* I think, I knew without doubt that, come what may, wherever that writing was coming from, that was where I had to be. I was fortunate in getting my basic training there at a time when it was functioning well as a magical initiatory fraternity.

One of the reasons for its vitality during that time was the presence of Margaret Lumley Brown, whose story I am enclosing with this. It has just been published in the United States and this is one of the first copies available over here. I think you will find her story a fascinating one, although you may have to skip over the last section for plainly she was not in your league when it comes to poetry – however, in other aspects of the pythoness's craft she was second to none.

When she was side-lined in the early 60s, nothing was ever quite the same again, although I have done my best to put a positive spin on this period in my DF biography. I think part of the trouble was that those then in charge wanted so desperately to be 'respectable' (which ain't easy in the esoteric field) and in a quest for unadulterated spirituality they all but converted themselves into a minor religious sect. However, there is no doubt that Arthur Chichester, the Warden at the time, did succeed in putting a bit of spiritual backbone and integrity into the system, which may well have been needed at the time. However, it was at the cost of making the patient magically anaemic.

Fortunately, as I was quite young during my magical apprenticeship there, I have survived all the old guard who were sedulously preserving this regime, and having also learned a thing or two in my wanderings in the wilderness, when the current inheritors of the dried up well sought for some informed guidance on how to strike water from the rock, I have been able to wield the necessary stick. All looks quite promising now, and there is some quite promising young blood in the ranks coming up, even if I do feel in much the same position as Moses upon glimpsing the Promised Land. Anyway, it has also been great fun, having the run of the archives, which has enabled me to get half a dozen of so books published from the gleanings of various bottom drawers (including a complete manuscript on esoteric healing that no-one knew existed) and of which the last one is that which you have before you.

How much of all this was pre-ordained, God only knows, or how much the result of someone pulling strings upon a higher plane. Certainly the way that Margaret Lumley Brown came our way again, in Braintree High Street, seems on a par with the chances of winning the national lottery or being struck by lightning. If given a choice of the three, I would stick with meeting MLB again!

She used once to do an 'esoteric review' as one approached the higher ranks of the Society, and the one she did for me, in 1959, is still producing active results in my life. It was a visionary vignette of myself in armour and chains in the middle ages, in what she felt was a very important incarnation that resulted in a particularly strong Higher/Lower Self contact in subsequent lives. I am still following that one up, which has been sufficiently productive as to motivate me to take a London external honours degree in French since I retired, and also to visit Poitiers and in particular the nearby little town of Lusignan, where the faery Melusine comes from (and allegedly built), and which is also the seat of the long dynasty of kings of Cyprus, Aphrodite's island, the first of whom was also King of Jerusalem. All this has sparked a line of enquiry where truth seems stranger than fiction, and which therefore I think I shall have to end up publishing as fiction – not that I fancy myself as much of a novelist, but needs must when the daimons (or whoever) drive.

It was very nice yesterday therefore to have a little extra bonus in the sight of a reproduction of a statue of Eleanor of Aquitaine that is lying next to a Blake drawing of her. I imagine it is a reproduction of the one at Fontevrault, where she is buried, and which I have not got round to visiting yet. She was, as I am sure you know, Queen of the Troubadour Minstrelsy, in reviving the ducal court at Poitiers, along with her daughter Marie of Champagne, the patron of Chrétien de Troyes … but it goes on and on, for the Countess of Flanders was involved too, whose husband, according to Chrétien, gave him a book containing the Conte del Graal – who in turn was part of a family that had gone back and forth to Jerusalem since even before the 1st Crusade. And so it goes – on and on and on and on. Needless to say, I had to be a little cautious in mentioning any of this stuff to the medieval specialists at Royal Holloway College.

Having got into this academic vein, I have now however embarked upon an MA in Imperialism and Culture at Sheffield Hallam, which can be done at a distance, and although they seem to react very kindly towards my work so far, I shall avoid any reference to Principalities and Powers in any dissertation upon Theories of Imperialism. I suppose this flurry of academic activity must suggest that I am a bit of a late developer educationally (it is not everyone who graduates at 70, I suppose), or maybe, like Merlin, I am living my life backwards. It was quite handy at examination time, the only time I went near the place, when university functionaries would assume that I was an Emeritus Professor rather than a student. (Didn't think I was that scruffy!)

Outside the halls of lower learning I am having something of a flirtation with Anna Kingsford, who seems to be a very neglected figure, considering what she did when she did, and against appalling odds. She was of course somewhat indebted to Swedenborg and Boehme but had some quite remarkable insights of her own as well as researching the Greek and Egyptian Mysteries. At least Mathers had the good grace to give high praise to *The Perfect Way* and dedicate his Kaballah book to her. And if a little more notice had been given to some of the things she wrote on the esoteric side of Christianity a lot of grief might have been later avoided in both the Golden Dawn and the Inner Light.

Ellic Howe, I am sure, knew a great deal about the Golden Dawn, but it seemed to me such a pity that, at any rate in his book, he seemed to delight in approaching it in such a destructive light. It seems a strange anomaly to have people so interested in a thing as to spend a great deal of time on it, yet with all the appearance of detesting it. Mind you, that seems to be much the fashion with all biography these days. My daughter Rebecca and John Matthews are currently laying plans to write mine, it appears, so at least, if they get on with the job fairly smartly, I shall be able to do a little discrete overseeing to avoid the worst excesses.

Even the academic world seems prone to a very subjective view of things, despite their claims to objectivity (if there indeed is such a thing). They seem to be taking a burgeoning interest in the esoteric world these days, although mostly from the historical viewpoint, where they are unlikely to be contaminated by higher things. I cannot say I have been at all impressed with some of the alleged research I have seen. But perhaps, coming as an outsider to the hallowed precincts of academe my expectations have been rather naïve and too high. Tolkien had little flattering to say about Oxford, and according to C.S. Lewis the teaching of wisdom (apart from Charles Williams' occasional lectures) was not really on the curriculum.

My next book is going to be on C.S. Lewis. Well it is not exactly a new book, but the rights of *The Magical World of the Inklings* have now reverted to me since Element Books went bust, and Sun Chalice are interested in republishing it in four separate volumes: one each on Lewis, Tolkien, Williams and Barfield. The Lewis one, which took the lion's share of the original volume, will be pretty much of a straight reprint, but I shall have to do some more original work on the others, who were squeezed out a bit in the original in order to make room for Lewis, all in under 120,000 words. I am quite looking forward to revisiting this trio.

One reason for this policy is that it seems that no-one of a later generation has heard of "the Inklings", which seems strange, and also a pity. However, once started on a series like this, who knows where it will end? At least I think I had better keep off Blake! All very well done already, and I still treasure those handsome Mellon lecture volumes you so kindly gave me many years ago.

Anyway, nice to hear from you, and I wish you well with your pursuit of spirituality in the land of my fathers on my great grandmother's side. Have been doing a little genealogical research on her, and it turns out her name was Amelia Johnson, which sounds Anglo-Saxon enough, but for the fact that a photograph we have shows her to have been very Indian indeed. It is still a puzzle how she came to be married to a British N.C.O. and to have given birth to her first child at the age of sixteen. Well, perhaps, best not ask!

At the other end of the genealogical scale, our daughter-in-law is Bulgarian, and she and our son Richard now live in Cathar country, as he works for British Aerospace in Toulouse. She was much diverted to learn that the Cathars had their origin in Bulgaria. However, have not followed this one up with any great diligence – there is already more than enough hot air rising from ancient sites for me to add to the flow.

At least the Temenos Academy seems set fair to keep the light of the spirit shining in the dark towers of academe.

106. To Mark Whitehead

31ˢᵗ January 2001

Dear Mark,

That is one hell of a Barfield site! He never asked permission from me, although it is possible that he may have done from Element Books, but as they exist no more we have no way of telling. Actually I am quite happy for him to have the stuff up there on the net, and there is plenty of stuff on there from which I can read, mark, learn and inwardly digest before embarking on a revamped version.

We can perhaps prevail upon him to give us some publicity when we are nearer publication, as he must be a focal point for all the Barfield buffs, and we need all the help we can get on this one as Barfield is not all that well known, except to fellow anthroposophists. Although he does have quite a high standing in certain American academic circles.

He wrote the foreword for my Inklings book. From which the publishers quoted on front and back of the cover:

Front: "more than outstanding" – Owen Barfield

Back: "because of the combination of information, understanding and insight on which it is founded, The Magical World of the Inklings is more than outstanding. It is not in the same league with anything else I have come across" – Owen Barfield

107. To the Revd Canon Anthony Duncan   *1ˢᵗ May 2001*

Dear Soul-Friend,

Many thanks for the free book. I don't get many of these now that I have drifted from the publishing world but I have to say that *Love Germinates* is more welcome, a better read, and worth much more to me than many a larger tome that has come my way for a considerable time. Your muse seems to improve with age and there is a great deal of distilled wisdom of experience within its pages that only old codgers like you and me begin to appreciate. I therefore find it somewhat bizarre that your *first* volume should have been entitled *Over the Hill*, which suggests that perhaps, like Merlin, you are living your life backwards.

I have been wondering about this phenomenon in my own life, having graduated only last year with a BA in French at age 70. However it might be just the result of being a 'late developer' – maturity was never my forte. Unfortunately, over the last few days, staying in France, I found myself unable to understand a word on French television. Reading a million and a quarter words of *À la Recherche du Temps Perdu* together with great gobbets of French literature from difficult medieval to incomprehensible modern has not seemed to convert into much skilful use of the vernacular. However, as it was mostly quiz shows and advertisements at which I uncomprehendingly gazed I don't feel that I missed too much and console myself with the high thought that I transcend all such vulgar stuff.

Anyhow, determined not to rest on my laurels I am now embarked upon an MA in imperial history and culture, and it's a pleasant relief to be able to study in English, or at least what passes for it in academic circles. All this I have to say is done by distance learning, which is just as well as I never could stand lectures – apart from my own, and even they could be a bit of a drag at times.

… …I ventured into biography last year with a book on Dion Fortune, *Dion Fortune and the Inner Light*, which was a fascinating experience, having been given the run of the Society of the Inner Light archives, although I would not care to do another biography, too much nit picking research for my taste. However, it was on the whole great fun to write and I even still enjoy reading it. A friend of mine made the rather backhanded compliment of considering it the best thing I have so far done, and "a compulsive read – not at all like your other books." !!!

I am currently going over *The Magical World of the Inklings* which was published ten years ago and is now out of print, Element Books having gone bust and not in a position, let alone the mood, to reprint it. However, Mark Whitehead has got very keen on reproducing it as four shorter books… …

...... This comes on top of a busy couple of years when I dug out, dusted down and refurbished half a dozen books out of Dion Fortune's bottom drawer, with editorial commentary where necessary. Details of all these, if you should be interested, are contained on my web site.

108. To Peregrin Wildoak
23rd November 2001

Dear Peregrin,

There is a lot still to be sorted out and understood about Masters and their identity. When I was going up through the grades of the SIL 1953-65 the principal contact, via Margaret Lumley Brown for the most part was, via Thomas More, who was reckoned to be a former incarnation of Thomas Erskine. My own main contact in the 1993-5 communications was More. After I rejoined the SIL in 1998 I started getting instructions, rather than communications, somewhat to my surprise via Erskine – who felt a very different contact indeed. Very much a sharp kind of 18/19th century lawyer than the more fatherly and pious Tudor contact. In my researches for the DF biography I came upon the information that DF had never used More, who came in via MLB some time in 1958. He was also held to have had a previous life as Thomas Becket, but no communications have ever come via that earlier source to my knowledge, although there are some odd synchronicities attached.

For instance, More's head is kept at St. Dunstan's church in Canterbury, just down the road from the cathedral of Becket's martyrdom. Also Henry VIII who cut off More's head went out of his way to desecrate and despoil Becket's tomb and shrine. St. Dunstan, for what it is worth, is associated with Glastonbury.

All this kind of mare's nest of associations suggests that in the deeper levels of occultism we are dealing with archetypes of the racial and national unconscious – even national neuroses or unresolved complexes – Mary Queen of Scots for instance comes up quite a bit in odd circumstances as part of the long standing controversy of the Stuart line. Not that I think we are dealing with spiritualist type contacts with the actual historical personalities, but that they provide a repository of objective inner power in some way. Something of this is dealt with in the communications I am currently sitting on.

The SIL got into the practice of referring to the Erskine/More/Becket contact as "the Chancellor" which is what each of them were in their time. Seymour of course reckoned to have got on to yet another Chancellor – Lord Eldon. The common denominator of all this is that the Chancellor of the kingdom is keeper of the Great Seal, which is the foundation of Law in the nation, its imprint having to be on any act of parliament with royal assent. It thus represents the enactment of the sovereign national will.

Of course this kind of thing is a far cry from the more popular kind of occultism that is retailed in the average bookstore. But it is at the root of events like the Drake weekend and so forth. Maybe you will have a simpler esoteric life in Australia where you are not sitting on this great archetypal compost heap. At any rate as far as the land is concerned. The blood lines will however I imagine have a part to play in the developing national psyche as it comes on stream in international politics in the 21st century.

As far as the UK is concerned, with the imperial past stimulating the growth of a multicultural society in Britain, and economic migration from the West Indies and Asia leading to sizeable minority cultures, together with the economic and political pull towards Europe, and all its old antagonisms, the inner plane state of group consciousness must be of considerable complexity.

So being a Master in the Planetary Hierarchy must entail a great deal more than sending messages of sweetness and light and wafting about on clouds over the Himalayas. This is one reason why I am currently doing an MA in Imperialism and Culture rather than Religious Studies or Anthropological Studies of the Esoteric Scene and their ilk.

109. To Libby Travassos Valdez   *25th January 2002*

Dear Libby,

Thanks for the card and initial sounds of enthusiasm.

The situation is as follows. The Society of the Inner Light, after having sat amassing funds and not doing much with them for the past decade or three have been told by the Charity Commissioners that they had better start spending some money on good causes that are in line with their articles of charitable association.

Amongst other things they have decided to get involved in publishing again, but most of Dion Fortune's works having been taken on by commercial publishers, they have turned to me and have issued me contracts for publication under their auspices of two volumes of collected articles, the Abbey Papers, and this very esoteric children's story culled from my bottom drawer: *Granny's Pack of Cards*. Additionally, the Warden has said that it would be very nice, if, being a children's book, it could be illustrated.

It must have been written all of fifteen years or so ago, and as I recall written under some inner pressure in the face of interior protests of mine that I was no good at this kind of thing. Having written it, I showed it to John

Matthews who approved of the esoterica but said that children didn't talk like that any more. I thought he was probably right, and so put it in a bottom drawer, but cannibalised the esoteric bits to go into the back of a current Tarot book *The Treasure House of Images* (Aquarian 1986). This may have preserved the esoteric guts of it but I rather feel removed the heart and soul of it along with the kids – old fashioned and prissy though their dialogue might be.

It has remained a very personal book, its protagonists having the same names, and much the same attitudes at their age, as my own children. And granny Berryman was quite a dab hand with the cards too (although not the Tarot), and the bit about the gypsy on Burnham sands is true. So knowing the ways of the commercial publishing world I have never been tempted to circulate it and have it mauled about by script editors and marketing directors and other forms of low life. It seemed best kept as a kind of cultural family heirloom.

However, the current Inner Light initiative changes all that. Not that it is likely to find favour with the book trade or the general public but at least it will see the dignity of print and may be of interest to those of an esoteric persuasion, if only as a literary curiosity from the pen of the master. Of course if it should take off like *The Chronicles of Narnia* or *Harry Potter and the Philosopher's Stone* I shall not complain, but I think winning the national lottery to be at slightly more favourable odds – and I don't even buy tickets for it.

Timewise, I have submitted the other works mentioned to the Society of the Inner Light in computer friendly format, but this one, having been written in the dark ages (in long hand with joined up writing) needs to be keyboarded onto a computer disc, and this I am currently doing. I have so far got up to page 22 and a copy of all that I have done so far I enclose. If you got involved in this thing it would be nice if you could complete the job by the end of the year, but another six months on top of that would probably be all right (before the SIL runs out of dosh or I shuffle off the jolly old mortal coil).

… … As to the number and type of illustrations, in my mind's eye I see certain scenes as lending themselves particularly to illustration, as typifying the contents of a chapter. For instance in the first chapter the kids in the loft with the Fool and the dog decorating the little doorway. But there could be more than one per chapter if this seems called for – where there is a major scene change. And some could be full page and some half or third page according to what kind of image has to be got in. So I think we are talking about a minimum of 24 illustrations and perhaps a maximum of 50. And we are talking black and white line of course.

As you will see, most are Tarot Trump derived, but I have not allowed this to limit my imagination into rigid occult convention and there are also visual cross references to other lines of myth, lore and legend. Roma currently has an eye infection which cuts down on her reading, so I have been reading to her, including excerpts from the book, and we find it comes over pretty powerfully, and not without a certain charm I feel.

If you take this on I suggest we follow our own heads on this one, having no-one else likely to take it upon themselves to say what is saleable or politically correct or anything else. Nor am I suggesting you do this for nothing. I am quite happy to pay you the normal commercial rate on receipt and acceptance of each of the illustrations you do, as and when you do them. Alternatively you can come in with me for a 50% split of my royalties, but I honestly do not recommend this as likely to be to your advantage.

I guess that's all for the moment. I had better get down to a bit more slogging on the keyboard so you can tell if it all ends happily ever after.

110. To Kathleen Raine   *17th February 2002*

Dear Kathleen,

Many thanks for your letter. I am very glad that the Society of the Inner Light can be of help to you and Temenos, there is no-one to my knowledge who has done more to deserve it. Not that the generosity is mine, I simply suggested you might be a worthy recipient of the Society's largesse.

It is very nice of you to invite me over for a chat. I recall your hospitality on three memorable occasions. The first time you gave me a couple of volumes of your Blake Mellon lectures that had recently been published, and which needless to say I still have, treasure and go back to from time to time. More importantly, you instilled into me a desire to study the romantic poets, from whom I have received much benefit, particularly from Coleridge.

The second time was when you laid on an excellent dinner for me and Gerald Gough, the former Librarian at the Inner Light (do many people know you cook so well?) And he also performed a path working. Not quite so memorable as Roma's back in Tewkesbury I think, but perhaps comparisons are odious in this respect. Although I recall to this day Roma evoking the figure of Persephone walking across the countryside with the flowers blooming as she came.

The third time was of course the christening party you hosted for John and Caitlín Matthews' baby, Emrys (now a rip roaring teenager and budding thespian I believe).

I would love to make it a fourth time at Paulton's Square, although it may be best to put it off to somewhat later in the year. The Tides are somewhat rumbustious just at the moment, with three sets of proofs to check and a couple of manuscripts to write.

Anyhow I am sure that those concerned will get under way with whatever mutual programming seems to everyone's advantage. It was very kind of Warren to give such a glowing opinion of my performance at his Oxford conference, although I tend to keep my lecturing commitments to a minimum these days. I find I can rise well enough to the occasion but it takes me a bit longer each time to recover from the effort.

I should say that scientology is not one of my particular enthusiasms, although I concede that a reading of my *Practical Guide to Qabalistic Symbolism* may give a different impression. That is because it was written in 1960/2 and gives a snapshot of what the seniors in the Society of the Inner Light were thinking at that time. This, together with one or two other observations in the book have become something of an albatross about my neck, but that is what goes with writing a book that is successful enough to reprint, but not in such quantities as would justify revision. Thus my remarks of forty years ago are preserved like a fly in amber. Anyhow, it has just been reissued in paperback in America and I believe they have added a new Foreword giving me a chance to update my views a little bit.

I rather agree with the remarks of the Tibetan lama you quote, that westerners tend to confuse wisdom with knowledge. However, wisdom does seem to be percolating into some circles of academe these days, if with some difficulty, and it seems to me that in this respect Temenos is a great standard bearer.

I recall feeling somewhat intellectually outgunned by the bevy of distinguished talent you amassed at the founding of the Academy. But I also recall your look of understanding at my remark that it was Wren who had sent me, which would have caused many present to give me some very odd looks I am sure. However there does seem to be a kind of inner sphere of influence that is associated with some characters associated with St.Pauls and Greenwich towards the end of the 17th century, who like to keep an eye on things, and not least the efforts of HRH.

Roma sends her love. She and Rebecca, whom you met at Vi Marriott's farewell party at the Young Vic, are quite the most gifted esoteric practitioners I know, but carry their wisdom so lightly. It is only old hacks like me who feel it incumbent upon themselves to go on burdening the world with esoteric verbiage.

Our other child, Richard, who was the baby in the cradle when you came to Tewkesbury[1], is now building aeroplanes in Toulouse, which provides a pleasant pied-á-terre in the sunshine for Roma and me from time to time. However, I am actively evading requests from the locals to "rencontrer les personnes qui se sentent en communion avec mes écrits, et échanger avec eux l'expérience qui leur a été transmise." Enough is enough!

[1] Actually 'the baby in the cradle' in 1969 was Rebecca.

111. To William Elmhurst   *24th April 2002*

Dear William,

David Williams has passed me your correspondence although I will not try to add to the masterly analysis of general principles that he has just sent you, but will confine myself to dealing with the specific questions you asked.

My experience of the Society so far, since rejoining it four years ago, is that David and his team have done a magnificent job in building things up from the parlous state in which they had apparently been left in 1990. Indeed the spirit within the Society is far more positive than ever I can remember it from my salad days, so to my mind the spirit of the Chancellor and the other inner plane adepti works effectively in many other ways than the passing of verbal communications.

When it comes to the latter I have to say this does remain, to my mind, vestigial at the present time, but on the other hand, with the new climate within the ranks, and the presence of some likely looking talent now within the group, it needs only a little sustained encouragement and guidance upon the right lines to get things back to as good as they ever were – and possibly even better.

I do not think that the Chancellor is particularly limited as to groups or individuals through which he is able to work, and so may very well have been a contact for Vera, but so also has he, I think, with lots of other people, consciously or otherwise. Therefore I am not sure that the Solar Quest material has a unique place in the scheme of things as far as the Inner Light is concerned, and I think you are better placed to be its custodian, as you have been the facilitator for its reception.

I was somewhat surprised to start getting some verbal communications myself shortly before I rejoined the Society but I will be surprised if I turn out to be the only one so favoured under the new dispensation. Anyway, some of this will be published later this year under the title of *The Abbey Papers* so you will be able to judge for yourself how you think it rates along the Tibetan's percentage scale.

Anyhow, I think there is a great deal to be gained by an exchange of information between groups. Time was when such interchange was severely discouraged, but although it can lead to some misunderstandings and difficulties, particularly upon the part of neophytes, this seems to me infinitely preferable to the state of mind of exclusive righteousness that can lead to abuses such as David has described occurred within the Society prior to 1990.

112. To Kathleen Raine   *3ʳᵈ October 2002*

Dear Kathleen,

Many thanks for your letter of September 18ᵗʰ although I have to say that it was not me who sent you a copy of *The Abbey Papers* so I presume it came from David Williams. I am generally very reluctant to inflict copies of my work upon friends, for reasons at which you hint in your remarks on the 900 page Yeats biography. Anyway, now that you *have* been sent a copy I hope that you will find it wholesome, uplifting and even pleasantly soporific bedtime reading.

Not that I feel wholly responsible for its contents. One is aware of great gobbets of one's mental content being regurgitated in this kind of work, but which nonetheless seems to be selected and rearranged by a higher level of intelligence and awareness inside or outside of oneself. I am by no means a poet but, from what I have read, the creative springs of poetry and other arts, including the magical, seem to have a common fount of inspiration. Indeed all the arts, truly pursued and expressed, are magical.

I sometimes wonder if poetry began to go into something of a decline when poets stopped invoking the muses at the beginning of their song. However the Pierian Spring seems capable of building up enough pressure to burst its banks into poetic consciousness when it wants to. I have heard poets talking in terms of a poem impressing itself upon them or building up within them until they were obliged to go into labour and deliver it. In my own experience this is identical with any form of imaginal work.

At the present I am embarked upon quite a mammoth process of gestation closely based upon Chrétien de Troyes and his Arthurian romances. Not an academic work of course although I felt it necessary to provide myself with a BA in French in order to attempt it. The motivation came, like the poetic or magical impulse, quite beyond my own workaday conscious mind, and indeed I was somewhat reluctant to attempt it, as it needs to be in fictional form, for which I feel I have no great talent. However, needs must when the daemon drives, and I am now, as the project matures, beginning to find it an enjoyable and instructive experience – a strange amalgam of 12ᵗʰ century cultural history and the Arthurian poetic impulse with its roots in the mythopoeic past. So let us hope that in due time it may prove enjoyable and instructive to others – although I shall be well past caring by then I fancy – and happy to leave to my heirs and successors the problem of how best to dispose of a quarter of a million words of typescript.

All of which sounds a bit self indulgent, but if only that were all. I also have the shade of Alfred Noyes hovering in the background ever insistently – whether figuratively or literally speaking is all one when it comes to getting words down on paper. Ours not to reason how or why!

Poor old Alfred has completely fallen out of public and academic consciousness these days, and in many ways not without good reason, but he was the most popular versifier (if no poet) of the 20th century in his day, and therefore an important social phenomenon. This does not prevent me finding him in many ways a somewhat irritating personality but what drew my attention to him in the first place was the realisation that a lot of the historical archetypes that seem to spring up in the course of one's magical experience are to be found in the works of Alfred Noyes – *Drake, Tales of the Mermaid Tavern, Robin Hood, Watchers of the Skies*, the *Song of Earth* – even early works such as *The Forest of Wild Thyme*.

From his autobiography it was therefore rather interesting to find that from childhood he felt he had a kind of faery companion, whom he called Shadow-of-a-Leaf, and that later in life Sir Oliver Lodge was convinced that he must be a natural psychic – although his efforts to convert Alfred to spiritualism fell on very stony ground. So, my other great project, pinching a title from the popular bard himself – *The Enchanted Island* – is to write an account of certain archetypes of the national unconscious with illustrations from my own experience and the works of Alfred Noyes. (Something of this line of country is to be found in *The Abbey Papers* if you get that far, most specifically in sections 40 & 57-60).

Whether I shall be able to get permission from Noyes' literary executors to quote extensively for such a purpose remains conjectural – I do not think he would have approved of me very much in life, whether or not his opinions may have changed in death!

His work does not enter the public domain until 2027, and I don't think I shall be able to hang around that long, even if successful in emulating your shining example of active and formidable longevity. But having written the book I shall not grieve too much about not being around on its eventual date of publication. I tend to lose interest in my progeny after they have been delivered – let others worry about the wet nursing.

Of course Alfred used to get in a frightful stew about all things he considered decadent and modern, from Marcel Proust to Edith Sitwell, and I find somewhat depressing, after his conversion to Catholicism, his squirming under the shadow of Vatican censorship over his biography of Voltaire. However, the old boy's heart was in the right place and he was by no means the shallow dabbler in Edwardian whimsy about Merrie England as modern critics assume him to be. But my concern is with the imaginal archetypes first and foremost and who can act as a vehicle for them.

Therefore I am looking forward to obtaining a copy of Peter Ackroyd's new book on images of Albion, although I may wait until it gets into paperback, just in case it does not live up to its promise. Ackroyd is another who seems to be able to pick up on the imaginal world, although on his off days he can be painfully mannered and pretentious. He also has a penchant for focusing on its seamier side – rather like Charles Williams – but this also has its validity, particularly in relation to big cities, such as London, as Blake well knew. The inner worlds are not alas all sugar and spice and all things nice, any more than the outer one, although we have a certain duty I think to try to alleviate the inner conditions that form the equivalent of old London smog, tuberculosis and cholera. Which is perhaps not best done in the ways Alfred Noyes tended to tub thump about it.

Anyway, on a far brighter side, I have just received a current listing from the Golgonooza Press in which I see you are well represented. And what good news to see that Routledge are reissuing *Blake and Tradition*. I should jolly well think so too – it should never have been let go out of print in the first place – but we live in barbarous times. The price looks pretty daunting so I don't envisage piles of them in the aisles of Waterstones but there should be no excuse for libraries not to replenish their shelves with something worthwhile. I of course am one of the lucky ones – I still have a copy of the first edition!

Well, can't bang on for too long. I have to go and polish the church brasses. (They are a little chary at allowing one so notorious as me to read the lesson or serve in any more overt way, but that suits me very well, I had quite enough of being dragged into PCC work and all that jazz when Tony Duncan was a curate at Tewkesbury!)

113. To Wendy Berg   *15th October 2002*

Dear Wendy,
Well you seem to have got the heebie jeebies and no mistake. There seems to be quite a divisive current running around at the moment which I think you may be picking up on. One element of this has been the bugbear virus which got into Jon Poston's computer and spread to all and sundry, including the SIL, some very trenchant comments of mine about SIL performance and prospects that I made just after the Vernal Equinox. However all are putting a brave face on it and not letting it rock the boat too much.

However, most of what you have to say I have to agree with, and it was for these reasons that I wangled you lot in. Whether or not this influx will prove successful is too soon to forecast, and a lot depends upon the individuals involved and what they make of the challenges facing them and the Fraternity as a whole. However, so far I am cautiously optimistic.

The thing to bear in mind is where the Fraternity is coming from, what its current resources are in terms of membership, and what is a reasonable rate of change.

For a whole generation, from the time I left, in 1965, to 1990 when David Williams took over as Warden, the regime was, in Mike Harris's memorable words, more like a Jesuit seminary than an esoteric fraternity. Those who have been in charge over the past decade or so realise the need for change but have not been entirely sure, for lack of adequate training, in which way that change should go and how to bring it about. This is one of the reasons why I have been taken back and given a fairly free hand to suggest and institute lines of growth.

The influx of members from the CIA and Avalon groups has been a pretty drastic operation, not too far removed from a multiple organ transplant, and it is only to be expected that symptoms of rejection will be experienced by 'old' and 'new' members alike. However these symptoms, acute and painful as they may seem from time to time, have to be overcome – and this is best done by thinking positive, and acting that way too.

I very much regret the feelings of off-handed neglect that you have experienced in visits to the House, and feel myself partly to blame for this. I could have arranged a better conducted tour of the establishment and effected more effective mutual introductions than I have, and will endeavour to do so in the future. Trouble is, I am run off my feet with administrative details on the days of meetings, and there is no great opportunity for socialising anyway.

On the more positive side, a lot depends on how one reacts to this seemingly unfriendly wall. The highly extraverted Sue seems to have overcome all by a commitment that most currently find astonishing, coming early, going late, spending days reorganising and refurbishing the garden, including an off-shoot from the Glastonbury thorn – she is of course a professional horticulturalist, which helps.

As to some of the other physical changes to the house, all is not as taken for granted as you might think. There is currently a great deal of work going on in recovering from years of neglect under the old regime. Thus garden walls are being rebuilt, a new porch installed, new roof on the studios, new carpets for same, car parking space organised, land slippage attended to, etc., etc. So whether or not knocking down interior walls is a desirable project for the future, it will need to wait a little while yet I imagine. However, a radical rethink of the use of existing rooms might well be worth consideration at some time.

As for the study course, this is an area that has long caused me some concern. As soon as I arrived back I did some urgent first aid on it, shortening it considerably and, with David Williams' permission and John Paternoster's help, made it a little more relevant than it was. However, it is still an area that needs drastic attention in my view, as it determines to a very large extent the type of people applying for membership, and the rate they come in. It had been my hope that Jonathan Poston, who had grizzled his way all through the Study Course himself (a determined chap when he gets going) might set to and possibly even rework it himself. Unfortunately he seems to have been diverted to Anglican pastoral studies. On the other hand I was somewhat gob-smacked by Wolfe who thought the course was wonderful!! If, as it seems, you have become involved as a supervisor, I suggest you do not take things lying down with John Paternoster, but let him know in no uncertain manner, how and why you think it lacking. If we can get a debate going on the matter so much the better – but rewriting it is a chore that I cannot spare the time for myself. (Been there, done that, too often in this life!)

This implies that, in general terms, I do not think that a general letter such as you have written to me, is likely to be productive of much positive change – but it is more a question of identifying what specific things need attention and concentrating on those, one at a time. By a series of separate battles the war might be won, but I thing a general statement of dissatisfaction on umpteen counts more likely to be counterproductive.

When it comes to the ritual side of things, there is no need to be dominated by current custom and practice. I think there are good reasons to be satisfied with the set-up of GM and LM lodges at the moment (and slow movement for change is taking place), but if you want to see rituals in a more open environment, why not suggest doing one in the downstairs robing room? I think John Paternoster is already using these rooms for meetings of Masonic friends.

As importantly, why not regard one function of the Avalon Group as an outrider to the SIL, laying on rituals of the type you prefer, and in residential circumstances if need be? The CIA have already on one occasion played host to three SIL junior members in this way, with what seems to have been beneficial results to all concerned.

In short, there are many ways in which the Fraternity falls short at the present time, but it is improving, and will only continue to do so to the measure that those who can see the way ahead grasp the challenges and make the changes happen.

However this will not happen wholesale overnight. I rather look upon myself, as I think does David Williams, as somewhat in the same position as Moses, who only survived long enough to see the chosen people enter the promised land. At 72 I reckon I have less then a decade to contribute actively to the Fraternity and lead it along the right lines. If it has achieved all you hope for it by 2010 then that will be enough for me, and I think that not an unreasonable time scale. I hope that you, along with most of the others of the old Gareth Knight gang, will be able to stay on board and contribute positively to that programme – but that is up to how you take the demons of disruption on.

114. To Alan Richardson   *21ˢᵗ October 2002*

Dear Alan,

I have never read Bill Gray's autobiography although what he might have said about me excites my curiosity considerably. I am quite sure it was not at all flattering, but then he did tend to live in a world of his own as far as relationships with the rest of humanity were concerned.

Anyway – yes I will be glad to help you all I can, because he was an important figure on the esoteric scene, if an idiosyncratic one. I will need to gather my thoughts a bit on this, because he was a complex man, and there is quite a lot to tell, and I want to be as fair and objective as I can. So give me two or three weeks and I will put something together for you which you can use as you wish. I respect your integrity.

I seem to be in the business of writing little thumbnail reminiscences of the great and good (?) I have met in my life, having just provided a sketch of Ernest Butler for SOL, for even Dolores seemed to know surprisingly little about him. But being a publisher and magazine editor (however small) puts one in an advantageous position I suppose in meeting people.

115. To Alan Pert   *28ᵗʰ August 2003*

Dear Alan,

Many thanks for your e-mails re Anna Kingsford. The approach I shall be taking is very much a metaphysical one, in much the same fashion that I did with Dion Fortune. This will not please everyone, particularly with a many sided character like AK, but it is the way I shape up to things, and for what I am best valued by my particular readership and the inner contacts whom I do my best to please. Although I could sympathise with the disappointment of one Australian reader who felt that it was not a proper biography at all as is generally understood by the term. No doubt much could be written about AK from the point of view of animal rights, women's rights, as well as metaphysical importance – let alone an attempt to cover all aspects as you hope to do – in which case 150,000 words would seem quite a modest requirement! Certainly the world needs a readable update on Edward Maitland's *Life* which is a fascinating read for those who are willing to put in the time to it, but whose leisured Victorian prose style demands a commitment which few seem able to raise these days.

I think there may very well be a strong AK current at work, and I am tempted to speculate about the old tradition of the tomb of Christian Rosencreutz, the archetypal figure of the western mystery tradition, being sealed for 120 years. Should this period be measured from AK's transition then we can perhaps look forward to the light shining forth to an astonished world in 2008 – the current interest of people such as ourselves being the first creakings of the casket being pushed open?!

From my own experience, AK made her presence felt in November 2000 when I set about writing and working a ritual aimed to update and supersede some of DF's Isis work – and for an important part of it used lengthy quotations from AK's *Illuminations* which just happened to come my way at a convenient time. This turned out to be a very memorable experience and to have a number of results in terms of new realisations being generated along with commensurate events. I had a persistent sense of AK in the background for some time afterward, accompanied by a lot of negative dream imagery to begin with, related to misuse of animals, and then the tune of "Love's Old Sweet Song" began to run persistently through my head, much as DF's Carstairs has been known to use "Roses of Picardy" as a call sign.

Going to the public library to seek information, on the course of which short journey I was met by a couple of synchronistic reminders of the former SIL pythoness Margaret Lumley Brown on the way, on consulting a book on 19th century popular music I discovered that "Love's Old Sweet Song" had been the smash hit of the year 1884, when AK and EM founded the Hermetic Society. This seemed to suggest that a genuine contact of AK might be trying to get through.

The impressions I received of this contact were of a very high level, and much beyond the historical personality of AK, as if coming directly from the Essential Self that projected that personality. Anyway it led me to write an article on AK which was published in the Spring Equinox edition of the *Inner Light Journal* (which I attach for your interest, although it is unlikely to contain anything you don't already know) and which was also included in a volume of my collected essays *The Wells of Vision* (SIL Publishing, 2002).

116. To Jonathan Poston   *24th January 2004*

Dear Jonathan,

Many thanks for the invitation to your ordination, which I do appreciate, but as you surmise, such occasions are not really my scene, and as you also intuit, I am pretty well hard pressed as to time and energy on various fronts. It seems that the IPA are concerned to squeeze the very last drop out of the old lemon before disposal into the ash can. If required on the day, I will no doubt be part of a visiting coach party on a higher plane, with guests from

Sirius and other pickup points, who will not put a strain on the mundane seating arrangements.

The high trapeze work on the Tree is great fun and causes all kinds of things to happen, but one is never sure exactly what. Being formless levels, you just pull the red switches and see what pipework down below seems most likely in need of lagging or replacement. The forces find their own forms to do what's needed. Strictly *entre nous* I got zapped very hard just before Christmas in such a way as to cause me to feel that after his sudden transition earlier this year our friend Tony Duncan has started getting himself (and others) organised at a new power base. Just what all this may portend God alone knows, and if past form is anything to go by, will no doubt keep His cards close to his bosom until the chips are down.

Yes April 3rd is my 74th birthday and I am just writing a working for the day, based on the Elemental Gates and Tides. Not that there is anything personal in the programme, but it seems a good opportunity to get in a bit of basic training on these lines. October sees my 50th anniversary of being initiated into the SIL and so I have put on a slot for the GM meeting in celebration – a dual working based upon Sirs Gareth and Bors.

No need to worry too much about informing me about GM attendance. Just come as and when you feel like it, although it eases my way slightly to know if you are intending to come at least a day before hand, so I know how many potato crisps to lay out. I imagine you have quite enough on your plate this year without too many trips to London. Your more active and regular aid might well be appreciated next year, when I shall be looking for other capable hands to take on running the GM work. At 75 years of age I intend to try to become more of an ornamental Elder and holy Sage rather than sweaty Head Chef cooking up things in the kitchen. Keep in touch, all the best.

117. To R. J. Stewart   *19th January 2005*

Dear Bob,
Good to hear from you. Things go very well with me, and I very much enjoyed a bumper meeting of the Company of Hawkwood in December as their guest, although I'll be content to make that my farewell performance from public workshops. Doing a bit of private work with the Inner Light and some leisurely writing on Arthurian legend and faery tradition, with a fair bit of French translation, keep me well occupied and contented. I have not seen your book that you mention by the way, and would be much obliged to receive a copy.

No problems for me in the article you have written but you might be interested to read my own memoir of Bill Gray that I wrote up for Alan Richardson, most of which in fact he published in *The Old Sod*. You will find a fairly detailed account of the working re Roy Bowers in there. I remember mentioning it to you over lunch at Malmesbury just before you left for the USA and being somewhat disconcerted over your completely different view of RB as compared to what I had been led to believe from Bill. Anyway I attach it for what it is worth.

As a matter of fact I have only just completed writing an article for the *Inner Light Journal* which concerns some of your own work quite closely. I also attach this in case there is anything in it that you feel erroneous or misleading or otherwise not to your liking.

As for a visit, Roma and I would be absolutely delighted to see you if ever you are down this way, and you are welcome to stay if you are in need of bed and board.

118. To Paul Dunne   *8ᵗʰ June 2005*

Dear Paul,

Thank you for the copy of your Carstairs article. The whole business of the identity of "Masters" seems very much in the air at the moment. It has been coming at me from various directions.

What you have to say seems to hold together well as a plausible theory although I have to say I find it difficult to apply in Carstairs' case owing to the familiarity I have built up with this particular contact over a number of years, both personally and via members of my former group. You could be right of course but when it comes down to practical magic what makes things work is believing in the reality of the contact at face value – whatever the ultimate metaphysics of it all might be. So it can get rather like pulling the wings off a butterfly to try to discover what enables it to fly.

I know Alan Richardson quite well and have discussed these issues with him although his main respondent over the possible identity of Carstairs at the time of writing *Priestess* was Alan Adams (pen name Charles Fielding), a contemporary of mine in the SIL in the 1950s and who later became head of the London Group, but who died in 1998.

119. To Jonathan Poston   *6th July 2005*

Dear Jonathan,

Many thanks for the service sheet and for the sermon. The latter gives me great encouragement for the future of the C of E if it is attracting new ordinands of this calibre capable of this level of clarity of communication – only hope he is appreciated by the punters. And glad to hear that the three ladies from your dark and heretical past made it to give you a kick start from the Divine Feminine.

Had forgotten about doing the Manchester gig, although now you remind me it comes back to me as the event when I decided I would do no more. Although I did do a nostalgic trip back to Hawkwood last December for John and Caitlín's 21st anniversary bash of the Company of Hawkwood that they launched a little while after I gave up public for private meetings there. It was a very heartening do, and a very lively crowd, many from Ireland but one or two from the USA as well, who seem to turn up every year for the annual thresh. I gave John the original horn that I blew back in days of yore for which he was touchingly appreciative.

I am I suppose trying to pass myself off as a grand old man these days, after a long career as a slowly maturing and now possibly decaying *enfant terrible*, and have comradely contacts with various old troupers in the business, who tend not to talk to each other, but seem willing to make an exception with me and even to solicit advice.

Have also recently got the message that I have probably written and spouted enough words for one incarnation, apart from the odd article, or one night stand. The SIL seems to be picking up enough steam also for me not to have to work quite so hard at shovelling coal into the boiler.

Talking of which, following a recent challenge from the Chancellor to spend some time evaluating inner plane communications from various sources with a view to sorting the wheat from the chaff the project rather blew back in my face when I came to review the *Abbey Papers* and was struck, to my astonishment, with the fact that they contain some pretty dynamic stuff and that some of it needs to be acted upon – particularly as it is now 12 years since I received it.

Anyway, all that can wait for a little while as we are off to Toulouse for a short break tomorrow to visit son Richard, who builds air buses. We recently spent a few days with Rebecca, who is doing some promising stuff on the musical scene it would appear – "folk rock" is a bit off limits for old jazz men such as myself but it seems a pleasant enough sound and it is quite amazing what they can do with computers nowadays. But as far as I am concerned the rot set in as soon as they started electrifying guitars and I guess I shall have to wait for another incarnation before I get swinging again.

120. To Jonathan Poston   *April 30th 2006*

Dear Jonathan,

You should be so lucky with just Arthurian tapes shouting at you from the shelf. I have just been lumbered with proof checking and indexing the *Arthurian Formula*, which is due to come out from Thoth later this year.

I have taken the opportunity to include as a lengthy appendix about 15,000 words of additional material from Wendy which I think should make a few people sit up and take notice. It pushes heavily on the faery connection, which happens to be the main thrust of the IGM work I have got going at the SIL at long last. Initial meeting was in January but we shall have a follow up on June 10th. It has certainly zapped up the voltage as far as Wendy and I are individually concerned. Have not been to any OGMs or LMs in the meantime as plenty to cope with, with "them" coming to us, without need to turn out on parade at Steele's Road. Indeed it seems as if I am being deliberately kept away for the time being – as you have experienced yourself in the past. The day Pat was raised to the pinnacle of the organisation I was booked to go off and give a lecture to local pagans, as it happens very close to where I was born, some 76 years ago. I attach a copy of my talk, although it will appear, I gather, in the next issue of the *Inner Light Journal*. Follows on from the Bristol job a month before, which also coincided with an SIL meeting.

Funny how all this stuff is tying up together in some strange way – although I suppose one should not be surprised if one really believed in all one likes to think. I think the animal element in the threefold alliance is something that well chimes in with you. Anyway, to close, I don't know if you have a copy of DF's *Esoteric Healing* book but it should be out again very soon in Thoth covers, smartly followed by *Pythoness*, my MLB book. Now there was someone who could really bloody mediate!

Then, with any luck, a new little book by me before year's end, on Dion Fortune's novels. And having got Tom Clarke at Thoth on the move, provided no other hangers on get in the way, we should see a new edition of *The Magical World of the Inklings* out again next year. In-between times I strive with some more *Cosmic Doctrine* articles, an IGM initiation ritual (well they did ask for it – although God knows when anyone will be ready for it) and of course the Great Work about the faery Melusine, Eleanor of Aquitaine, Chrétien de Troyes and various other 12th century goings on. I am beginning to wonder if it is not in some way an autobiography coming out about 800 years late! Well better late than never I suppose.

121. To Alistair Munro   *27ᵗʰ December 2006*

Dear Alistair Munro,

Many thanks for your letter. I don't know whether or not to envy you Christmas in high summer. Although with the central heating breaking down in the midst of a cold snap a couple of weeks ago I must confess I did have certain unseasonal longings.

Glad you liked my Inklings book, which I hope to get back into print some time in the next year or two, with a little expansion on the Barfield and Tolkien sections. I felt immensely flattered that Barfield greeted my MSS so generously when it was sent to him prior to publication – and not a little relieved as he can be a highly perceptive critic and philosopher way out of my league. The extra bit on him will cover his children's book *The Silver Trumpet* which I had not been aware of when I first wrote the book – and being an extremely modest man he never even mentioned it in his comments.

The Tolkien section will cover *Smith of Wooton Major* and related Elemental connections as far as possible in the limited space available – one could of course go on *ad infinitum* about Tolkien and his works. But as you may have gathered from the gist of my talks over the past year, posted on the web site, the Elemental connection seems to me of considerable importance in human thinking about now. One reason for spending time talking to pagan audiences, who whatever their theological shortcomings, have their attention focused upon a relevant spiritual issue.

Not that I imagine your new vicar would find grasping that very easy. This of course was Anthony Duncan's great strength – brought about largely by coming to terms with the fact of being naturally unusually psychic as well as being a down to earth and sensible kind of guy. And helped (or hindered) by long discourse with me at a crucial period in both our lives.

Your suggestion about telling the story of our connection strikes a certain chord with me – and might be worth spending some time on for an article for the *Inner Light Journal* and the web site. We really knocked sparks off each other over a fairly lengthy period that commenced with one of his first jobs as curate at Tewkesbury Abbey being giving confirmation classes to yours truly. The upshot of this was two books, *The Christ Psychotherapy & Magic* by him, and *Experience of the Inner Worlds* by me, both published around 1975. (Seems like another life ago!)

Sorry to hear of your vicar's lack of sympathy for your views. I have been fortunate down my way as my local one, on being tipped off that he had a black sheep in his flock, announced from the pulpit that he had no intention of turning *anyone* away from his church. I suppose maybe your chap feels that you might be spreading a little heresy consciously or unconsciously if you have a prominent role in the local ministry.

I avoided all that by simply taking on something innocuous and that nobody else wanted to do – namely cleaning the altar brasses. To which I perhaps was able to impart a certain esoteric shine. Who knows? I do know that on occasion I had a very powerful Christ contact whilst going about this humble business – although it was not something that I felt that I could impart to anyone else in the congregation, clerical or lay, without being thought a bit weird. But there is a time and place for all this kind of thing and as ever the need for wise discretion.

Freemasonry itself does not seem at all anti-Christian to me – it seems to me to be largely good old fashioned 18th century deism – so I suppose what Tony Duncan might have described as sub-Christian (rather like the modern pagans in a way, who are on the whole a very decent crowd). A prominent mason I know however, who is also a member of the SIL, was telling me recently that he has been somewhat concerned by one or two elements within the movement who are rabidly anti-Christian. Same thing happens with the pagans for that matter – although they would be horrified to realise themselves to be narrow minded bigots. I just plough on and state my case and blissfully ignore them, without deliberately treading on any toes.

As to magical battles or whatever ahead – the one that exercises me at the moment is what Bob Stewart has called the Threefold Alliance – which has been back of my talks over the past year and which are posted on the web site.

122. To Mike Omoleye   *31st May 2007*

Dear Mike,

Thank you very much for your letter of 7th May and I must apologise for not responding to your letter of last September. I put it on one side in order to reply to it as soon as *The Arthurian Formula* was published, but when this in turn was delayed, I regret that by the time it appeared I had filed and forgotten your letter. I am sorry about that. The VCD was also safely received but unfortunately I cannot make it play on my equipment.

Anyway, along with this letter I am posting a copy of *The Arthurian Formula* and in a separate packet a couple of cassette tapes containing a recording of *The Immortal Hour*. As the latter may be somewhat difficult to understand if relying entirely on listening to the singing I have included with the book a printed copy of the libretto.

It is a very ancient story from Irish Celtic mythology of a faery maiden called Étaín who wanders into the human world and marries Eochaid, the High King of Ireland, but is then called back to fairyland by her faery husband Midir. It thus has a certain resonance with the theory about Queen Gwenevere that is expounded by Wendy Berg in Appendix 3 of *The Arthurian Formula*.

Anyway, plenty there for you to get your teeth into. As also appears to have been the case with *Principles of Esoteric Healing*, although I regret that I cannot come back with simple answers to your questions – for the most part your guess is as good as mine on these various subtle points. There was very little supporting material in the files that I had to work from, indeed they were all in a great muddle, as it had not been realised that they were in fact material that originated from Dion Fortune. They had been worked over by a qualified medical doctor who was a member of the Society (you may have met him perhaps – Dr Edward Gellately). He did a fair amount of research based upon them in conjunction with Margaret Lumley Brown, but was not at all book publishing minded and so in the end just left a great wodge of this material in a file that was marked with his name, which until I came along and realised what it was, had been assumed to be rough notes for a book by him.

Thank you for the copy of your lecture. Obviously you are doing sterling and much needed work with your Divine Society, although it must seem like a struggle against overwhelming odds at times. Recognition of the importance of the ancestors is a matter that is much in need of emphasis these days I think.

I do not know why you have not received copies of *The Inner Light Journal* over the current year – and I must say I was very pleased to see you featured as a contributor in a recent one. It may be due to a radical reorganisation of the Society at the beginning of this year, when David Williams stepped down as Warden, having reached the age of 75, and handed over to Pat Arthy. She strikes me as a very good choice I must say. But at the same time they decided to undertake a considerable amount of physical changes with office locations, so possibly organisation of the overseas distribution of the journal has suffered as a consequence. Anyway, I have sent a note to Pat to ask her to look into the matter, so hopefully you will shortly receive any missing copies.

Roma and I are coasting along quite happily in spite of not getting any younger and I do not do as much travelling about as I used to do. I attend the SIL only for more important meetings and have cut down my public lecturing to just one appearance this year. Having just about come to the end of editing books by Dion Fortune (there are none left to do!) I am taking my time to write a final book of my own, largely inspired by certain elements in *The Arthurian Formula*, and provisionally entitled *The Faery Gates of Avalon*. The thesis being that the ladies of the Arthurian legend are very often as important as the knights, insofar that they lead the knights into their adventures and test them on the way, which very often turns out to be a quest into the world of faery if you read the signs aright.

Apart from that, a couple of books are in the pipeline with Thoth Publications. One is an overview of Dion Fortune's fictional work, called *The Occult Fiction of Dion Fortune*, and the other a record of some inner contacts I had shortly after rejoining the Society which will be called *The Temple Papers*. Actual publication date unclear, as there is quite a queue of manuscripts awaiting publication at Thoth Publications, but the fiction book should be out fairly soon and I will send you a copy as soon as it appears.

123. To Alan Richardson

August 30th 2008

Dear Alan,

Delightful young lady editor at Llewellyns asks if you know of any writers who might have new stuff in them? Thanks for the thought Alan, but not for me. I am indeed embarked upon a fairly weighty project on the faery Melusine, but when finished will be more appropriate for some niche publisher such as R J Stewart.

However, thinking about your own track record as a biographer, you might think about approaching them with a biography of Gareth Knight! I was just thinking the other day, that I have moved and shaken quite a lot of things (and people!) over the past 50+ years of my esoteric career. SIL 1953-64, founding the prototype of the SOL with Ernest Butler in 1964-73, founding Helios Books to publish Regardie and Gray, meeting Gray, Regardie, Doreen Valiente, Margaret Bruce, the Crowthers and many of the burgeoning neo-pagan crowd when editing *New Dimensions* 1963-5, founding and running the GK group from 1973-1998, rejoining the SIL to liven things up since 1998 and getting the old DF stuff into print. Its something that might appeal to Llewellyn as *New Dimensions* was launched by them originally, and indeed Carl Weschcke, who owns them, and whose son Gabriel now runs them, first commissioned me to write the *PGQS* and thereby spawned Gareth Knight. I wonder what karma he's got coming to him as a result!

I have lots of documentation and correspondence stored up in my garage and loft, but I really cannot be arsed to think in terms of an autobiography. If anyone is going to do the job I would as soon that it was you as anyone else – someone who knows what's what and can cut through the bullshit.

Anyway, think about it. The thought only crossed my mind on receiving your e-mail.

124. To Paul Dunne   *26ᵗʰ September 2008*

Dear Paul,

Many thanks for the run down on the Glastonbury meeting. I put out a few feelers, including to yourself, not having heard from anyone since the event, and Mike Harris having got a bit jittery beforehand as to whether it would break even financially this year. Fortunately it seems to have done so, and he is now sounding quite up-beat about a follow up for next year, though I think it likely to be held in the smaller venue of the Town Hall.

Like you said, the Assembly Rooms have a rather strange kind of ambience, some of it quite good and hallowed with age but also some rather 'iffy' undertones. Like Alison said (whose psychic perception I respect) it could maybe do with a good spring clean. Mind you, I think much the same could be said of a lot of Glastonbury – and what with the druggy culture and what have you, as fast as one mess is cleared up another is likely to take its place. Bit like superintending a public toilet – but don't quote me on that!

The theme for next year, I am told, is likely to be "successors to DF" which will give Mike and Wendy a chance to plug their groups no doubt, and I have no problem about that. However as their one time mentor in the GK Group I feel the time has come to take a back seat in dealings with the general esoteric public, having done my share over the years. My main concern before I finally succumb to the ravages of time is to do a bit of esoteric research, resulting in another book or two, supplemented by a few IGM SIL meetings and related *Journal* articles.

Incidentally I liked your faery article very much and hope that despite being crowded out of the next issue they might find space for it in the new year. Actually I think you have the material for a couple of articles here, and if it were me I would have cut it off just before the Fiona MacLeod verses, the material of which is worthy of separate treatment – although I have to say that despite great respect for what she/he writes about, I find his/her writing actual writing a bit depressive – too much misty moisty late 19ᵗʰ century Celtic twilight for my taste, so if I were writing it I would tend to paraphrase rather than to quote directly. But that's up to you mate.

Harking back to the Seminar, I am somewhat relieved to hear that the music was a high point, as I had been personally a bit dubious about that innovation myself. As for the 'open forum' discussion, these can always turn out to be a bit of a bummer – especially in a place like Glastonbury. Needs pretty ruthless and even charismatic chairmanship. Anyway, thanks for your feedback on the event. Of the others I have received Mike and Wendy were very up beat – Jonathan more luke warm.

125. To Dolores Ashcroft-Nowicki   *17ᵗʰ October 2008*

Dear Dolores,

Many thanks for your news. You put me to shame with your global travelling. What a great trouper you are! And what a long way have all come since the 1960s – and I think it can be proclaimed as very much a success story, so I hope your autobiography will serve as something of a stimulus to the up and coming generation of budding Aquarians.

Apart from being a bit creaky in the knee joints, so that walking any distance is a bit of a chore rather than a pleasure, and popping pills for high blood pressure, I cannot complain healthwise. However I have called a halt to all public appearances as I just cannot work up the enthusiasm for them. I am in the fortunate position of being able to go up to the SIL whenever the fancy takes me (about three or four times a year) and lay on a bit of magic in a controlled environment with a few trusty colleagues.

Apart from that my current destiny seems best played out behind a keyboard. Have just completed indexing and proofing *The Faery Gates of Avalon* which is a close analysis of the faery elements in the early Arthurian romancer Chrétien de Troyes, and am in the throes of coming to terms with another faery book – probably entitled *Melusine – Faery Guide and Goddess*. These to be published by Bob Stewart with whose work I find a lot of sympathy these days.

Have not been tempted into any tilt into autobiography although I have told Alan Richardson that if he wants to make a play at a biography I will not stand in his way as long as it does not involve being waterboarded. I think though that he already probably has quite enough on his plate. I have been quite amused by his recently set up new website and was also much impressed on meeting him at the Glastonbury DF Seminars, the first two of which I attended. By the way, it would seem to me very appropriate if you were on the panel at next year's event, the theme of which, I gather, is to be on those who took up the torch from Dion Fortune. I will put an elbow nudge in the appropriate rib cages if you think it might interest you. Shall not be there myself, although one or two of my latterday sidekicks such as Wendy Berg and Mike Harris will almost certainly be.

Thank you, by the way, for the photos. Despite being quite tempted by some of the attractive totty that you appear to have assembled, and your generous offer of transportation to your Gathering of Lights, I would however prefer to keep to my reclusive comfort zone, as I get the impression that my energies need to be concentrated on mediating the enthusiasms of the current inner mob, who can be quite demanding. But many thanks for thinking of me and for your invitation and I am sure that it will all go swimmingly well without my curmudgeonly presence.

126. To Katie Belle   *16th January 2009*

Dear Katie,

It just occurred to me that putting test questions to communicators might be unproductive on account of it putting up a kind of subliminal barrier – on the theory that inner communication is a delicate business which requires an attitude of faith on each side to make and keep the connection. I think the best way of validation is to see what comes and then question the results afterwards.

Don't be intimidated by the quantity of stuff that came through MLB, although I must say it looks pretty formidable when it is all collected together. But it was just a matter of going one step at a time. I found it helpful to sit with a pad and pencil, visualise the contact, and then formulate a question and write it down, then wait to see if an answer came into my head – either by words or ideas or even pictures. Don't be afraid if it seems to be just your own subconscious or semiconscious mind – just write it all down uncritically – for evaluation afterwards.

It is very similar to creative writing really. Imagine you are writing dialogue in a play. Or a conversation between two characters in a novel. Just let it flow. Even if it's rubbish no harm is done, you just tear it up afterwards.

It is helped by having someone pretty high powered and expert on the inner, which you may well have. MLB certainly was. In fact that was how I got started, back in 1993 when I started getting a scenario pushed into my head persistently. It seemed quite ridiculous. In what seemed like the saloon bar in the Queen's Hotel at Burnham-on-Sea I was present in a crowd of people who were about to set off to a vicars and tarts fancy dress party. I kept getting this coming through with the impulse to imagine I was there and write down what happened and I would learn something to my advantage. Eventually I did, just to get rid of it or prove it to be a lot of old cobblers. When I did so, the party goers went off, leaving one chap there who seemed dressed up in somewhat old fashioned army officer's uniform. He was feeding money into a slot machine, or trying to, and asked for my assistance. When I went over I saw that he was trying to use old money – big pre-decimal pennies. I accidentally knocked against him, I think, and he appeared to be suffering from some old war wound or something, as he was obviously pained. I realised then it was David Carstairs. Went with him to his room which happened to be room number seven. When we got there and opened the door, who should be sitting there but a couple of the Masters who first contacted Dion Fortune. They asked me to take time to sit regularly and take down what they told me. Again – thinking this all to be subconscious hokum I tried it – sitting down with a pad and pen to write down what might come. And lo, words started to flow. But at about two or three times the speed it takes me to write off my own resources. This went on for a period of ninety days, sitting down regularly and writing for about an hour each time, and the result was *The Abbey Papers* which were eventually published.

That was in 1993. Then five years later came this MLB stuff, which was a direct result of a couple of ladies at the SIL asking me to help them develop communication skills, which I did by sitting with them in the lodge for an hour or so once a week and seeing what we might pick up – which was not much I have to say. Until MLB came through in this dream to start this series of chats with me at home – which I have tentatively called the *Temple Papers*. I was a bit dubious about publishing them, but then I discovered that despite the fact that they contain some quite interesting stuff the SIL intended to do nothing with them but file them in the attic. I felt that they deserved somewhat wider exposure, and so approached Thoth, who were very keen but so far seem to be somewhat ineffective. Ah well, publishing was ever thus.

I also have an interesting record of MLB's first attempts at getting communication through back in 1946 – just after DF died – when she was thrown into the deep end, so to speak, and although thought to be psychic (as she no doubt was) had never done any formal communication work. She was given a room to herself at the SIL HQ and told to develop herself in these skills as best she might in time to give an address to the assembled members at the Summer Solstice meeting in about three months' time. This she did, obviously with some potent help from the inner, but it was quite hard graft for her. Sitting for an hour, twice or three times a day, waiting to get something through, which might well be nothing – certainly to begin with. But then she blossomed forth remarkably. I wrote a book about her in the end, called *Pythoness* – but you probably have quite enough to ready without my chucking that at your head.

127. To Jonathan Poston

Dear Jonathan,

Nice to hear from you again. The Steiner seems to have downloaded OK and I have printed it off in order to read later. Don't care much for trying to absorb deep stuff straight off the screen.

I know exactly what you mean about how anthroposophists tend to come across – and even Owen Barfield, whom I admire greatly – is not entirely free from that strange intellectual aura – which I must say I regard as a defect rather than as evidence of superior evolutionary status or wisdom. Not even bloody Steiner was perfect – something they need to take on board.

That said, I too have been having quite a strong rapprochement with the Steiner teachings. It arose out of reviewing the old public Hawkwood events and until now I had not realised how important the 1984 one was, where Roma distinguished herself with the Crystal Boat visualisation, and Bob Stewart was also there. The theme of the weekend was *The Flaming Door* which is the title of a book by Eleanor C Merry, subtitled *the mission of the Celtic folk soul.*

Having a copy of the book on a neglected shelf I started to read through it and was much taken with it, as an excellent exposition of the general Steiner teaching – which is often so difficult to comprehend from the diabolical translations of his lectures. So went on to purchase and begin to read other books of hers, *Easter, Spiritual Knowledge,* and *The Ascent of Man* – which in turn has led to my having Steiner's own *Knowledge of the Higher Worlds* as a bedside book. Have to confess that I tried to read the latter many years ago and thought it just a load of evasive waffle, but coming to it again find it a very precise manual of spiritual exercises. Not that I intend to give up a life time's dedication to my own version of going about things esoteric. I have however got out my old book on *Projective Geometry* by Olive Whicher which gives some practical drawing exercises which are quite mind expanding and fun to do. *The Plant Between Sun and Earth*, which she wrote with George Adams gives some mind blowing theoretical background to it with evocative pictures.

This is a lot to have come out of my current literary effort which is an autobiography. I had long put off the idea of such a project as of little point but it suddenly came to me a few weeks ago that on the contrary it was something that could be of value to the outer world that goes rather further than just personality chat. As someone put it to me recently, it has been quite a remarkable life, all things considered, and I had never quite realised just how many things I had started off and people I had launched on their way. Now I come to write about it, it turns out to be a very tangled skein, but also quite educative for me, in seeing how different strands worked out over the course of years. So I suppose it is also a bit of advanced homework in preparation for the Judgment Hall of Osiris when I take my finals for this incarnation.

I agree that the *Hallowquest Tarot* of the Matthews is a fine piece of work, although personally I have tended to get my kicks out of Bob Stewart's *Dreampower Tarot*, which is regrettably out of print.

Part of my homework for the autobiography has been ploughing through past correspondence with both Stewart and the Matthews, going back nearly forty years. And I still have all those Lodge Reports on file to tackle next. Blimey! I shall need a twenty year extension on my current life span to absorb all that lot, digest it, and render it into pithy amusing but instructive anecdote to the next generation – most of whom seem to come off another planet anyway, but that's their problem, not mine. One of the advantages of advancing age is that you tend not to give a fuck about too much any more! Brings great freedom of expression and self regard.

Something for you to look forward to.

Anyway, thanks for calling in. Hope all is well with you and your nearest and dearest. Rebecca seems to be doing well with her music, which she reckons has an esoteric slant to it. I came across an old interview she did for the Macjams website about a year ago, in which she was described as a "Psychedelic Renaissance Woman"! One of her replies that caught my eye was *"Yeah! I am naturally rebellious, and I get it from my dad, who has achieved so much in his life on the basis of his wits and bloody-mindedness."*

Was it Robbie Burns who wrote *"O would some power the giftie gie us, to see ourselves as others see us?"* Well, out of the mouths of babes and sucklings also cometh forth truth. So much for me to ponder there! Is there a title for an autobiography in there somewhere I wonder.

128. To Katie Belle
March 27ᵗʰ 2009

Dear Katie,

No, you are not in the least naïve or ignorant in what you say and feel about ritual. As so often, you put your intuitive finger on the pulse with devastating accuracy.

I suppose I could qualify as having done as many rituals of many different kinds as anyone in the world, and in the right circumstances I have found it an excellent way of bringing certain people on. However there is a great deal of glamour and misinformation that hangs about it – also a great deal of unnecessary complication – a doubtful legacy we have from our 19th century Masonic forebears. The Golden Dawn and heavy Qabalah type stuff reminds me somewhat of a bloody great ornate wedding cake – all silver gilt and cardboard and indigestible decoration all of which tends to obscure something the size and attractiveness of a measly stale bun in the middle – and without too many currants at that!

It is that inner pattern which is more important than outer accessories. You have already been formulating this in the Melangell work. Central sacred spot, which marks the cross ways of the four cardinal directions (with whatever persona or symbols you wish to associate with them) plus the vertical element of heavens above and earth powers below. That stable format provides you with an inner sacred space or even space ship with which to travel the universe.

Of course a certain minimum of ritual action can help – which is probably not always recognised as ritual action – that is to say, rather like the Keepers of the Planetary Flame formula, just sitting before a dedicated artefact like a stone, crystal, light, picture or what have you. Whatever you feel comfortable with, and which brings your wandering superficial twittering mind, by association of ideas, into a suitable receptive and dedicated state.

I see that Stewart and Dolores have written little books on cord magic, which I think is also a popular wicca device, and that also seems a good approach to individual ritual, although not one that I feel I particularly need.

I have to say that I found Bill's thoughts about having a full scale ritual to tap into someone's past lives in order to access magical powers somewhat and somehow distasteful. I have come across some unfortunate results of this kind of approach in the past, which gave me quite a bit of trouble at the later Hawkwoods. Fools rush in where angels would make sure they had shit-proof thigh boots on first.

Apart from my ritual capers at the SIL and GK group and the relatively short lived Hawkwood experiment, a great deal of my esoteric work – and arguably some of the best, has been done in dual meditational visualisation. Roma and I did some pretty good stuff (for instance the account of the H.G. Wells contact in *The Wells of Vision*) but more importantly and extensively than that, my own face to face conversation or instruction from inner contacts. Any of this I could send you but you don't really need it – for I suspect you are quite capable of making contacts of this type on your own.

129. To Wendy Berg

16th June 2009

Dear Wendy,

Many thanks for your letter. I could not agree more with your assessment of the current state of affairs at the Society of the Inner Light; however, ever the optimist, I live in hopes of improvement and their coming on stream at some time at the Greater Mystery level in the way to which you and I have become accustomed.

I think that green shoots are present, but whether I live to see them push very far above the surface remains to be seen. In any case I feel I have done all that I reasonably can to get things moving in the right way, and in this respect I would like to thank you heartily for your support in the past, which I know has not been easy. However, that's what sorts out the men from the boys, or whatever the feminine equivalent of that is! In that respect you have proved that you have real balls, my dear!

My own role is somewhat at a distance, as it has been brought home to me that laying on stuff for them is not in their best interests. Rather, a vacuum has to be left that hopefully they may learn to fill. And if they fail to rise to the challenge then at least I have left behind a raft of ritual for them to work with until such time as someone comes along who can light their own torch and carry them into the future in a more dynamic way.

For the time being I have agreed to lay on three workings per year, to give them something of a spur for the other occasions. I am pushing the limits for them by making these more or less spontaneous and unscripted jobs, and followed up with a journal article to help the contact filter down. You will I presume shortly receive reports of the latest effort, on the Tarot, and I have already written an article summarising it, a copy of which I will e-mail to you so you don't have to wait for the Autumn journal.

For the September meeting I shall probably follow up on a dream that Pat had that concerned a kind of roll call or review of the whole Fraternity and its members going right back into the past, and also onto the inner planes. At the same time, spurred on by what you say in your letter, I may well take the opportunity to lay on the line just what is expected of them if they presume to regard themselves as Greater Mystery initiates.

On the credit side, it has to be said, I think, that at the Lesser Mystery level they lay on a good show, possibly superior to anything else that is on offer these days, which indeed has come on quite strongly over the past few years as a result of getting a GM grade going, in however low key a form. There does seem to be a 'trickle down' effect. In this respect John Selby has I think been a good influence, and I am somewhat concerned to learn that he does not seem to be in the best of health of late. He has had the advantage of having been through the old SIL 'boot camp' regime as well as the GK Group experience.

As regards the latter, I am most encouraged to hear your news about how its incarnation as the Avalon Group is doing so well. I am in the process of writing my autobiography, which is quite an educative process, reviewing how various seeds I have sown have flourished, whether in the form of individuals or groups.

Is it ten years since I passed on my sword to you? Blimey, how time flies! Yet I have quite a few other decades to review since I first enrolled on the SIL Study Course in 1953. Quite a lot to load onto the balance against the feather of Ma'at when the time comes to take my finals!

Anyway, if spared, I very much look forward to seeing you again on 5th September.

130. To Gillian Bourne   *8ᵗʰ July 2009*

Dear Gillian,

Thanks for your positive reaction to what I have written so far. If it comes across in a readable way then thanks are due to Katie who helped me to find the right tone when I made my first attempt at it. I originally cast it more in a third person lodge report kind of way but she insisted that she expected more than that from a biography. She wanted to know first and foremost what it was like at the time for the person involved and the acid test was for it to be sufficiently gripping to keep her from falling asleep as she sat by the fire with her dog on a winter's evening. So although the intention of the book is to be an esoteric rather than a popular read, as I write I keep firmly in mind that I have to keep Katie awake (never mind the dog!) but without dumbing it down too much.

There is indeed a sort of biography of Margaret Lumley Brown which I edited, entitled *Pythoness* and published by Thoth Publications. It contains the story of her own early life, that she originally wrote in fictional form, together with specimens of her work – articles, mediumship and poetry. A truly remarkable woman. I don't know whether she put rose petals in her tea caddy, I never looked, but it would not surprise me if she did.

As for Bill Gray, a bit of an unpleasant character to get on with (Katie reckons most ritual magicians are like that) but important nonetheless in his idiosyncratic way. Both Bob Stewart and I – and indeed others – learned a great deal from him – although this entailed having to put up with a lot. His biography *The Old Sod* written by Alan Richardson and Marcus Claridge (distilled from an original quite libellous autobiography I understand) is worth reading in spite of everything. And one reason why ritual magicians of his ilk, and time at which he lived (which is also an important factor), can be such bombastic cynical bastards is what they had to put up with, in holding together some kind of self esteem in a world much less sympathetic than that of today to the things they held most dear and felt obliged to devote their lives to. Having said that though, I personally do not find myself particularly at home with his work – but the best of it has been filtered down by the likes of Bob Stewart and myself and no doubt others. So think yourself lucky you did not have to drink direct from the somewhat noxious fountainhead!

I do not recall ever having seen an obituary of Tony Duncan, and I am not sure than many people would have sufficient personal knowledge or breadth of perception to write one. All I knew of his death was when his wife Helga wrote to tell me. Apparently he just dropped dead, quite unexpectedly. Not a bad way to go I suppose, but a pretty devastating shock for his nearest and dearest. He had had, some years before, a slight heart problem, and it seemed it just stopped beating one day. He of course was a much more pleasant person to get on with than Mr Gray. I think he has a stained glass window dedicated to him somewhere – I might even have contributed to it. I still exchange Xmas cards with Helga.

Well, if you like what you have read so far of the autobiography, I am happy to reveal that you ain't heard nothing yet! The next few chapters concern ten years of a quite remarkable series of public workshops I did at Hawkwood College between 1979 and 1989 – the full significance of which I am only just beginning to appreciate myself as I go over my notes of them. Fortunately I have kept fairly detailed records which I suppose may wind up some day in some university archive to provide PhD fodder – but it is I feel important to get out an esoteric overview on the whole shooting match – hence the autobiography – which may act as some kind of practical guide and encouragement to others who seek to tread the Way rather than debate about it in what the Shropshire Pixie would regard as a "swottish" kind of way.

And in this respect I must say I am getting quite a bit of wisdom and encouragement myself from Tomberg's *Meditations on the Tarot*. Some of his definitions must seem very idiosyncratic to his fellow Catholics – but in his own take of them he often makes extremely good sense and even inspired good sense. I am now about halfway through, and quite gobsmacked by his definition of 'virginity' which is right on the ball esoterically, whatever a member of the Catholic Truth Society might make of it. Pity in a way that the Society of the Inner Light did not have the opportunity to read him back in the 1960s – or indeed Duncan and I.

No, I am not a Reverend. Could never take on an ambience of authority – divine or otherwise.

131. To Dolores Ashcroft-Nowicki   *19th August 2009*

Dear Dolores,

Thank you for your understanding. And I will look forward to seeing a copy of the book when it comes out. Gazing at a computer screen will never take the place of the printed page I think, and I already spend several hours a day doing just that by way of duty, so I try to avoid it for anything not essential. No tweeting or face-booking for me, thank you very much, let alone reading novels, however promising!

Most of my efforts currently are going into an autobiography, which I always swore I would never do, as to start looking backwards instead of forwards seemed like an invitation card for the grim reaper. However, it has been borne upon me by a few well wishers that some kind of record of my life and hard times would be of value to a new and probably feckless generation, so I feel I must do something for posterity even if posterity has never done much for me. Actually it is turning out to be quite an eye opener, as I realise the meaning of certain episodes in my life which I was too busy living through at the time to appreciate any finer or inner nuances.

All this involves wading through a massive archive which seems to have accumulated over the years. Correspondence and lodge reports going back to the 1950s in some cases. I suppose much of this will end up in some university archive for academic nerds of the future to sift through in pursuit of increasingly obscure doctorates. (Wonder if I can get a good price for it while I am still active and compos mentis enough to enjoy spending the money!?) The autobiography may well serve as a general guide through the turgid mass.

132. To Paul Dunne   *10th December 2009*

Dear Paul,

Many thanks for your letter and copy of your article, which has in fact now appeared in the latest issue of the *Inner Light Journal*. It goes a bit further than your recent article in *Quest* (with which I broadly agreed) but I have to say that I call into question some of the points that you develop within this longer effort.

To begin with I very much doubt if there is a "one and only true" system of correspondences of Tarot to Tree of Life, in or out of the Golden Dawn. This for two reasons.

The first is that the historical development of the Tarot does not accord with this assumption when submitted to accurate scholarship. I cannot go into all of this here but it is plainly and painstakingly laid out in a couple of books which should be in the library: *A Wicked Pack of Cards, The Origins of the Occult Tarot* by Decker, Depaulis and Dummett, and *A History of the Occult Tarot 1870-1970* by Decker and Dummett.

The second is that from my own esoteric experience <u>various</u> attributions will work very well or at least well enough for specific purposes. This was the first lesson I learned after writing *A Practical Guide to Qabalistic Symbolism*, after which a number of pretty competent people let me know alternative correspondences to the one I used – which was indeed the GD system as published by Crowley, Regardie and others. I already knew that leading French occultists such as Dr Gerard Encausse (Papus) follow Eliphas Levi's published system, which is at variance to the Golden Dawn – and could all those Frenchmen be deluded I asked myself? In any case I have found the published GD system to work pretty well for me – as demonstrated in some of my later books and articles – although I have also branched out with bright ideas of my own – which also work. I do not publish anything that doesn't!

I learned about W.G. Gray's system after I left the SIL in 1965, as I worked with him for a time and indeed published some of his books. I did not take to it particularly at the time, thinking it too idiosyncratic, but I have later worked with R.J. Stewart's system of correspondences, which closely follows although is not identical with Gray's, and have found it very good in its way, particularly as developed in his *Dream Power Tarot* which is closely connected with Planetary Being work, although he does not say so in so many words. Nonetheless I do not consider the system to be the one and only true – and Gray, an irascible old sod, had nothing but contempt for the Golden Dawn – as for much else!!!

Gray's approach to path working was different to any that I have come across in so far that he did not go from one end of a Path to the other, but regarded the Sephiroth as the two pillars on either side of the pictorial emblem, so one went down the Path at right angles so to speak. That is probably the reasoning behind his allocation of Trumps to Paths, although Stewart provides rather different ones.

As for A.E. Waite, he deserves more credit than he is sometimes given, and his set of cards drawn by Pamela Coleman Smith has had an enormous influence, but I don't see any evidence for thinking that he had another system of correspondences in mind other than the published Golden Dawn one. Nor do I see a link with Gray's set up.

My considered opinion of Tarot Trumps is that they are part of the common stock of western symbolic consciousness (via the Planetary Being if you like!) and so more or less arbitrary but none the worse for that. It follows that pretty well any Trump will fit any Path. This gives a great deal of freedom for personal experiment, although I am conscious that it might lead the occasional armchair nerd trying to catalogue 22 x 22 = 484 secret gateways to inner knowledge. But that is what turns certain people on!

When it comes to Maiya Tranchell Hayes, as with the Golden Dawn in general, a lot of faded glamour still hangs about that we could probably do without. I was interested to read in Alan Richardson's recent book on Aleister Crowley and Dion Fortune that she felt her branch of the Golden Dawn headed by Brodie Innes was a bit of a busted flush as early as the nineteen twenties, and it seems to have been a progress of gradual disillusionment for her ever since, capped by Regardie publishing the whole GD works in 1937, at which she more or less gave up and buried her robes and implements at the bottom of the garden.

She obviously sensed a kind of resurgence in 1940 when invited to join up with DF but it seemed to me that it served only to knock DF and her contacts off balance for a time. The positive element that came from it was the *Arthurian Formula* which was a staple of advanced work in the fraternity for some years, along with the opportunity for DF to do some work with the Spiritualist movement for a time, as Maiya, who knew everybody, was a useful link to Charles Cammell who edited *Light*. However, nothing much came of it in the end. Most of this is recorded in *Dion Fortune and the Inner Light*. The work was not aborted by DF's death, for Maiya had slung her hook by then, I imagine having realised that she was not going to be able to take over the place as she might have hoped. Just as Crowley had dreams of taking over the SIL after DF's demise. Fat chance! Such are the penalties of success. People who missed their own bus want to jump on the bandwagon.

The Earth, Sea, Moon, Sun, Star symbolism is pretty obvious stuff corresponding to the central pillar Sephiroth of the Tree of Life. So I cannot say I detect any great secrets being pursued here, and much the same goes for DF's novels. Sure, they tie up more or less with Sephirothic principles, but their sequence (as well as their style) seems at variance with any theory of a master plan for a New Order having been in anyone's mind.

So all in all, I guess I have to disagree with your summary of events, which, if I may say so, is because to my mind you tend to take a number of disparate facts and weave them into a fabric of assumptions and presumptions to your own design. Mind you, this can make a fascinating read, and some people seem to make a very good living at it, as in *Holy Blood and Holy Grail* or *The Da Vinci Code* and all that stuff. So maybe you have missed your vocation! About the only way of making big money out of occultism I think.

I did detect however beneath the froth some good points you made about the Planetary Being, as in your analysis of DF's article in *Quest*. And work with the Planetary Being seems to me the important work for the future – in which we do not really need to stir up the ghosts of yesteryear.

133. To Libby Travassos Valdez   *10ᵗʰ December 2009*

Hello Lib,

So how are things going then? I assume you are back online otherwise you would not be reading this – or perhaps I am just sending this into a black hole in cyber space, whatever that is. Anyway, to go back a few moons, when first I wandered into your floral web site with all its other delights, we had a little chat and then you said you were going off somewhere for some unspecified period. I waited and waited but nuffink did I hear from you any more, but anyway it appears that you are back. Are you still rescuing animals and things?

It has been a bit of a sod of a year, not just in general terms of the banks going bust with greed, or the planet heating up because everyone wants to drive a 4x4 or fly off to Ibiza every other weekend, or politicians being revealed as petty crooks – but everyone seems to have their own unique bit of hassle. Not that it is all bad. I am getting a bit arthritic in the knee joints but it has the advantage that I can carry an offensive weapon about with me in the form of a blackthorn cudgel posing as a walking stick. It also gives me the excuse not to go anywhere I don't want to – so being able to play the age card (80 next year) is almost as great a benefit as having a bus pass. Not that I use buses very much. We have a new car. Well a new second hand one. I had thought the last one would be our last – and it chuntered on gamely for 12 years, but we realised that as we are running out of good legs with which to press the pedals, an automatic transmission job might be a good move. And so it is, although it has been quite traumatic on occasion learning how to cope with the beast. I mean it should be a lot easier, and technically it is, but if you have been used to changing gears manually for donkey's years, you can feel a bit distrait when the car starts doing things for you – Aaaaagh – I'm not in control!!!!!

Nonetheless I am being very productive on the writing front. Beavering away at no less than two books and with contracts signed for both of them. One of them I have been stewing over for years, ever since visiting Lusignan and getting mugged by the faery Melusine. It is a follow up to my one last year *The Faery Gates of Avalon*, which was about the Arthurian romances of Chrétien de Troyes and how it was the ladies rather than the knights who were the key players, as they were faery ladies introducing the blokes to fairyland. This one is more specific to the Melusine legend, which is not greatly known in the Anglophone world (my learning French a few years ago is coming in useful – I wondered at the time why I did it – now I think I know). The other one is going to be my autobiography, which someone convinced me was worth having a shot at – to let the world know what magic was like at the sharp end. I am about halfway through it, just about up to 1986 with most of the Hawkwood stuff behind me. But I'm putting off the rest until the Melusine book is done (which I – and a rather pushy lady on the inner – think to be more important). Anyway I might chicken out and arrange for posthumous publication – not that it aims to make any enemies. But you know what people are!

Apart from that I am still playing the piano with the big band on a Monday night. I have been at this a number of years now, which has been rather a strange spectrum of experience. When I started it I was an amateur playing along with mostly ex-professional musicians, and so felt a bit challenged. As the years have passed, the ex-pros have died off and their place taken by increasingly raw amateurs, in fact by now not far off beginners, so I find myself one of the best in the band now – and feeling a bit superior to people who can't read very well, or play in time or in tune. Not that I have improved very much, if at all. I think in anything you reach a peak at which you are not going to improve to any great degree. And with me that happened a good while ago.

Although the magic stuff is something I flatter myself you probably can go on getting better at. Not that I do a lot these days. Wendy seems to be doing well with the old group, and whilst I have been giving a helping hand to the Society of the Inner Light over the past decade or so, I have recently given up attending meetings (you can get fed up with negotiating London Transport stairs – just as once I got fed up with driving up and down to Hawkwood half a dozen times a year). So it is all done with mirrors and candles and bits of fetish bric a brac in the privacy of my own home nowadays. Or the occasional walk down the park to talk to the trees.

134. To Carl Weschcke   *14ᵗʰ July 2010*

Hello Carl,

Think of a person and they appear. Wow! You are really on to something there! What could I have done with powers like that in my younger days. Although I suppose Dr Faustus got there first with Helen of Troy.

Seriously though, yes you have my address right and I will appreciate reading your book even if I don't approve of it. Seems a bit of a come down becoming a writer after the dizzy heights of being a publisher I have to say – but it is a congenial occupation and indeed quite compulsive once you get into the swing of it. At any rate I continue to scribble and seem likely to do so until I am prised away from the keyboard and carried off feet first. At least I don't have to write it all out in long hand and then type it up with three carbon copies like in the days of *A Practical Guide to Qabalistic Symbolism*.[1]

I am glad to hear Llewellyn continues well in spite of the savage commercial climate of the past year or so – elsewhere esoteric publishing seems to have gone to hell on a hand cart. With one of my more successful books, on the Goddess, published by Inner Trads International, bookseller returns even exceeding current sales. First time I have ever had a negative royalty statement!

Your mention of Louis Culling made me smile as I look back on him with considerable nostalgia. When I first set up publishing with Helios Book Service, and when I could only afford to publish very slim books, he, along with Israel Regardie, was one of my first authors, with a little book on the I Ching.

Sorry to hear of your comparative immobility but knowing you I doubt if you let it cramp your style very much. I am getting a bit creaky in the knees and ankles but I get around reasonably well within a quarter of a mile radius and with the excuse to carry a blackthorn cudgel which passes as a walking stick. Which is quite reassuring at a time when some of the youth of our country sport ill-controlled pit bull terriers as fashion accessories. No doubt I will have it taken off me if I try to board an aeroplane but as I am quite a stay-at-home these days I doubt if that eventuality will arise.

All the best to you and yours.

[1] Carl had originally commissioned me to write *A Practical Guide to Qabalistic Symbolism* back in 1961.

135. To John Matthews

26th *July 2010*

Dear John,

So pleased to hear you liked the Melusine MSS. I thought about including *The Wandering Unicorn*[1] in the bibliography but decided against it as I felt it a bit too apocryphal. Great piece of writing of course! Maybe I should change my mind and make a note of it at proof stage.

I continue to beat my head against the walls of the faery castle without much positive result. I feel some approach that deals with realities on two (or more?) levels is called for. To this end I have been re-reading James Branch Cabell's *The Cream of the Jest* once more, and also contemplating some of Peter Ackroyd's work. But neither approach seems to open the door, rattle the key in the lock as one might!

Although in the original communication I sent you there seems to be a caveat about getting too concerned with historical human characters – I still feel at the back of my mind that there is something highly significant to be discovered there. To this end I attach two chapters of the Melusine book that I suppressed in the end, for various reasons. Partly because they seemed somehow to miss the boat and partly because I felt it would not go down well with many readers to associate faery with the crusades. All very politically incorrect! However, you might as well have a look at them. Bob has seen them, as I did not delete them until after I sent him the full manuscript – and he agreed that they would be best left out (at least it makes the production cheaper!!!) but reckoned they rang some bells for him in regard to his visit to Jerusalem some time this year.

What nags at me is the close approximation of some very feisty 12th century women who seem almost like faery characters. Not only Eleanor of

Aquitaine (who has a close association with Melusine, as having built many of the castles and other real estate accredited to the faery) but women in Outremer from the notorious Agnes de Courtenay (mother of the Leper King) to the four times married Isabella of Jerusalem – and one or two more Byzantine and Antiochan princesses one could mention. To do justice to this would require a bloody great fictional saga such as I have not the talent or the time left me to write.[2]

There again, is another level of reality at the imaginal level with Bors and the other Graal heroes. I have been looking back at all Bors' life story as recorded by Malory and there is quite a mine of possibilities for him, who was responsible for letting the Arthurian court know what had happened on the quest, and being deputed to spread the word to the rest of Logres – I wonder if a discovery of faery was included in his undertaking that task. In the end he ended up being crowned a king. A faery king??? If any of this sets your creative juices flowing, feel free to follow it up.

Well, I have dumped quite enough in your lap for one morning. Hope you can make more of it than I have so far!

[1] by Manuel Mujica Lainez (Chatto & Windus, 1983)

[2] Not withstanding this downbeat opinion, the chapters in question are being recast and greatly expanded in fictional form under the title *The Faery and the Queen* – although in light of current interpretation of these words it should be said that the two protagonists, Melusine of Lusignan and Eleanor of Aquitaine, were gay ladies in the *old fashioned* sense of the word, each producing no less than ten children in the course of their remarkable lives.

136. To Peregrin Wildoak   *14th November 2010*

Hello there Peregrin,

I passed on your thanks to Rebecca who it turns out is a great fan of your blog[1] and has recommended me to spend some time on it too. In so doing I was particularly interested in your remarks about Golden Dawn type grading systems – about which much nonsense is written and even more believed! It puts me in mind of an ironic remark put to me by the former Warden of the Society of the Inner Light, Arthur Chichester, to the effect that one could very often calculate a person's 'grade' by seeing how they expressed the traditional 'vice' of the relevant sephirah.

Putting my own gloss on this (as much from self inspection as of anybody else) it struck me that you could regard Yesod as a standoffish independence from the common herd of humanity; Hod as an obsession with reams and reams of the printed word; Netzach as the englamoured glow of being on the road to becoming a great initiate; Tiphareth the vainglory of thinking you had made it to the ranks of adepthood; Geburah a critical disapproval of anyone outside your chosen clique; Chesed self satisfied pontificating to any prepared to listen.

But then comes Daath – the Janus faced – which spells disillusion in its negative aspect or dis-illusion (i.e. freedom from same) in its positive – when you face the supernal or truly spiritual realities of Binah-Chokmah-Kether a three-in-one which is perhaps best expressed as Faith, Hope and Charity. Beyond which lies the undefinable Glory of the Brightness – which I must say seems a far cry from the concept of Negative Existence favoured in some quarters.

As for any ways you can help. Well anything to spread the word on the output of Skylight Press would always be appreciated. Speaking of which you could also give yourself a treat by taking a look at the remarkable Rebecca's *In Different Skies* and *This Wretched Splendour*. I know I am the child's father, which rather puts me out of court as an impartial critic I suppose, but I honestly believe that the greatest and most unexpected achievement of my life is to have produced such a true chip off the old block with superior talents in many ways, both literary and esoteric. I guess I am very lucky.

Yours ever, GK

[1] Magic of the Ordinary, found at http://magicoftheordinary.wordpress.com

A GARETH KNIGHT BIBLIOGRAPHY

A Practical Guide to Qabalistic Symbolism (Helios Book Service, 1965; reissued by Samuel Weiser, 1986; paperback edition by Red Wheel Weiser, 2001)

Occult Exercises and Practices (Helios Book Service, 1969; reissued by Aquarian Press, 1976; Sun Chalice Books, 1997)

The Practice of Ritual Magic (Helios Book Service, 1969; reissued by Aquarian Press, 1976; Sun Chalice Books, 1997)

Experience of the Inner Worlds (Helios Book Service, 1975; reissued by Samuel Weiser, 1993; Skylight Press, 2010)

The Occult, an Introduction (Kahn & Averill, 1975)

A History of White Magic (Mowbray, 1978; reissued as *Magic and the Western Mind* by Llewellyn Publications, 1991; reissued under its original title by Skylight Press, 2011)

The Secret Tradition in Arthurian Legend (Aquarian Press, 1983; reissued by Samuel Weiser, 1996; R.J. Stewart Books, 2010)

The Gareth Knight Tarot Deck (U.S. Games Systems Inc, 1984)

The Rose Cross and the Goddess (Aquarian Press, 1985; reissued as *Evoking the Goddess* by Destiny Books, 1993; later as *Magic and the Power of the Goddess* also by Destiny Books, 2008)

The Treasure House of Images (Aquarian Press, 1986; reissued as *Tarot and Magic* by Destiny Books, 1991)

The Magical World of the Inklings (Element Books, 1990; reissued by Sun Chalice Books in 2001-2 as four separate books: *The Magical World of C.S. Lewis*; *The Magical World of J.R.R. Tolkien*; *The Magical World of Charles Williams*; *The Magical World of Owen Barfield*; revised and expanded edition published in one volume under the original title by Skylight Press, 2010)

The Magical World of the Tarot (Aquarian Press, 1991; reissued by Samuel Weiser, 1996)

Dion Fortune's Magical Battle of Britain (Golden Gates Press, 1993; reissued by Sun Chalice Books, 2003)

An Introduction to Ritual Magic [with Dion Fortune] (Thoth Publications, 1997)

The Circuit of Force [with Dion Fortune] (Thoth Publications, 1998)

Magical Images and the Magical Imagination (Sun Chalice Books, 1998)

Principles of Hermetic Philosophy & The Esoteric Philosophy of Astrology [with Dion Fortune] (Thoth Publications, 1999)

Spiritualism and Occultism [with Dion Fortune] (Thoth Publications, 1999)

Merlin and the Grail Tradition (Sun Chalice Books, 1999)

Dion Fortune and the Inner Light (Thoth Publications, 2000)

Principles of Esoteric Healing [by Dion Fortune, edited by Gareth Knight] (Sun Chalice Books, 2000; reissued by Thoth Publications, 2006)

Pythoness: the Life and Work of Margaret Lumley Brown (Sun Chalice Books, 2000; reissued by Thoth Publications, 2006)

Esoteric Training in Everyday Life (Sun Chalice Books, 2001)

Practical Occultism [with Dion Fortune] (Thoth Publications, 2002)

The Abbey Papers (Society of the Inner Light, 2002)

Dion Fortune and the Threefold Way (Society of the Inner Light, 2002)

The Wells of Vision (Society of the Inner Light, 2002)

Granny's Magic Cards (Sun Chalice Books, 2004; reissued as *To the Heart of the Rainbow* by Skylight Press, 2010)

Dion Fortune and the Lost Secrets of the West (e-book published by ritemagic.co.uk, 2006)

The Arthurian Formula [with Dion Fortune, Margaret Lumley Brown and Wendy Berg] (Thoth Publications, 2006)

The Occult Fiction of Dion Fortune (Thoth Publications, 2007)

The Faery Gates of Avalon (R.J. Stewart Books, 2008)

Melusine of Lusignan and the Cult of the Faery Woman (R.J. Stewart Books, 2010)

INDEX

References given are to **Letter numbers**, not page numbers.

CPSIA information can be obtained at www.ICGtesting.com
Printed in the USA
BVOW070338251111

276776BV00003B/129/P